C000070532

NORFOLK MISCELLANY

NORFOLK MISCELLANY

PAMELA BROOKS

breedon **books**
PUBLISHING

For Gerard, Christopher and Chloë,
with all my love.

First published in Great Britain in 2009 by
The Breedon Books Publishing Company
Limited, Breedon House, 3 The Parker Centre,
Derby, DE21 4SZ.

© Pamela Brooks, 2009

ISBN 978-1-85983-692-7
Printed and bound by TJ International Ltd,
Padstow, Cornwall.

All Rights Reserved. No part of this
publication may be reproduced, stored in a
retrieval system, or transmitted in any form, or
by any means, electronic, mechanical,
photocopying, recording or otherwise without
the prior permission in writing of the copyright
holders, nor be otherwise circulated in any
form or binding or cover other than in which
it is published and without a similar condition
being imposed on the subsequent publisher.

Contents

1. All about Norfolk 9
Location, Location, Location 9
Government 12
Media 13
Norfolk sport 14
Norfolk weather 16
Norfolk trees and flowers 17
Norfolk wildlife 21
Norfolk birds 22
Norfolk insects 23
Travellers' tales 23

2. Norfolk through time 26
Prehistoric Norfolk 26
Roman Norfolk 28
Saxon Norfolk 31
Norfolk under the Danes
and Vikings 32
Norfolk and the Norman Conquest .33
Mediaeval Norfolk 34
Tudor Norfolk 36
Stuart Norfolk 38
Norfolk in the 18th century 39
Norfolk in the 19th century 40
Modern Norfolk 43

3. The Coast and the Broads . . .46
The Coast 46
The Broads 51
A wherryman's list of the 48 reaches 53
Other waterways 55
Floods 56
Lighthouses 56
Piers 58
Fishermen's lore 59
Unusual visitors 59
Famous mariners 60
  Thomas Allison, Arctic navigator . .60

Henry Blogg,
lifeboatman extraordinaire 61
George Manby, inventor
and lifesaver 62
Sir Cloudesley Shovell, commander-in-
chief of the British fleet 64
Robert Tinkler,
cabin boy on the *Bounty* 65
George Vancouver, naval officer
and hydrographer 66

4. Churches and Cathedrals 67
Round-tower churches 67
Thatched roofs 68
Dedications 68
Churches great and small 69
Bells 71
Bench-ends and poppy heads 72
Brasses 74
Fonts 74
Glass 76
Graffiti 77
Lecterns .77
Monuments and memorials 77
Roofs 79
Screens 80
Wall paintings 81
Curiosities 83
Strange tales 86

5. Castles and Abbeys 89
Castles 89
Abbeys, monasteries and nunneries . .96

6. Epitaphs 101
Lost epitaphs 101
The sea, the sea 103

Strong personalities 104
Medical matters 106
Wordplay 107
Families 109
Love and loss 111
Accidents 112
Sad tales 113
Memento mori 114
Murder most horrid 115
More than an epitaph 116

7. Norfolk Folk 119
Charlotte Atkyns,
the Norfolk Scarlet Pimpernel 119
Henry Cable –
from convict to colonial settler 120
Howard Carter
and the discovery of Tutankhamun 121
Joseph Clover,
the father of modern anaesthetics ..123
John Coan, the 'Norfolk Pigmy' ...124
Sir Astley Cooper – surgeon,
anatomist and bodysnatcher 124
Harold Davidson,
the Prostitutes' Padre 126
Pablo Fanque, the first black circus
proprietor in Britain 126
Robert Hales, the Norfolk Giant ..127
Robert Hearne,
comedy legend 'Mr Pastry' 128
Margery Kempe, visionary 129
Mary Mann,
the Norfolk Thomas Hardy 130
Harriet Martineau,
writer and political thinker 131
Robert Marsham,
the father of phenology 133
Thomas Paine,
author and revolutionary 133
Humphrey Repton, landscaper 136
Amy Robsart, the queen's rival 137
Anna Sewell,
author of *Black Beauty* 139

'Turnip' Townshend,
politician and agriculturalist 140
Saint Walstan 141

8. Why is it called that? 143
Place names 143
Pigg's Grave 145
Stewkey Blues 145
Grimes Graves 145
Lothingland and King Edmund ...145
King's Lynn 146
Seven Burnhams by the Sea 147
Salthouse 147
Diss and its mere 147
Feltwell Anchor Corkway 148
California and the gold rush 148
Buildings 148
Syleham lights and lantern men ...149
Sporting names 149
Markets and spaces 149
Yarmouth Rows 150
Paths, roads and tracks 151
Little Switzerland 152
Hellfiregate and Wicked Hampton .152
Heartsease 153
St Edmund's Point 153

9. Notable buildings 154
Follies 163
Ice houses 164
Water pumps 164
Windmills 167
Mills great and small 168
Bridges 170
Crime and punishment 171
Market crosses 172

10. Rebels and rogues 175
The Burston School Strike 175
Duellists 176
 Sir John Heydon and
 Robert Mansfield, 1600 176

CONTENTS

Thomas Berney and
Thomas Bedingfield, 1684 177
Sir Henry Hobart and
Oliver le Neve, 1698 178
Smugglers 179
Pirates 182
Bodysnatchers 183
Wife-sellers 185
And a nasty taste... 186

11. Particular to Norfolk 187
Food and drink 187
Clothing and shoes 189
Animals and birds 191
Whifflers and Old Snap 193
Wherries 194
Cosseyware 195
Jack Valentine 195
Harry Carriers and Swills 195
Norfolk brands 196
A bit of a mardle 198

12. Norfolk and the arts 200
Norfolk on film and TV 200
Actors and comedians
with a Norfolk link 203

Norfolk music 203
Norfolk and the fine arts 204

13. Pioneers and record-breakers ...206
The King's Lynn Mart 206
Boulton and Paul's aircraft 206
The Pulham Pigs 207
Postal codes 207
Medical pioneers 208
Pioneers in science and industry ...208
Literary firsts 209
Norwich firsts 210
The first anti-aircraft rocket 211
The first lottery 211
Boats 211
The first bowler hat 212
Food for thought 212
Windmills 213
The first recorded steeplechase 213
The first turnpike in England 213
Record-breakers 214

14. This and that 217

Selected bibliography 223

Preface

I love little books of interesting facts – so I was delighted when my editor at Breedon suggested that I wrote the *Norfolk Miscellany*.

Norfolk is an amazing county with so much history, from its people to its buildings, to its flora and fauna and everything in between. Whether your family has been here for generations or you've recently moved to the area, I can guarantee there will be some facts in here that you didn't know.

There are some obvious gaps here, particularly the people of Norfolk; where are the big stories about Cavell, Fry and Nelson? The answer is, I have already covered them in my previous books for Breedon, and I didn't want to cheat my readers by just rehashing what I've written before. I've therefore used this as the chance to tell some of the less well-known tales about our county.

This is also the place where I would like to say thank you. First of all to my husband Gerard and my children Christopher and Chloë, for coming exploring with me and not complaining whenever I hijack family outings for work purposes. To my wonderful agent Dot Lumley, as always, for her support and encouragement. To Michelle Harrison and Steve Caron at Breedon, for giving me the chance to do what I love most – ferreting around in archives and exploring quiet corners to discover interesting things about my home county. And last, but certainly not least, thanks to all the people who helped me with information: the staff of Norfolk County Library and Information Services (particularly the Heritage Centre, and Ann at the Costessey branch), Kate Jackson Bedford (for films and TV) and Carol Twinch (for her expertise on St Walstan).

Pamela Brooks,
January 2009

Chapter 1

All about Norfolk

Location, Location, Location

✳ Norfolk is bordered by Suffolk to the south (where the rivers Little Ouse and Waveney form a natural boundary), the fenlands of Cambridgeshire and Lincolnshire to the west and the North Sea to the north and east. It has 90 miles of coast, 250 miles of waterways and 6,329 miles of roads.

✳ It's the largest county in East Anglia, and the fifth largest of the 34 non-metropolitan counties in England. The Office for National Statistics' figures for 2007 show that Norfolk has an area of 537,070 hectares (2,074 square miles). Nikolaus Pevsner, the renowned historian of art and architecture, has said that the county measures 68 miles east to west and 41 miles north to south.

✳ Around 80 per cent of the land in Norfolk is used for agriculture; 8 per cent is mineral workings, lakes, rivers and fens; 5 per cent is taken up by towns and villages; and 7 per cent is woodland and forests.

✳ According to the historian Christopher Barringer, Norfolk was the most densely populated English county from around 1000 until 1600. Although it has the seventh largest population in the country, with 840,700 people (at mid-2007 estimates), it has the 10th lowest population density, at around 1.57 people per hectare (compared with Surrey, the highest at 6.61, and Northumberland, the lowest at 0.62).

✳ Unsurprisingly, **Norwich** is the most densely populated area of Norfolk, with 33.19 people per hectare. According to Bill Wilson, over 25 per cent of people in Norfolk live within eight miles of Norwich Castle. Official government statistics show that 38 per cent of the population live in the conurbations of **Norwich**, **Great Yarmouth** or **King's Lynn**; 18 per cent live in the market towns; 40 per cent live in a parish containing more than 300 people; and the remaining 4 per cent live in a parish containing fewer than 300 people.

✳ Around one in five of the population is aged over 65, and one in 10 is aged over 75. According to recent statistics from the government, the average age of people in Norfolk is 43 (coincidentally, the author's age at the date of publication!).

✳ The name 'Norfolk' comes from 'North folk'.

✳ The first printed map of Norfolk was in Christopher Saxton's *An Atlas of England and Wales* in 1579. The original map was drawn in 1574 and it remained the basis of Norfolk maps until the early 1700s. James Corbridge published the first large-scale map of Norfolk in 1730; and a one-inch scale map was drawn by Thomas Donald and Thomas Milne, published in 1797 (and known as *Faden's map* after the publisher, William Faden). Andrew Bryant carried out surveys between 1824 and 1826 and published his map in 1826, showing parish and hundred boundaries. The first Ordnance Survey map of the county was published in 1838, based on surveys carried out in 1816 and 1817. The Norfolk Record Office contains what may be the oldest surviving plans of fields in England: two sketches of fields in Shouldham, dating from 1440–41.

✳ The highest point in Norfolk is Beacon Hill, south of **West Runton**, standing at 103m (338ft) – Ordnance Survey map reference TG 186413.

✳ The lowest point in Norfolk is thought to be **Hilgay** Fen, which is just below sea level in places.

✳ **Norwich** is the most easterly city in the UK, at longitude 52.38N and latitude 01.18E. From the middle of the 14th century until the middle of the 18th it was the second city of England. The next largest population centres in the county after Norwich are **Great Yarmouth**, **King's Lynn** and **Thetford.**

✳ The county can be roughly divided into eight types of soil:

a small amount of marshland on the north coast between **Hunstanton** and **Salthouse**, and more to the west of the county around **King's Lynn**;

the peat fens in the west of Norfolk (part of the Fens) – there are also mudflats at the edge of the Wash;

the 'smeeth', around 6,132 acres of unenclosed common in the northern fens;

Breckland in the south west of the county;

the 'good sands' – roughly in a triangular area, with **Morston**, **Hunstanton** and **West Lexham** as the 'points' of the triangle;

loams and broadlands in the east of the county;

heathland around **Norwich** and **Holt;**

clay for much of the rest of the county.

✳ There are many marl pits in the county. Marl is a mixture of clay and carbonate of lime, which was excavated and used to improve the texture of enclosed lands in the 18th and 19th centuries. (See also **Little Switzerland** in Chapter 8).

✳ The county contains 20 national nature reserves and 10 local nature reserves. Some (such as **Blakeney Point** and **Brancaster Staithe**) are owned by the National Trust; some (such as **Berney Marshes**) are owned by the RSPB; and some (such as **Foxley Wood**) are owned by the Norfolk Wildlife Trust.

✳ The Norfolk Wildlife Trust (NWT), established in 1926, is the oldest of a national network of wildlife trusts, and its first reserve was set up in **Cley** Marshes in 1926.

✳ The largest village green in the country is at **Old Buckenham.**

✳ **Hunstanton** is the only east-coast resort that actually faces west. It's famous for its three-tiered striped cliffs. The top layer is white chalk from the upper Cretaceous era, the next is red chalk (iron-stained limestone) and the bottom layer is carrstone.

✳ The common at **Thompson** is famous for its pingos (shallow pools) and is one of the best-preserved pingo sites in Britain. There are about 300 pingos on the common. They were formed about 9,000 years ago in the last ice age and are home to rare water beetles and dragonflies. There is an 8-mile circular walk around

Cliffs at Hunstanton.

the pingos, known as the Great Eastern Pingo Trail. There are other pingos in the county at **Foulden, East Harling** common and **East Walton.**

✳ **The Wash** is the largest marine embayment in Britain, with the second largest expanse of intertidal sand and mudflats in the country.

✳ **Norwich** market is the largest open-air market in England and is open six days a week.

✳ The Norfolk and **Norwich** Millennium library is the busiest in the country – more than a million and a half people used it in 2006–07.

Government

✳ The county contains 540 parishes. Historically, it was divided into 33 hundreds: Blofield, Brothercross, Clackclose, Clavering, Depwade, Diss, Earsham, North Erpingham, South Erpingham, Eynesford, East Flegg, West Flegg, Forehoe, Freebridge-Lynn, Freebridge-Marshland, Gallow, North Greenhoe, South Greenhoe, Grimshoe, Guiltcross, Happing, Henstead, Holt, Humbleyard, Launditch, Loddon, Mitford, Shropham, Smithdon, Taverham, Tunstead, Walsham and Wayland.

✳ In 1974 the Hundreds were replaced by the districts of North Norfolk, South Norfolk, West Norfolk and East Norfolk.

✳ Norfolk is now divided among seven district councils: Breckland, Broadland, Great Yarmouth, King's Lynn, West Norfolk, North Norfolk, Norwich and South Norfolk. At the time of writing there are proposals for a unitary government.

✳ Norfolk Rural Police Force was founded on 22 November 1839 and was one of the first county forces to exist. Originally it was divided into 12 areas with 12 superintendents and 120 constables. In 1968 the county police force merged with **Norwich** City Force and **Great Yarmouth** Borough Force, and became known as the Norfolk Joint Police. The name changed to Norfolk Constabulary in 1974. The police force is divided into Central Area (with its headquarters in Norwich), Eastern Area (with its headquarters in Great Yarmouth) and Western Area (with its headquarters in King's Lynn); there is also an Operations and Communications Centre at Wymondham.

✳ Norfolk's police force was the first to use helicopters when three armed prisoners went on the run from Norwich prison in May 1947. There were only two civil helicopters in the UK, and one of their test pilots – Squadron Leader Peter Garner – was the son of Superintendent Garner of the Norfolk police. Superintendent Garner, after a demo flight across London, believed that helicopters would be useful in helping the police to make arrests. Westland Aircraft Ltd, a helicopter firm, allowed the Norfolk police to use their helicopter in the search for the prisoners, making Inspector George Brunson of Norfolk Constabulary the first police helicopter observer in the UK. The runaway prisoners were duly recaptured.

✳ Norfolk County Council is divided into 84 electoral divisions, each with one councillor. The councillors are elected every four years, and within the council a chair, a vice-chair and 10 cabinet members are elected.

✳ The Diocese of Norwich is one of the oldest dioceses in England, dating back to **Dunwich** (in AD 630), **Elmham** (AD 673) and **Thetford** (AD 1070). It became the Diocese of Norwich in 1094, and covered Suffolk until 1914 when the Diocese of St Edmundsbury and Ipswich came into being and took over the 355 Suffolk parishes. There are 577 parishes in the diocese.

Media

✳ The transmitter at **Talconeston** is 150 metres tall. It was one of the first VHF radio masts built by the BBC, and it's thought that a JCB excavator was used for the first time in Norfolk during its construction. It was commissioned in 1956 and replaced a temporary 230ft aerial erected in February 1955. From 1966 it began transmitting TV to Norwich and those living within a 15-mile radius; it serves an estimated 1.25 million people. The National Grid Wireless wants to replace the mast with a 206-metre-high mast for digital TV.

✳ BBC Radio Norfolk (broadcasting on 95.1FM, 95.6FM, 104.4FM and DAB digital radio) began broadcasting in September 1980 from Surrey Street, **Norwich**. It moved to its current location in the Forum in June 2003. Its programme *Today in Norfolk* was nominated for Breakfast Show of the Year in the Sony Radio Academy Awards 2004, and the station itself was shortlisted for Station of the Year (for stations with an audience between 300,000 and one million people) in the Sony Radio Academy Awards 2006. It was also nominated for the Best Radio Programme in the Creative Awards East 2008 for both *Breakfast with Stephen Bumfrey* and *BBC Voices*.

✳ Anglia Television was formed by a consortium on 11 September 1958, with capital of £110,000. Its first studio was in the former Agricultural Hall on the

Prince of Wales Road, **Norwich**. It first went on air on 27 October 1959. The station ident (or logo) of the silver knight was the first 3-D ident in independent television and was used for 30 years until it was replaced by a modern abstract forming the letter A. The station's most famous programmes include the natural history series *Survival*, the drama series *Tales of the Unexpected*, the rural heritage programme *Bygones* and the quiz show *Sale of the Century*.

Norfolk sport

✳ **Norwich** City Football club was formed in June 1902 at the Criterion Café in White Lion Street. It officially became a professional club on 3 March 1905. The original strip was blue and white, and the players were nicknamed 'The Citizens'. However, as people began calling them 'Canaries' they changed the strip to canary yellow and green in 1907 (and, of course, have a canary on the badge). The club's first ground was at Newmarket Road (and is still used by Town Close House School) and its first home game was against Harwich and Parkeston on 6 September 1902. In 1908 the club moved to a new ground, the Nest, which was an abandoned chalk pit in Rosary Road. Thousands of tons of earth were moved before the pitch could be laid and the stands and steep terracing were put up to hold crowds of up to 25,000 people. The site was redeveloped after the war and is now the site for Bertram Books' offices; there is a scale model of the old ground at the Bridewell Museum in Norwich. The Canaries moved to Carrow Road in summer 1935 – and it took less than three months to build the new stadium. In 1962 they became the second football club to win the League Cup, and in 1972 they were promoted to the First Division. In 1985 they won the League Cup at Wembley.

✳ Norfolk County Cricket Club was founded in 1827. One of its earliest star players was Fuller Pilch, who was called 'the best batsman that has ever yet appeared' by sports writer Arthur Haygarth in 1862. In 1834 his individual scores in a match against Yorkshire were more than the whole of the opposing team's total! Over the next 100 years the club won the Minor Counties Championship several times. Other famous cricketers who played for the county include the Edrich brothers (Bill, Eric, Geoffrey and John), G.B. Raikes (who was also capped four times as a goalkeeper for the England football team) and Michael Falcon (unique in having captained his team from before World War One until after World War Two).

✳ Speedway started in Norwich in 1930 at The Firs Stadium in **Hellesdon**. The stadium was converted to a dirt track the following year, and the first Norwich team was captained by Arthur Reynolds (real name Fred Leavis –

he was freelancing at the non-League track in Norwich under an assumed name!). The track licence was taken over by Pakefield in Suffolk in 1935, but then in 1937 star rider Max Grosskreutz decided to switch from riding to team management and took over at Norwich. As well as being manager, he was the chief coach and mechanic, building all the team's bikes. The city team did well, moving up to the First Division, but the real magic started when Swedish rider Ove Fundin joined the team in 1955. Fundin became world champion the following year, and the sport went from strength to strength, drawing crowds of up to 25,000. Sadly, the club closed in 1964 and the site was sold to a housing developer.

✳ Norfolk has seen several boxing champions, including Jem Mace (often known as the father of modern boxing), who was born at **Beeston-next-Mileham**. In 1918 the Lads' Club was founded in **Norwich** and several top boxers trained there, including middleweight Ginger Sadd, welterweight Jack Forster and British lightweight champion Jon Thaxton.

✳ Former boxer Jackson Williams, born in **Norwich**, changed sports to become an ultra-marathon runner. His achievements include running an incredible 3,086 miles coast-to-coast across America in 95 days during 2007, and one of his earliest runs – at the age of just 17 – was from London to Norwich in just three and a half days.

✳ **Norwich** cyclist Emma Pooley won a silver medal in the women's time trial in the Beijing Olympics 2008 – and also became the Sports Personality of the Year in the Norfolk Sport Awards 2008.

✳ Matthew Pinsent CBE, the quadruple gold Olympic medallist rower, was born in **Holt**.

✳ Racing driver Martin Brundle was born in **King's Lynn**. During his Formula One racing career he was on the podium as runner-up 10 times. He was also World Sports Car Champion in 1988 and won the Le Mans 24-Hour Race in 1990.

✳ Marksman Mick Gault OBE, born in **Dereham**, was named the Norfolk Sports Personality of the Year at the inaugural Norfolk Sports Awards in 2007. He is also England's most decorated Commonwealth Games competitor, winning 15 medals in four games.

✳ Norfolk's Chrissie Wellington was the first British athlete to win the Ironman World Championships in Kona, Hawaii, in 2007. She completed the triathlon of a 2.4-mile swim, a 112-mile cycle and a 26.2-mile run in nine hours, eight minutes and 45 seconds – and, despite getting a puncture, she shaved over two minutes off her time in the 2008 championship and kept her title.

✳ Jody Cundy, who grew up in **Walpole St Andrew**, is a Paralympic triple gold medallist and world record holder. He won the 100m fly gold in the pool at the 1996 Atlanta and 2000 Sydney Games (setting a new world record both times), and when he made his debut as a cyclist in May 2006 he won a gold medal and set a new British record, following up with a gold medal and world team sprint record in the Paralympic World Cup. He topped that with two gold medals in the 2008 games in Beijing, beating his own world record by three seconds to win gold in the kilometre competition and also taking a gold in the team sprint.

Norfolk weather

✳ Norfolk is one of the driest areas of Britain, though it has also seen some of the worst flooding in the past (see chapter 3).

✳ The highest temperature recorded was 36.2°C at **Hillington** on 9 August 1911.

✳ The lowest temperature recorded was -18.9°C at **Santon Downham** on 23 January 1963 (though the winters of 1683–84 and 1739–40 were colder overall). This was also the snowiest year, when Santon Downham recorded 64 days of snow on the ground. Snow has also fallen in Norfolk as late as July, back in 1888.

✳ The driest year recorded was 1921, when just 10.5 inches of rain were recorded at **Outwell**.

✳ The sunniest year recorded was 1911, with 2,000 hours of sun.

✳ The wettest year recorded was 1912, when 40.74 inches of rain were recorded at **Norwich**. The wettest day also occurred in that year, on 26 August, when 7.31 inches of rain fell at **Brundall** and there were major floods throughout the county.

✳ The strongest wind was measured at **Cromer** on 3 January 1976 at an amazing 108mph.

✳ The aurora borealis has been seen over Norfolk – as mentioned in the diary of Revd Benjamin Armstrong, vicar of **Dereham**, on 9 March 1861.

✳ It was so cold in February 1929 that the sea froze at **Hunstanton**. The winter of 1607–08 was also extremely cold, and it was recorded that rivers at **Great Yarmouth** froze for 40 days.

✳ On 12 January 1987, temperatures dropped below -7°C and birds were washed ashore at **Bacton** covered in ice.

✳ It was cold enough to play a cricket match on the surface of **Diss** Mere on 20 February 1827. As well as cricket matches, people went skating and played tenpin bowling, and the *Norfolk Chronicle* estimated that 1,500 people had been on the mere during the day. There was another cold snap in the winter of 1890–91 with Diss Mere again the centre of celebrations, including 30 musicians in the Rifle Band who played music on the ice on 3 January 1891.

✳ In the Fens you might discover your windows covered in a thick black dust after one of the 'Fen Blows'. It happens when there is a lot of rain followed by a very dry period, leaving the ground cracked and dusty. When the wind blows sharply it causes a soil storm, similar to a sandstorm in a desert.

Norfolk trees and flowers

✳ Six thousand years ago the most common tree in Britain was the lime. In Norfolk three varieties of lime are found: the Large-leaved (*Tilia platyphyllos*, which is rare), the Small-leaved (*Tilia cordata*, found in ancient woods) and their hybrid, the common lime (*Tilia x europea*, which tends to be used in avenues).

✳ Wood from ash trees was used as part of the process of curing herrings in **Great Yarmouth**.

✳ The ash woods at **Ashwellthorpe** were used to make broom handles at the Briton Brush factory in **Wymondham** until the 1970s.

✳ The scientist and collector James Edward Smith was born in **Norwich** in 1759. At that time you could only study botany as part of a medical degree, so he studied for a medical degree in Edinburgh. He bought Carl Linnaeus's collection of nearly 3,000 books, plants, minerals, insects and manuscripts for 1,000 guineas, and founded the Linnean Society at his home in London in 1788. He was its first president until his death 30 years later. He wrote several important books on botany, including *Flora Britannica*, and contributed an incredible 3,348 items on botany for Abraham Rees, the editor of the *Cyclopaedia* or *Universal Dictionary*. After his marriage in 1796, he moved back to Norwich.

✳ The area around **Little Walsingham** was once renowned for producing saffron. At **Stiffkey** Hall there were rooms set aside for drying saffron. However, the saffron industry faded after about 1760.

✳ The first ever cricket bat willow (*Salix alba 'Caerulea'*) was first found in Norfolk in the 1700s, and was subsequently planted in Suffolk and Essex. It is a variety of the white willow, which was used to make baskets and eel traps. It was first used in cricket bats in the early 1800s because of its lightness and durability, and was also used for false legs.

✳ Matted sea-lavender *(Limonium bellidifolium)* is only found in the saltmarshes of the Norfolk coast. At **Blakeney** you can also see the other types of sea-lavender found in Norfolk: common sea-lavender (*Limonium vulgare*), lax-flowered sea-lavender (*Limonium humile*) and rock sea-lavender (*Limonium procerum*).

Bluebells in Foxley Wood.

✳ At the Fairhaven Garden Trust in **South Walsham**, the King Oak tree is said to be more than 950 years old. The Trust is also famed for the largest collection of naturalised *candelabra primulas* in the country; the best time to see them is the last two weeks in May.

✳ The **Bale** Oak was reputedly 36ft in circumference when it was cut down in 1860, at a grand old age of 500, and one branch was said to be 75ft long. According to the 18th-century historian Francis Blomefield, the hollow trunk was so large that 10 to 12 people could stand in it, and at one point it was used as a pigsty and as a cobbler's shop.

✳ At **Feltwell** there was a huge oak to the south-east of the village, which gave its name to Oak Street. It's said that Charles II (who was known to visit **Methwold**) sat under it, as did Cromwell – though obviously not at the same time! According to folk legend, people used to drive a nail into the tree to transfer the pain of their toothache to the tree.

✳ **Winfarthing** also had an enormous oak, near Lodge Farm. According to *White's Directory* of 1883, it was 'probably the largest in England except the one at Cowthorpe, in Yorkshire' measuring 70ft in circumference at the roots and 40ft in circumference in the middle of the main stem. The directory adds that the oak was known as 'the Old Oak' at the time of the Conquest and was believed to be more than 1,200 years old. The hollow shell finally crumbled in 1953.

✳ **Foxley** Wood is 6,000 years old and is listed in the *Domesday Book*. The 123-hectare site is renowned for its bluebells in late spring and has 'rides' cut through it for transporting felled timber. As well as bluebells, the wood contains dog's mercury, early purple orchid, herb Paris, lily of the valley, meadowsweet, water avens and fleabane. Bark was stripped here and used for the tanning industry until well into the 19th century.

✳ **Wayland** Wood near **Watton** is a 34-hectare reserve of ancient coppiced woods owned by the Norfolk Wildlife Trust. It's the only place in Norfolk where the Star of Bethlehem (*Gagea lutea*) grows.

✳ **Thursford** Wood contains some of the oldest oaks in the country, which may be anything up to 500 years old. The oaks here were pollarded originally to protect them from grazing cattle and deer, which prolonged their lives.

✳ The **Hethel** Old Thorn is one of the smallest wildlife reserves in the country, at only 0.025 hectares. The hawthorn itself (*Crataegus monogyna*) dates from the

13th century and is the oldest hawthorn on record in East Anglia. There is a legend that the thorn originated from a staff carried by Joseph of Arimathea. A more factual record is that the hawthorn was once one of the largest in the country and its trunk measured more than 12ft in circumference in the mid-18th century.

✳ The **Breckland** forests were cut down in prehistoric times, and the area is known for its light, sandy soils and flint. Its climate is different, too: it is colder in winter and hotter in summer than the British average temperature. During the 15th to the 19th centuries many warrens were set up in the area and there are remains of a warrener's lodge just outside **Thetford**. The area was first called 'Breckland' by W.G. Clarke in 1894.

✳ **Thetford Forest** was planted just after World War One. The 20,000-hectare site is the largest lowland pine forest in Britain.

✳ The fragrant orchid found at **Booton** Common is one of only a few sweet-smelling orchids in Britain; the fen orchid, found in the Broads, is a nationally protected species.

✳ **Roydon** Common is the largest remaining heath in West Norfolk. The eastern section used to suffer from outbreaks of fire caused by sparks from passing steam trains before the railway running across the heath was dismantled.

Seal pup at Blakeney Point.

✻ The Breckland speedwell (*Veronica praecox*) is mainly found in Breckland.

✻ *Hookeria lucens*, a genus of moss, was discovered in **Holt** in 1810 by William Jackson Hooker (later Sir William). Hooker was born in **Norwich** in 1785. In 1820 he was appointed Regius Professor of Botany at the University of Glasgow and in 1826 started publishing the *Botanical Magazine*. In 1841 he became the first director of the Royal Botanic Gardens at Kew; he opened the gardens to the public and also set up the first official guidebook.

Norfolk wildlife

✻ Red squirrels are almost extinct in southern England as they have no immunity to the pox virus carried by grey squirrels. One of the few places to find them is in **Thetford** Forest. There is also a red squirrel breeding programme at **Pensthorpe** and at **Banham**; kittens born there are eventually released into the wild in Anglesey.

✻ Of the 16 species of bat found in the UK, 13 of them can be found in Norfolk. **Paston** Great Barn in Norfolk is home to one of only seven British colonies of the barbastelle bat (*Barbastella barbastellus*), and out of the three breeding sites known in the country this is the only building used as a maternity roost.

✻ **Blakeney Point** has the largest colony of seals in Britain, with around 500 grey seals (*Halichoerus grypus*) and common seals (*Phoca vitulina*). Almost 10 per cent of the UK's seals are found in **The Wash** and on the north Norfolk coast.

✻ **Syderstone** Common is one of only two inland sites in the UK where the rare natterjack toad (*Bufo calalmita*) is still found. As they need both chalky water and sandy soil in which to thrive, natterjacks are more usually found on coastal dunes. The males emerge from burrows at dusk and call in a chorus to attract females; their call can be heard over a distance of several kilometres and they are thought to be Europe's noisiest amphibians. Natterjacks can be identified by the yellow stripe running the length of their back and by the fact that they run rather than walk or hop. It is illegal to handle, disturb or photograph natterjack toads and great crested newts without a licence.

✻ Four of the UK's six reptiles can be found in Norfolk: the adder, the grass snake, the slow-worm and the common lizard. Some of the best places to see them are in the NWT reserve at **Roydon Common**, the dunes between

Waxham and **Horsey** and the NWT reserves at **Ranworth**, **Hickling** and **Upton Fen.**

✳ The pool frog (*Rana lessonae*) was reintroduced to a location near **Thetford** under special permission from Sweden in 2005, and researchers studying recordings of mating frogs across Europe discovered that the frogs had a 'Norfolk accent'! The pool frog was originally found in East Anglia, but fenland drainage and damage to its habitats caused the population to decline to just one site in Norfolk and it became extinct in the 1990s. The pool frog is legally protected.

Norfolk birds

✳ **Breckland** is home to the rare stone curlew. There are only 254 breeding pairs in the UK and nearly three-quarters of them are in Breckland and Suffolk. **Weeting** Heath is recognised as the best place in the UK to see the stone curlew.

✳ As Norfolk is so close to the continent, more rare birds visit the area than any other county in the country. The Norfolk coast is known as a birdwatchers' haven, from the RSPB reserve at **Snettisham** right through to **Great Yarmouth**. Around 150,000 pink-footed geese from Iceland and Greenland arrive to spend the winter in Norfolk. Some of the best places to see the pink-footed geese are **Snettisham, Brancaster** and **Wells.**

✳ The bittern, which is one of the rarest breeding birds in the UK, is found mainly in Norfolk. Its 'booming' call is very distinctive and best heard at dawn or dusk between April and June. The best places to see bitterns in Norfolk are **Hickling** Broad, **Cley** Marshes, **Strumpshaw** Fen and **Titchwell** Marsh.

✳ The UK's largest colony of little terns breeds on **Great Yarmouth**'s North Beach each year. The RSPB sets up special viewing areas to see them between May and August.

✳ The **Pensthorpe** Conservation Trust has breeding programmes for the corncrake, eight species of crane, the lapwing, the redshank, the scaly-sided merganser and the turtle dove. Pensthorpe is also the location for the BBC's *Springwatch*, and has the only cranery in the UK – a purpose-built facility where visitors can see the largest collection of cranes in the UK.

✳ Marsh harriers (*Circus aeruginosus*) are found mainly in Norfolk, particularly at **Titchwell** Marsh and **Strumpshaw** Fen. They became extinct before the 20th century, and, although a breeding programme was successful in the 1920s, as a result of pesticides the population declined to just one recorded breeding pair in 1971. The population is growing again but they are mainly migrant from Holland.

Norfolk insects

✳ The Set-aside Downy-back beetle (*Ophonus laticollis*) is one of the rarest of Britain's 4,100 species of beetle. It's found in Breckland, as the light chalky soil and plants producing lots of seeds provides its perfect environment. Its name comes from the field margins or 'setaside' where it was found at **Croxton** Hall Farm, near **Thetford**.

✳ Rare butterflies found in Norfolk include the white admiral, the purple hairstreak, the meadow brown and the ringlet at **Foxley** Wood; the silver-studded blue at **Kelling** Heath; and the swallowtail in the Broads.

✳ The Victorian lepidoperist Margaret Fountaine, born in Norfolk, was an expert on butterfly life cycles. She spent 50 years collecting butterflies in 60 countries, and died from a heart attack at the age of 78 while collecting butterflies in Trinidad. Her collection of 22,000 butterflies is now in **Norwich** Castle Museum, and her sketchbooks of butterfly life cycles are kept at the Natural History Museum in London.

✳ The rare ground beetle *Nebria livida* is found at **Sidestrand** and **Trimingham**, under clay blocks at the bottom of the cliff.

✳ The only site in the UK where the planthopper bug *Chloriona vasconica* can be found is at **Brancaster**.

✳ **Thompson** Common is famous for rare water beetles, including the lesser water boatman (*Corixa punctata*).

✳ The cliffs at **West Runton** are a stronghold for the rare rove beetle *Bledius filipes*.

✳ At the time of writing, the Norfolk Wildlife Trust is hoping to reintroduce one of the rarest water beetles – the Oxbow diving beetle – to the mere at **East Wreham** Heath.

Travellers' Tales

✳ Many comments have been made about our county, including:

I am still reeling with delight at the soaring majesty of Norfolk – John Betjeman, 1974.

It is a region large and spatious, and in maner all throughout a plaine champion [flatland], unlesse it be where there rise gently some prety hils, passing rich, exceeding full of sheepe and stored with conies, replenished likewise with a great number of populous villages. For beside XXVII mercate townes, it is able to shew villages and country townes 625. Watered with divers rivers and brooks, and not altogether destitute of woods – William Camden, *Britannica*, 1607.

Oh! rare and beautiful Norfolk – John Sell Cotman, letter to Dawson Turner, 1841.

Very flat, Norfolk – Noel Coward, *Private Lives*, 1930: spoken by Amanda. (And we who live here know differently! Gas Hill in **Norwich** is reputedly as steep as Steep Hill in Lincoln).

There are few places in England where you can get so much wildness and desolation of sea and sandhills, wood, green marsh and grey saltings as at Wells in Norfolk – William Henry Hudson, *Adventures Among Birds*, 1913.

All England may be carved out of Norfolk. Here are fens and heaths, and light and deep, and sand and clay-ground, and meadows and pasture, and arable and woody ... so grateful is this shire with the variety thereof – Thomas Fuller, *History of the Worthies of England*, 1662.

I am a Norfolk man and Glory in being so – Horatio Nelson, 1802, on being made a Freeman of the Borough at **Great Yarmouth.**

What a coast this is, with its salt marshes and lavender, its channels, dunes, bays and crumbling Ice Age cliffs, lonelier and wilder than its Suffolk neighbour, arctic, melancholic, beautiful, treacherous, with sandbanks and quicksands, storms and floods, and never-ending erosion – Peter Sager, *East Anglia: Essex, Suffolk and Norfolk* (Pallas guide), 1994.

A fine old city, truly, is that, view it from whatever side you will; but it shows best from the east, where the ground, bold and elevated, overlooks the fair and fertile valley in which it stands – George Borrow describing **Norwich** in *Lavengro*, 1851.

Norwich is a very fine city, and the castle, which stands in the middle of it, on a hill, is truly majestic – William Cobbett, *Rural Rides*, 1821.

What a grand, higgledy-piggledy, sensible old place **Norwich** is! – J.B. Priestley, *English Journey*, 1933.

Thetford is famous for its setters; nearly all the rich people here keep them, as the whole district is an excellent one for shooting – Duc de la Rochefoucauld, *A Frenchman in England*, 1784.

Yarmouth is an antient Town, much older than Norwich; and at present, tho' not standing on so much ground, yet better built; much more compleat... the finest Key in England, if not in Europe, not inferior even to that of Marseilles itself – Daniel Defoe, *Tour through the whole Island of Great Britain*, 1727.

(on the Brecklands) Here we feel in touch with man in his early days, with all that is primitive and prehistoric... the heathland road on which one may wander for mile after mile without seeing any human being, seems as though its only fitting user would be a skin-clad hunter with his flint-tipped arrows – W.G. Clarke, *In Breckland Wilds*, 1937.

...this corner of England which once it holds your heart is more lovely than any place on earth. Beautiful with a hint of secrecy which haunts it, as the memory of a dark and tender sadness clouds the brilliance of a summer day – Lilias Rider Haggard, *A Norfolk Notebook*, 1946.

Long miles of sinuous, gleaming river, marshes gay with innumerable flowering plants, wide sheets of water bordered with swaying reeds, yachts or wherries, boats, fish, fowl and rare birds and plants, and exquisite little bits of paint and sketch – G. Christopher Davies, *Rivers & Broads of Suffolk and Norfolk*, 1929.

If the rest of Britain sank beneath the waves, and Norfolk was left alone, islanded in the turmoil of the seas, it would, I think, survive without too much trouble... Norfolk is a proud county of unique individualism. It has always stood alone and aloof from the rest of England – James Wentworth Day, *Norwich Through the Ages*, 1976.

Yarmouth, sir... the strangest place in the wide world: one hundred and forty-six miles of hill-less country between it and London... I shall certainly try my hand at it – Dickens, in a letter to his biographer, John Forster, 1848.

Chapter 2

Norfolk Through Time

Prehistoric Norfolk

❋ One of the oldest known creatures discovered in Norfolk is the **West Runton** mammoth (*Mammuthus trogontherii*), which died more than 600,000 years ago, aged around 40. It's possible that the mammoth was unable to get up again after a knee injury, and its bones have been found to have hyena teethmarks on them. A large bone was found exposed in December 1990 after cliffs eroded at West Runton. It took specialists two years to dig out a quarter of the mammoth, and it was finally excavated in 1995 from under 20 metres of cliff. At 85 per cent complete, it's the best-preserved example of a mammoth in the world and the biggest elephant skeleton found in Britain. In its lifetime it would have been as tall as a double-decker bus and weighed in at 10 tons (about twice the size of a modern African elephant); it was one of the largest animals to live on the land apart from the largest dinosaurs.

The site of the discovery is known as the **West Runton** Freshwater Bed, which is basically mud deposited from a river before the ice age. Other finds during the excavation included animals that became extinct in Britain many years ago (including a rhinoceros, a sabre-toothed cat and a wolf), as well as voles and stoats. Pictures of the mammoth from the Norfolk Museums and Archaeology Service were used on the cover for a set of stamps issued in March 2006.

❋ During the ice age the glaciers stopped in Norfolk. There's a ridge in **Morston** showing where the last glacier to arrive in East Anglia stopped and began to retreat. The **Cromer–Holt** ridge was also formed by glaciers, and in the sandy soils there are erratics (pebbles and boulders transported by glaciers) from as far away as Scotland and Scandinavia.

❋ The earliest known settlement in Norfolk was in 400,000 BC. Norfolk contains the earliest known Neanderthal hunting camp, thought to be 50,000 years old, discovered at **Lynford** Quarry in 2002. The finds included tusks up to 8ft long, large teeth and partial skeletons from at least four mammoths, along with eight Neanderthal flint hand-axes (one is inside a mammoth skull still attached to a tusk), teeth from a woolly rhinoceros and reindeer antlers. Flint implements have been found in more than 200 sites across the county. Twenty-eight Neanderthal flint hand-axes were found on the seabed off **Great Yarmouth** in 2008, indicating that at some point part of the bed of the North Sea was actually dry land.

✳ When the ice sheets moved, the settlers moved south. As the ice retreated again, people moved back. Settlements dating from 6500 to 3500 BC have been found at **Hellesdon, Kelling Heath, Sparham** and **Lyng**.

✳ Neolithic man-made clay pots and pottery have been found at **Sparham** and **Spong Hill**. The settlers grew barley and emmer (wheat), and also ate crab apples and hazelnuts. They kept pigs, sheep, cows and goats. Long barrows were built for the dead and some have been found at **Ditchingham, West Rudham, Harpley** and **Felthorpe**.

✳ The henge monument at **Arminghall** dates from 3250 BC and is the most important henge outside Wessex. It was discovered during a survey of crop markings by Wing Commander Gilbert Insall in 1929, and from the air it looks like a horseshoe of eight huge posts within a ditch. It was partially excavated in 1934. Originally, the outer ditch was 1.5 metres deep and the inner ditch was 2.3 metres deep, with a bank between them; the timbers were one metre in diameter.

✳ The earliest evidence of organised industrial workings in Norfolk are the flint mines and pits known as **Grimes Graves**. The site covers 90 acres and there are 500 shafts (some of which are 12 metres deep, with some connected to others by galleries), as well as 1,600 shallow pits. The shafts and pits were all excavated with antler picks. Work started at the end of the third millennium BC. Grimes Graves is the only Neolithic flint mine in Britain that is open to visitors.

✳ Seahenge was discovered at **Holme-next-the-sea** in late 1998 when tides uncovered the peat beds. It's a circle of 55 posts thought to be 10 feet tall, with an upturned oak root in the middle. Dating showed that the timbers were felled in 2049 BC. It is the only structure of its kind in the UK to be discovered almost intact. We still do not know what it was used for, although one theory is that the tree root was used like a table and a body was placed on it for birds and animals to pick clean before the bones were buried; another theory is that it was a calendar. Seahenge has been preserved and part of it is now on display at **King's Lynn** Museum. It has the earliest metal tool marks on wood ever discovered in Britain; marks from 50 different axes were found on the timbers. There was a second henge at Holme, earlier than the one now preserved, but most of it has been washed away.

✳ During the Bronze Age round barrows were built for burying the dead. Over 1,000 sites have been found in Norfolk. One of the largest groups is at **Salthouse,** named Gallows Hill, Three Ha'penny Hill and Three Farthing Hill. The barrows are 6ft high and 25 yards across and originally would have had a 6ft ditch around them.

✳ There are five known hill forts in Norfolk – at **Warham, Holkham,** Bloodgate Hill in **South Creake, Narborough** and **Thetford.** The fort at Thetford was reused in Norman times as the ditches around the castle motte. The best-preserved fort is at Warham, which is the only one of the forts with a double ditch. It is open to visitors, as are the forts at Thetford and Creake.

✳ At Micklemoor Hill, **West Harling,** there is an Iron Age site. It was excavated in the middle of the 20th century. It had three enclosures, which included two circular houses and one with a rectangular building.

✳ More Iron Age torcs and bracelets have been found in Norfolk than in the rest of Britain put together. Other incredible finds in the county include the **Snettisham** treasure, which is the richest Iron Age hoard found to date in England and includes the largest collection of Iron Age gold and silver neck rings found anywhere in Europe. The first discovery was made in 1948 during deep ploughing. The farmer originally thought he had found part of a brass bedstead and it stayed at the side of the field for a week! When more finds surfaced they were taken to Norwich Castle and the importance of the treasure was realised. There were further finds in 1950, 1964, 1968 and 1973. Squadron Leader Hodder was metal detecting in the area in 1990 and discovered the treasure. The Snettisham hoard includes 75 complete torcs, fragments of another 100 torcs (all made from electrum, an alloy of gold and silver), bronze bracelets and coins (including Gallo-Belgic coins dated to 70 BC).

Roman Norfolk

✳ Norfolk was part of Iceni territory. Iceni coins have been found at Gallows Hill in **Thetford,** along with a hoard of jewellery, including 22 gold rings set with semi-precious stones, a set of 33 silver spoons (many of which bear inscriptions to the woodland fertility god, Faunus) and a jewellery box made from shale.

✳ In AD 60 Prasutagus, the king of the Iceni, died. He was supposed to leave all his lands to the emperor, but instead he left Nero only half, dividing the rest between his daughters. The Romans promptly seized Iceni property, publicly whipped his wife, Queen Boudicca, and raped their daughters.

Boudicca led a revolt in AD 61, which led to the Iceni marching on Colchester (Camulodunum) – which had a Roman garrison of only 200 men, compared to Boudicca's army of 100,000 – sacking and burning it. They also burned St Albans (Verulamium) and London (Londinium). However, the Romans regrouped, and, despite the fact that Boudicca's army outnumbered them hugely, the Romans had better firepower, strategy and discipline. They defeated the Iceni at a battle somewhere north of St Albans. The Roman historian Tacitus reported that 80,000 Britons died, but there were only 400 Roman fatalities.

✤ It is generally believed that Boudicca either fell ill or took poison and died. Her grave is rumoured to be at various sites, including an urban myth that she is buried under platform nine at King's Cross Station! Other contenders for the site of her grave include a barrow on Hampstead Heath and a barrow on the heath at **Garboldisham**.

✤ Norfolk then became part of the Roman Empire and a new capital was built at **Caistor St Edmund** (Venta Icenorum, meaning 'Marketplace of the Iceni'). It began as a few houses of wattle and daub, but the forum (market place) and law court had been built by about AD 125, followed by a

The remaining town walls at Caistor.

View of the walls from the middle of Caistor Roman Town.

bathhouse later in the century. Pottery and glass were made at the town. The walls were built in the third century, enclosing an area of 35 acres (and, according to 19th-century historian Walter Rye, the largest Roman camp in England). The remaining walls are 19ft high and 11ft thick.

✳ Another Roman settlement grew up at **Caister**, near Yarmouth. At **Brampton** there was a major pottery centre with over 140 kilns, and a Roman bathhouse was also found in the village. A pair of dolphins, which were believed to be the carrying handle of a Roman centurion's helmet, were found and their image is part of the village sign.

✳ Smaller settlements were built at **Walsingham/Wighton**, **Toftrees**, **Billingtree**, **Kempstone**, **Narford**, **Fincham**, **Denver**, **Hockwold**, **Brettenham**, **Threxton**, **Crownthorpe**, **Scole**, **Long Stratton**, **Needham** and **Ditchingham**. There was also a villa at **Appleton** which had a tesselated mosaic floor; during excavations in the 1940s archaeologists discovered the skeleton of a newborn baby under the floor.

✳ The Romans built three Saxon shore forts – one at **Brancaster** (Branodunum), one at **Caister** and one at **Burgh Castle** (Gariannonum). Nowadays, Burgh Castle is four miles inland, but in Roman times it was a seaport. Some historians think that there also might have been a fort at **Cromer** that has been lost to the sea.

✳ The oldest trackway in the county is the **Icknield Way**, which runs from **Hunstanton** via **Thetford** to Salisbury Plain. Part of the Icknield Way was incorporated into **Peddar's Way**, which starts at **Thetford** and runs for 63 miles to **Holme-next-the-Sea**, where it joins the **Norfolk Coastal Path**, running to **Cromer**. Other Roman roads in the county include the **Pye Road** (from **Norwich**, roughly where the A140 now runs from Norwich to Ipswich) and **Stone Street** (which ran from **Caistor St Edmund** to Bungay).

✳ A rare Roman amulet with a Greek and Latin inscription on a gold sheet, appealing to the gods Iao and Abraxis, was found in **Billingford** in 2003 – one of only four known amulets in the whole country. A lead tablet containing a Roman curse (to the thief who stole things from Brumasius, including some leggings) was found at **Caistor St Edmund**.

✳ Perhaps one of the oddest finds in the county was a Roman coin in **Bacton** in 1971 – found inside the stomach of a 3½lb cod!

Saxon Norfolk

✳ In the Saxon period, Norfolk and Suffolk became the kingdom of East Anglia. Settlements grew up mainly along streams and rivers in central and north coastal areas. An Anglo-Saxon cemetery containing over 2,000 cremations has been found at **Spong Hill**, near **North Elmham**, and sunken huts have been found at **Witton**.

✳ There are two earthworks from the Saxon period which possibly acted as boundaries: the Foss Ditch and the Devil's Dyke. The Foss Ditch runs for seven and a half miles between the River Wissey and the Little Ouse River. The Devil's Dyke (also known as Bircham Ditch) ran from the Iron Age fort at **Narborough** to **Beachamwell**. It's mentioned in the charter of Ramsey Abbey in 1053, and Pevsner dates it to between the fifth and seventh century.

✳ According to Bede, Raedwald (one of the Wuffing kings of East Anglia) was the first High King of Britain after defeating the king of Northumbria at the Battle of the River Idle in 617. Raedwald was baptised in Kent in 605 and is believed to have set up a temple which included altars to his ancestral god as well as altars to his new god. He died in 625 and is thought to have been buried in Mound One at Sutton Hoo in Suffolk.

✳ Later Saxon settlements include **Norwich** (at Fishergate) and **Thetford**. Thetford is unique because it's the only major Saxon town in England which was completely abandoned as the inhabitants moved to the other side of the river. The original town was rediscovered in 1968 beneath some allotments on the Bury Road.

✳ St Fursey founded a monastery at Cnobheresburg (in the ruins of the fort at **Burgh Castle**) in about 630, and Withburga founded a nunnery at Dereham in the 640s. There was also a settlement at **North Elmham** and the chapel there (dating from the 680s) was built upon and fortified by the 'fighting bishop' of Norwich, Henry Despenser, in the 14th century.

✳ Saxon coins, pottery, metalwork and even writing implements have been found across the county.

✳ The remains of the oldest timber hall in East Anglia were discovered in **North Elmham** in 1969. On the same site one of the largest Saxon halls in the country was also excavated – 60ft long by 25ft wide.

✳ The Saxon burial ground known as **Spong Hill** in North Elmham is one of the largest in England; the nearest comparable one is in Lincoln.

✳ Evidence of successful surgery in Saxon times has been found in the county, including a woman's skull found at **Oxborough** in 1990 which showed signs of trepanation (an operation to relieve pressure on the brain). There were also signs of a successful surgical operation on a man's left leg, from a skeleton found at **Grimston** in 1955.

Norfolk under the Danes and the Vikings

✳ The Vikings invaded Norfolk in 838 and again in 869, when the Danes occupied **Thetford** during the winter. In 870 King Edmund was killed at Hælgelisdun (probably at Hoxne, in Suffolk, although some historians argue that it was **Hellesdon**, near Norwich).

✳ In 1990, archaeologists discovered a 200ft defensive ditch in Calvert Street, Norwich, which they believed may have been dug by the Vikings to protect a mint after the English recaptured Norfolk in 917.

✳ The Danes sacked **Norwich** and **Thetford** in 993. After the massacre of the Danes in 1002, Sweyn Forkbeard took revenge by sacking Norwich and Thetford in 1004. Ulfcytel and his army met them at **Wretham** Heath to try to stop them returning to their ships, and although they were unsuccessful they fought well enough for Ulfcytel to be nicknamed Snillingr ('The Valiant') and East Anglia became known as Ulfcytel's land. In 1010 Ulfcytel fought Sweyn's ally Thorkell the Tall at the Battle of Ringmere, and was finally killed at the Battle of Assendun in 1016.

✳ There are few traces of the Danes in Norfolk, apart from place names ending in -by (meaning a farm), -thorpe (meaning a small hamlet), -thwaite (meaning meadow) and -toft (meaing plot of land). Most of the place names in the county with -by endings occur in the island of **Flegg**.

✳ There are two known Scandinavian burials in Norfolk – a female at **Santon Downham** and a male at **Middle Harling.**

✳ Viking remains in Norfolk include a gold Thor's Hammer from **South Lopham** (one of only six found in the county – two of the other five are made of lead, one of silver, one of gold and silver and one of gold alloy); a gold ingot found in **Norwich** during excavations before the Forum was built; a trefoil brooch at **Taverham**; a wooden Viking or Danish spade at **Bawburgh**, similar to those seen on the Bayeux tapestry; and a Viking ship at **Great Yarmouth**, which was discovered in 1886 and re-exposed in 1911.

✳ **Thetford** was an important town in the late 10th century and even had a mint. However, after the Episcopal See was moved from **Thetford** to **Norwich** in the late 11th century, **Thetford** declined in importance.

✳ The earliest written evidence of **Norwich** is on coins minted in the 10th century. 'Norvic' is seen on coins from Aethelstan's reign (924–39). The town was called 'Northwic' in the *Anglo-Saxon Chronicle* when Sweyn sacked it in 1004. It's also known that burgesses in the time of Edward the Confessor (*c.* 860) sent a present to the king, along with their taxes, of six jars of honey, one bear and six dogs to bait the bear.

Norfolk and the Norman Conquest

✳ The Normans arrived in 1066. Ralph de Guader was made the Earl of Norfolk after the Conquest; he rebelled against William I in 1074 and left Emma, his countess, to hold **Norwich** Castle. She was forced to surrender the castle and obtained terms to leave the country.

✳ The *Domesday Book* commissioners visited Norfolk in 1086 to list the new king's possessions. The book lists 62 'tenants in chief' as well as the king, the 'king's free men belonging to no estate', the 'king's men in demesne' and annexations. There were 731 settlements in Norfolk, along with plenty of sheep – so the wool-producing industry that would become so important in mediaeval times was already in place. It was recorded that 5,000 people lived in **Norwich**, 4,000 in **Thetford** and around 400 in **Yarmouth**. The *Domesday Book* also stated that 98 properties were destroyed to make way for the earthworks of Norwich Castle.

✳ There were over 250 mills in the county at Domesday, but they were likely to be watermills; windmills were only introduced in the 12th century.

Mediaeval Norfolk

✳ Two of the major landholding families in the early mediaeval period were the de Warennes and the d'Albinis. William d'Albini built **New Buckenham** Castle and **Castle Rising** Castle in the mid-12th century, and William de Warenne fortified **Castle Acre.**

✳ Herrings were incredibly important to **Great Yarmouth**'s economy. In mediaeval times an annual fish fair was held on the Denes and lasted from Michaelmas (29 September) to Martinmas (11 November). Defoe described the fair in the 18th century, saying that 'the land was covered with people, and the river with barques and boats'.

✳ Three herrings were included on the town's coat of arms, adopted when **Great Yarmouth** was given a charter in 1207/08.

✳ **Great Yarmouth** and **King's Lynn** were both very important ports in mediaeval times. When King John taxed imports and exports by sea he collected only £6 19s from Norwich in 1203–04, but he collected £54 15s 6d at Yarmouth and an incredible £651 11s 11d at King's Lynn. Great Yarmouth was ordered to send six ships to fight the Scots at Berwick in 1301, while King's Lynn handled provisions for the northern garrisons and sent three ships. Both ports declined in importance in the 15th century due to the effect of the Hundred Years' War on trade.

✳ **Blakeney** was also an important port: it sent two ships to Berwick in 1301, and provided ships for Edward III at the siege of Calais during the Hundred Years' War. Blakeney was the only Norfolk port with a customs house other than **Great Yarmouth** and **King's Lynn** from the 14th to the 16th centuries.

✳ **Norwich's** city walls were built between 1297 and 1334, making it the largest area within a walled city in the country – including London.

✳ In 1349 the Black Death came to Norfolk. It's thought that as many as 58,000 people died in the county. The plague was particularly bad in **Great**

Yarmouth, whose population decreased from 10,000 to only 3,000. Plague hit the county again in 1361, 1369, 1375 and 1391, and there's an inscription in the church of St Edmund's, **Acle,** referring to the plague (see page 83).

✳ More than a hundred settlements in Norfolk that were named in the *Domesday Book* had disappeared by the year 1500.

✳ There were problems with animals too. In the 14th century there were frequent outbreaks of murrain (an infectious disease which caused fever and death) in sheep.

✳ During the Peasants' Revolt of 1381, a group from Bury St Edmunds threatened to burn **Thetford** on 14 June 1381. Another group, led by the **Felmingham** dyer Geoffrey Litester, went to Norwich. There they killed Sir Robert de Salle at Mousehold, beheaded the JP Sir Reginald Eccles and looted the city. Litester's rebels took the town charter at Yarmouth, and burned court rolls at Norwich and St Benet's Abbey. However, after Wat Tyler was killed in London and it became clear that the king's concessions would be overturned, Litester sent his men to negotiate terms. The Bishop of Norwich, Henry Despenser, had them beheaded and chased Litester's rebels back to **North Walsham** before hacking them down in the church where they'd taken sanctuary – Despenser knew that it hadn't been consecrated yet and that sanctuary rights were therefore invalid.

✳ One of the largest surviving blocks of 'ridge and furrow' (strip-farming land) in Norfolk, around 19 hectares in total, is at **Hilgay.**

✳ There was a major fire in King's Lynn in 1421. The Trinity Guildhall burned before the snow could put out the flames. Margery Kempe (see page 129) describes the fire in her autobiography.

✳ Sir Miles Stapleton of **Ingham** was appointed to care for the signal beacons in **Norfolk** in 1427. These were designed to warn of any imminent French invasions during the Hundred Years' War.

✳ The letters of the Pastons – a Norfolk family who had humble origins and yet who rose within three generations to become courtiers – are one of the great treasures of Norfolk. They are a huge collection of family letters dating from the 15th century, and were discovered at **Oxnead** three hundred years later and saved by the historian Francis Blomefield. The letters give an insight into what life was like during the Wars of the Roses

– including legal disputes, fashion, food, politics, marriage and running a household – and also give details of sieges at **Gresham** Castle and **Caister** Castle. The collection includes the first known valentine letter, from Margery Brews to John Paston the Younger.

Tudor Norfolk

✳ **Norwich** was hit by severe fires in 1507. The first, which started in Tombland, lasted for four days and burned more than 700 houses, and the second, which started in Colegate, lasted for two days and burned more than 350 houses. In May 1509 the city's rulers ordered all new buildings had to be roofed with 'thaktyle' and not thatch. There are now only five buildings remaining within the old city walls which were originally thatched.

✳ The Tudor period saw the Dissolution of the Monasteries, between 1536 and 1540. The only one not technically dissolved was St Benet's, near **Horning** (See chapter 5). This had a huge knock-on effect on the ownership of land, and also on alms-giving and hospitals; the poor, instead of being looked after by the religious houses, now had to be dealt with by the authorities.

✳ Robert Kett, an elderly, law-abiding landowner from **Wymondham,** was an unlikely rebel. However, when people started pulling down his fences in 1549, he took up the cause of social justice. From all over the county, men marched to Mousehold Heath in **Norwich** to join him. He drew up a list of 29 requests to the king, which included an appeal for an end to enclosure and rack-renting, the introduction of standardised measures, that priests should preach properly and teach the children of the poor, and asked that 'all bond men may be made free, for God made all free with his precious blood shedding.' However, the rebels were defeated by the Earl of Warwick's forces and Kett was hung from the walls of Norwich Castle. In 1949, 400 years after the rebellion, a commemorative plaque was put on the castle walls 'in reparation and honour to a notable and courageous leader in the long struggle of the common people of England to escape from a servile life into the freedom of just conditions.'

✳ Elizabeth I visited **Norwich** in 1578 as part of her Summer Progress and stayed for five days. Before her visit the city was renovated: houses were rebuilt, the streets widened and the pillory and cage removed from the market place. The city gave her a gilt cup worth £100 (equivalent to a little over £20,000 in today's money) and entertained her with masques and pageantry. In response she knighted the mayor and promised never to forget Norwich.

✳ The plague was prevalent in the county during Tudor times. **Great Yarmouth** was hit badly in 1544, 1556 and 1579, as was **Norwich**. The 1579 epidemic wiped out almost a third of the population and the mayor of Norwich issued a proclamation 'for avoidynge the encrease and spreadynge of the infection of the plague within this Citie'. If someone in your house was affected by the plague, you weren't allowed to go 'into anye streete market or shop or open place of resort within the cytee or the liberties or the suburbes' until the plague had been gone from your house for at least 20 days, unless you carried a white stick two feet in length. If you carried a white stick, you weren't allowed to go to sermons, lectures or the guildhall – if you did, you'd be set in the stocks until 8pm that day, or you'd have to pay 5 shillings (the equivalent of just under £10 in modern terms).

✳ In the Elizabethan shipping survey of 1582, **Blakeney** had 36 ships – four more than **King's Lynn**. **Wells** had 19, and petitioned for a customs house in the 1590s.

✳ During the 15th century trade was poor and Nicholas Sotherton, the Mayor of **Norwich**, decided that the weavers from the Netherlands might be able to teach the city weavers new techniques and revive the cloth industry. The Protestant weavers were being persecuted by the Spanish at the time, so Sotherton arranged for 30 families to join the city. These weavers were known locally as the 'strangers', and because they used Sotherton's house as a staging post the house became known as Strangers Hall. By 1583 there were 4,500 'Strangers' in the city.

✳ In 1599, after a bet with Shakespeare, Will Kemp danced from London to **Norwich** in nine days – backing himself at odds of 3 to 1. The journey actually took a month because he had 'rest days', but the times that he danced were the only ones that were counted for the purpose of the bet. When he reached Norwich, the city whifflers (see page 193) parted the crowds for him so he could dance through to the market place; Kemp was impressed by the music provided by the city waits, saying, 'Few cities in our realm have the like, none better… Besides their excellency in wind instruments, their rare cunning on the viol and violin, their voices be admirable.' He ended his journey by leaping over the churchyard wall at St John Maddermarket – and landed with one foot on the skirts of a girl, ripping her petticoat off. His gravestone in Southwark mentions his feat: 'Welcome from Norwich, Kempe all joy to see, Thy safe return morriscoed lustily.' On the 400th anniversary of his dance, the 127-mile route was danced as a morris relay by morris clubs in the eastern region, with each club completing a 'leg'. They managed to do it in only eight days and, unlike Kemp, didn't stop for any rest days.

Stuart Norfolk

✴ Plague hit Norfolk again in 1603, and nearly 3,000 were buried in Norwich alone. 1625 was another bad year for plague as people in **Norwich** had to keep their dogs and pigs indoors or they would be killed, and the Black Tower was used as a hospital for the infected poor. Nearly 1,500 people died from the plague in the city during this period.

✴ In 1620, a group of Puritans left England for America on the *Mayflower*. More than a quarter of the passengers were from Norfolk, including the ship's physician, Dr Samuel Fuller, from **Redenhall** (who died of smallpox in America); his brother, Edward Fuller, with his wife and son (Edward was one of the 41 men who signed the Mayflower Compact which was the agreement that the colony would be governed by the will of the majority); Desire Minter from **Norwich** (aged only 15, who was looked after by John and Katherine Carver); and Thomas Williams from **Great Yarmouth** (who died in America during the first winter).

✴ Hingham in Massachusetts was founded by Revd Robert Hobart, who was born in **Hingham**. Other settlers from the village included Samuel Lincoln, whose great-great-great-great-grandson was Abraham Lincoln, the 16th President of the United States.

✴ The first attempts to drain the Fens were made in 1630 by Francis, the fourth Earl of Bedford. He had a royal charter to turn the Fens into summer grazing and so hired Dutch engineer Sir Cornelius Vermuyden to work on the drainage. Work ground to a halt during the civil war, but in 1651 the first Denver Sluice was built across the River Ouse.

✴ During the English Civil War, Norfolk was mainly on the parliamentarian side and Norwich supplied Cromwell's Maiden Troop. Although no major civil war battles were fought in the county, there were two major incidents. The first was the siege at **King's Lynn** on 13 August 1643, when Sir Hamon le Strange declared support for the king. Parliamentary forces, under the leadership of the Duke of Manchester, blockaded the town. By September, Manchester had won West Lynn and bombarded the town across the river. In mid-September le Strange still refused to surrender, so Manchester simply cut the water supply and the rebels were forced to give in on 19 September. The other notable incident was the 'Great Blowe' of 1648 in **Norwich**, where the city thought that its much-loved royalist mayor would be taken to London and marched on Committee House (now the site of the Bethel Hospital), where the county arms were stored. When a shot from inside the building killed a boy in the crowd, the crowd stormed the building. Gunpowder had been spilled through Committee House and when it caught light 98 barrels of gunpowder went up. The explosion destroyed Committee House and blew out the windows of St Peter Mancroft Church, St Stephen's Church and many neighbouring houses: forty people were killed. After an investigation, 108 rioters were tried in the Guildhall on Christmas Day 1648. Twenty-six were fined, seven were imprisoned, two were whipped and eight were hanged in the castle ditches.

✳ Charles I's death warrant was allegedly signed at **Great Yarmouth** in the Nelson Room at Elizabethan House. Miles Corbett of **Sprowston,** the MP for Great Yarmouth, signed the warrant; in 1649 he was hanged at Tyburn for regicide.

✳ The plague hit Norfolk again in 1665; it was the last serious plague in Norwich. There was also a severe food shortage that summer, but it was relieved by herrings from **Great Yarmouth.**

✳ **King's Lynn** was still a flourishing port in Stuart times. It had the best system of inland navigation outside London, and in the 17th century Lynn imported more coal than any other port between Newcastle and London. However, the harbour began to silt up towards the end of the 17th century.

Norfolk in the 18th century

✳ Much land was enclosed during the 18th century: this meant fencing off 'common land' (which was actually owned by one person, but others had rights of grazing on it). In Norfolk more than 300 Enclosure Acts were passed, the third-largest number in England (after the West Riding of Yorkshire and Lincolnshire). More than 400,000 acres were enclosed in the 18th and 19th centuries – the majority between 1793 and 1815 – almost a third of the county.

✳ Roads were also turnpiked and improved in the 18th century. In the later years of the century stagecoaches were developed. They stopped at 'staging posts' where they could change their horses. The coaches tended to stick to the improved roads where they could travel at up to 10mph. Between 1766 and 1823, nine turnpike roads were made to Norwich. The city's mediaeval gates soon came to be seen as constricting trade, so they were demolished between 1791 and 1810 and the streets widened.

✳ Medicine in the county received a boost when the Norfolk and Norwich Hospital was opened in 1771 for the relief of the sick, the lame and the poor. Previously, the only hospitals between **Norwich** and London were at Shotesham and Bury St Edmunds. The first outpatient was treated at the hospital on 25 July 1771, and the first patient was admitted to the wards on 7 November 1771.

✳ The 18th century also saw the beginning of the financial services industry in **Norwich**. The first Norwich bank was opened in 1756 by Charles Weston; Gurney's bank was set up in 1775 and today is part of Barclays; and Norwich Union Fire Insurance Society was founded by Thomas Bignold in 1797. Its earliest known policy covered the house and shop of blacksmith Seth Wallace in **New Buckenham** in 1797. Their most expensive claim in the first seven years of the company was for £27 (the equivalent of nearly £2,000 today).

✳ In 1785 and 1786, the first records of aviation in the county come from reports of manned gas balloon flights made from Quantrell's Gardens (off St Stephen's Road) in **Norwich.**

✳ Olaudah Equiano, one of the earliest anti-slavery campaigners, wrote his autobiography about being kidnapped in Africa and made a slave at the age of 11. He stayed in **Norwich** for several months in 1794, and the eighth edition of his book was printed in the city.

Norfolk in the 19th century

✳ The 19th century was the peak of rabbit production in the county. The industry was concentrated in the Brecklands, where warrens had been set up 500 years earlier. Around 2,400 rabbits were sent each day to London. The skins were then sent to **Thetford** and Brandon where they were made into felt. The banks of the warrens were up to 2 metres high and were made of turf; one warren at Thetford had an 8-mile circumference.

✳ During the Napoleonic wars the authorities believed that there were more likely to be diversionary raids in Norfolk, rather than a huge invasion. **Weybourne** (because of its deep inshore waters) was considered the most likely place. **King's Lynn** was protected by St Annet's Fort, and the area between King's Lynn and **Hunstanton** was protected by the Wash. The plan was to flood the saltmarshes between Hunstanton and **Sheringham**. The town of **Cromer** had a small battery and so the cliff paths were destroyed. **Great Yarmouth** also had a harbour fort. After the war had ended all the coastal defences were disarmed and the river course changed, leaving St Annet's fort inland. The fort at Yarmouth was made unsafe by the river so it was demolished in 1833.

✳ The end of the Napoleonic wars meant unemployment, reduced wages for agricultural labourers and falling corn prices. The situation was compounded by the demands of church tithes (the equivalent of 10 per cent of the harvest, demanded in cash), increased mechanisation and failed harvests. Eventually, the economic situation led to the 'Captain Swing' riots and machine breaking of the early 1830s, with protests in around 150 parishes, including **East Tuddenham, Rougham, Haddiscoe** and **Swanton Abbot**. In **North Walsham** the magistrates issued a statement saying: '*It is their opinion* that such disturbances principally arise from the use of Threshing machines, and to the insufficient Wages of the Labourers. The Magistrates therefore beg to *recommend* to the Owners and Occupiers of Land in these Hundreds to *discontinue the use of Threshing machines, and to increase the Wages of Labour* to Ten Shillings a week for able bodied men, and that when task work is preferred, that it should be put out at such a rate as to enable an industrious man to earn Two Shillings per day.'

✳ In 1834, the Poor Law Amendment Act meant that the county was divided into poor law unions with a workhouse. The unions (with the name of the town/village containing the workhouse in brackets) were:

Aylsham (**Aylsham**)
Blofield (**Lingwood**)
Depwade (**Pulham St Mary** Magdalen)
Docking (**Docking**)
Downham Market (**Downham Market**)
East and West Flegg (**Rollesby** – the house, which is now a hotel, has an inscription over the door: 'For the Instruction of Youth, the Encouragement of Industry, the Relief of Want, the Support of Old Age, and the Comfort of Infirmity and Pain')
Erpingham (**West Beckham**)
Forehoe (**Wicklewood**)
Freebridge Lynn (**Gayton**)
Great Yarmouth (**Great Yarmouth**)
Guiltcross (**Kenninghall**)
Henstead (**Swainsthorpe**)
Loddon and Clavering (**Heckingham**)
Mitford and Launditch (**Gressenhall**)
Norwich (**Norwich**)
King's Lynn (**King's Lynn**)
St Faith's (**Horsham St Faith**)
Swaffham (**Swaffham**)
Thetford (**Thetford**)
Tunstead and Happing (**Smallburgh**)

Walsingham (**Great Snoring**)
Wayland (**Rockland**)

Some of these workhouses were new buildings erected specially for the purpose, but other unions used existing buildings. After the unions were abolished in 1929 some of the buildings became hospitals while others became private homes. The Gressenhall workhouse is used as a museum.

✳ Norfolk was one of the last English counties to embrace the railways. The first railway line built in Norfolk was the **Norwich** to **Yarmouth** line, which opened on 30 April 1844. It cost £10,000 per mile to build (the equivalent of just over three-quarters of a million pounds today). The line connected to the London-Brandon railway in July 1845, and the fastest train from Norwich to London took four and a half hours. Many of the smaller lines in the county were lost in the Beeching cuts of the 1960s, although some heritage lines have been brought back: the North Norfolk Railway travels between **Sheringham** and **Holt**; there's a narrow gauge railway between **Wells** and **Walsingham**; the Bure Valley Railway runs between **Aylsham** and **Wroxham**; and another service runs between **Wymondham** and **Dereham**. Some abandoned railway tracks have become foot and cycle paths, such as the Weaver's Way (from **Cromer** to **Great Yarmouth**) and Marriott's Way (from Norwich to Aylsham).

✳ The textile industry in Norfolk collapsed owing partly to cheap imports and partly to competition from Lancashire and Yorkshire, who had cheap coal at their disposal and could undercut Norfolk manufacturers. The industry was partly replaced by leather working and shoe manufacturing: in Norwich there were 220 firms making shoes or working leather by the mid-1800s.

✳ Brewing was also an important industry in Norwich. It's said that the city once had a pub for every day of the year, but there were far more than that – in 1845 there were 505 pubs. In 1836 there were 27 breweries, but the industry soon became dominated by a few large companies and the number fell to 12 in 1858 and seven in 1878. The largest brewer was Steward and Patterson, whose output was even bigger than any of the London firms.

✳ The first department store in **Norwich** was Jarrolds, which opened in London Street in 1840 with a business involving bookselling, printing and medicine.

✳ The manufacture of mustard, starch and indigo became important in the city. Colman's moved their business from **Stoke Holy Cross** to Carrow in 1856 and there were 2,500 employees by 1898.

✳ During the 19th century, as improvements were made to education, 64 new schools were built between 1816 and 1840.

Modern Norfolk

✳ The first black mayor in Britain was Dr Allan Glaisyer Minns, who was elected Mayor of **Thetford** in 1904. He was born in the Bahamas, trained at Guy's Hospital in London and became the medical officer for Thetford workhouse and Thetford cottage hospital.

✳ Norfolk was one of the first places bombed in air raids during World War One. On 19 January 1915 the first people to die in air raids in England were 72-year-old Martha Taylor and shoemaker Sam Smith in **Great Yarmouth**, and 14-year-old Percy Goate and 26-year-old widow Alice Gazeley in **King's Lynn**. Another Norfolk name to hit the headlines during the war was **Swardeston**-born nurse Edith Cavell, who was executed by the Germans in 1915 for helping prisoners escape from occupied Belgium to neutral Holland. Nearly 8,000 servicemen were admitted to the Norfolk and Norwich Hospital during the war, and the *Eastern Daily Press* Ward, funded by money raised by the newspaper, was opened in 1915 for 60 soldiers.

✳ Between the wars, sugar beet became a major crop in the county, and there was a move away from sheep farming to dairy farming.

✳ The shoe industry expanded rapidly. By 1931 nearly 11,000 people were employed in boot and shoe manufacture and in 1935 they produced six million pairs of shoes – an incredible 16 per cent of the British output.

✳ Norwich was particularly badly hit during World War Two. During the war there were 1,443 alerts (an average of one a day) and Norwich was raided 46 times. The worst raids were in 1942 when the Luftwaffe High Command decided to hit the places in Britain that were marked in *Baedeker's Guide* as having great historical significance. This was in reprisal for the assassination of Heydrich, Himmler's deputy, in Czechoslovakia. Norwich was one of the cities featured in Baedeker and the Baedeker raids would cause 60 per cent of deaths in Norwich due to air raids during the war.

On Monday 27 April 1942, during the course of two hours, the Luftwaffe dropped 185 bombs weighing a total of more than 50 tons. Two days later, 112 high explosive bombs and incendiaries weighing a total of 45 tons landed on the city. There was another serious raid on 27 June, during which bombers dropped around 850 incendiaries on the cathedral. The hospital was badly hit and the nurses' home, the main operating theatre and four wards were destroyed.

By the end of the war, 2,000 of the city's 35,000 houses had been completely destroyed, 2,600 had been seriously damaged and another 25,000 had had damage. The last siren sounded on 27 March 1945. The cost of repairs, according to the city engineers, was £1,060,000 – £280,000 of this was for materials and haulage. Repairs had to be made to 23,450 ceilings, 2,300 chimney stacks and 19,850 doors and window frames – and an incredible 610,000 feet of glass was used to replace shattered windows.

✳ Norfolk was home to many USAAF bases during the war, including Buckenham (where James Stewart was based) at **Old Buckenham, Wending, North Pickenham, Shipdham, Deopham Green, Snetterton, Tibenham, Thorpe Abbotts, Hardwick, Seething, Hethel** and **Rackheath**. Joint airfields with the RAF were at **Bodney, Watton, East Wretham, Fersfield, Attlebridge, Horsham St Faith's, Oulton, Foulsham** and **Sculthorpe**. Some of the airfields have been reused; Lotus Cars is at the former base at Hethel, and a racing circuit is at Snetterton.

✳ The first World War Two memorial to be erected in Britain was the cross at St Mary's Church, **Great Bircham**.

✳ In the 1950s agriculture was still an important part of the county's economy, but modern farming methods meant there was less employment.

✳ The 31 January 1953 saw what has been described as the worst peacetime disaster that Britain has ever known – a storm in which 307 people were killed, 32,000 people were evacuated and thousands of livestock were drowned. It was the greatest storm surge ever recorded in the North Sea, reaching 2.97 metres at **King's Lynn**, where over a fifth of the town was flooded. There were 80-foot waves at Mundesley, and the sea defences around the coastline couldn't cope. Fireman Fred Sadd in **Gorleston** was awarded the George Medal for his bravery during the rescues, and American serviceman Reis Leming from Washington State, who saved 27 lives in **Hunstanton**, was also awarded the George Medal.

✳ The University of East Anglia opened in 1963 and since then it has been the first university in the world to establish a Climatic Research Unit, the first UK university to offer a masters programme in creative writing (graduates of which include award-winning authors Ian McEwan and Kazuo Ishiguro) and has recently established the first new pharmacy programme in the UK for 30 years as well as a new medical school.

✳ Heritage has been developed in the county since the 1970s, including listed buildings and Sites of Special Scientific Interest (SSSIs). Special mention here should go to conservationist Wilhelmine (Billa) Harrod. She wrote the *Shell Guide to Norfolk* in 1957, a record of the county's heritage, and in 1970 she stepped in to save mediaeval churches in Norwich from being demolished. She was the founder of the Norfolk Society Committee for Country Churches, which became the Norfolk Churches Trust, and as a result of her determination, many churches in the county have been preserved.

✳ Gas and oil from the North Sea have played an important part in the region's economy in the second half of the 20th century. The gas terminal at Bacton is the largest gas terminal in the UK and receives gas from offshore fields, processes it and then transmits it to the National Tramission System for use throughout the UK. It connects to Belgium via the Interconnector gas pipeline, and to the Netherlands via the BBL pipeline. The Shell terminal takes gas from the SEAL (Shearwater Elgin Area Line) pipeline, which, at 474km long, is the longest pipeline on the UK continental shelf.

✳ In 2001, the Norwich Millennium Library and The Forum opened at a cost of £63 million.

✳ Norwich hosted the BA Festival of Science in September 2006 – one of Europe's biggest public science events – which included exhibitions, debates and hands-on experiments. Some of the issues explored included the impact of climate change, the development of families, medical research and the food of the future.

✳ In July 2007 Norwich joined the World League of Historical Cities – the first city in England to be admitted.

Chapter 3

The Coast and the Broads

The Coast

✳ The Norfolk coastline stretches for 90 miles, from **the Wash** in the north to **Hopton** on the Suffolk border in the south. Due to changes in sea level cliffs have eroded and dunes have moved, so it's possible that the coast of North Norfolk in Roman times was up to a mile further out to sea.

✳ Three-quarters of the coast in North Norfolk is designated as an Area of Outstanding Natural Beauty.

✳ In Roman times there were forts at **Caister** and **Burgh Castle** on opposite sides of an estuary that came within four miles of **Norwich**, and **Flegg** was an island.

Wells beach.

✳ The sea off the coast of **Cromer** was formerly a forest.

✳ Geographical historian Peter Murphy states that in Roman times the River Nar was tidal and there was a settlement on the **Terrington** silt beds.

✳ **The Wash** is the UK's largest natural embayment and it was known as *Metaris Aestuarium* in Roman times. It's a Special Protection Area bordering the North Norfolk coast. It's home to nearly 80 per cent of the country's English common seals, and is said to be the most important estuary for birds in the UK.

✳ Several barrier schemes for **The Wash** have been proposed. In 1949 and 1966 there were proposals for a barrier to form a freshwater reservoir and Europort; in 1972 there was a feasibility study regarding freshwater for rivers and improving navigation for sea locks; and in 2008 there were proposals to build a tidal barrier.

✳ One famous character associated with **The Wash** is King John. In October 1216 he was travelling towards Newark via Wisbech when his retinue and baggage train decided to take a short cut over the causeway crossing the Wellstream. It is not entirely clear what happened, either some of the train was stuck in the quicksand and held up the others, or perhaps they misjudged the time of the tide, but the whole train was lost – including all John's treasure – and is thought to lie somewhere between **Walpole Cross Keys** and Sutton Bridge just over the border in Lincolnshire. People have tried to find the treasure, including American treasure-hunters who paid local farmers 2s 6d an acre to help them search for it in the 1930s, but it remains lost.

✳ There's a rather odd saying about **Blakeney** in Vincent Stuckey Lean's *Collectanea* of proverbs (published posthumously in 1901):

> The Blakeney people
> Stand on the steeple
> And crack hazel-nuts
> With a five-farthing beetle.

✳ Back in the 1960s, there were secret plans to build a British rocket site – and **Brancaster** made the shortlist. In the first instance, it was reasonably close to the British space industry centres at Hatfield, Stevenage and London, and secondly, it was thought that the rockets would have a clear path across the North Sea. However, as each rocket would have shed at least two stages during the flight, the risk to the oil rigs in the North Sea was too great.

✳ **Caister** was developed as a new seaport in about AD 125, as it was the shortest sea crossing from the Rhine.

✳ The entire village of **Cley** moved in 1612 after a severe fire. It was embanked in the 1640s by Sir Henry Calthorpe, which ruined the harbour. In 1822 Thomas Telford was asked for his advice on the problem of silting in the Cley channel, but his advice was ignored and the channel eventually silted up.

✳ Jane Austen referenced **Cromer** in her novel *Emma*, 1816: 'You should have gone to Cromer, my dear, if you went anywhere. Dr Perry was a week at Cromer once, and he holds it to be the best of all sea-bathing places. A fine open sea, he says, and very pure air.' The bathhouse at Cromer was built in 1814, although bathing machines had been introduced in the 1790s. In the 1880s and 1890s writer Clement Scott dubbed the area around Cromer 'Poppyland'. And in 1724, Daniel Defoe, in *A Tour Thro' the Whole Island of Great Britain, divided into circuits or journeys, vol.1*, said of Cromer: 'A market town close to the shore of this dangerous coast. I know nothing it is famous for (besides it being thus the terror of the sailors) except good lobsters.'

✳ In 1605 the village of **Eccles** petitioned the king for funds to restore their church. The petition stated that after the storm the parish had been reduced in size from 2,000 acres to 300 acres, and only 14 houses were left out of the original 80.

✳ The rare Natterjack toad is found in the Norfolk Wildlife Trust reserve of **Holme** Dunes.

✳ There were once plans for a Butlins holiday camp at **Holme**.

✳ **Hunstanton** has the only chalk cliff in Norfolk and is also the only east coast resort that faces west. St Edmund's chapel – of which only a ruin remains – may have been a beacon originally. There is a legend that says Edmund was saved from drowning there and built the chapel in thanksgiving.

✳ Roger Le Strange was born in **Hunstanton** in 1616, brother of Hamon Le Strange who tried to capture King's Lynn for the royalists during the civil war. In 1663 he started publishing a weekly sheet, *The Public Intelligencer*. This was one of the earliest newspapers in the country, so Le Strange is also known as 'the father of the Newspaper Press'.

✳ There's a very obscure 17th-century prophecy about **Weybourne**: 'There shall come out of Denmark, a Duke, and he shall bring with him the King of Denmark and 16 great Lords in his company, by whose consent he shall be crowned King in a town of Northumberland, and he shall reign three months and odd days. They shall land at Waborne stone. They shall be met by the Red Deare, the Heath Cock, the Hound and the Harrow. Between Waborne and Branksburn [possibly Brancaster], a forest and a church gate, there shall be fought so mortal a battle, that from Branksburn to Cromer Bridge it shall run blood. There the King of Denmark shall be slaine, and all the perilous fishes in his company.'

✳ Another saying is that: 'He who would all England win, must at **Weyborne** Hope begin.' This is because there are deep inshore waters at Weyborne where troops and stores could easily be unloaded.

✳ King John gave **Great Yarmouth** a charter in 1207/08. Herrings were so important to the economy that the town's original coat of arms had three herrings on it; they were changed to lions in the 1300s. 1913 was a record year for herrings – over 1,200 million were caught.

✳ Dickens described **Great Yarmouth** as 'the Norfolk Gridiron' because of the way the town was laid out in rows. The passageways, which were between 2ft and 6ft wide, connected the town's three main north–south streets and expanded during the herring boom of the mid-1550s. The first written reference to Yarmouth's row houses was in 1198, and in 1598 Nash said there were 'seven score' rows. Most of them were destroyed during World War Two.

✳ **Great Yarmouth** was a leisure resort as well as an important port. A bathing house was set up in 1759, and at the Great Exhibition it was said that the town had 'long been celebrated for the great purity and bracing quality of the air.' The Pleasure Beach opened in 1887 and contains the world's oldest still-working wooden roller coaster, which was built in Paris in 1929 for the Colonial Exhibition and moved to Yarmouth in 1932. The earliest ride recorded at the Pleasure Beach was a 'Switchback', which was built in 1887. It was taken down and moved to Huddersfield in 1909.

✳ **Great Yarmouth** was involved in early communications advances; at one point there was signalling apparatus on the west tower of the south gate called the 'commercial telegraph', which sent signals to **Norwich**. In 1807 an order from the Admiralty office in London was received at Yarmouth in 17 minutes. In today's era of almost instant communication that seems like a huge wait, but in 1807 the post from Norwich to London went just once a day and the teams of horses needed to be changed frequently, with stops of 10-20 minutes at a time. Even in 1838, when the roads and carriage suspensions had been improved, the Royal Mail coach left Norwich at 4.30pm and reached London at 7am – 14 and a half hours after its departure.

✳ **Great Yarmouth's** town walls are among the best-preserved in the country.

✳ There was a training site on the beach at **Sea Palling** during World War Two.

✳ The cliffs at **Trimingham** are among the fastest-eroding clifflines in Britain and also contain some of the youngest chalk in the country.

✳ Sir William Wodehouse established a duck-catching device at **Waxham** in 1620, and the 18th-century historian Francis Blomefield has said he was the first person in England to build a decoy. Broads historian Tom Williamson believes that the decoys at **Acle** and **Hemsby** were built at around the same time, with the one at Flixton (which is shown on a map of 1653 and is probably the earliest representation of a duck decoy in England) being built about 30 years later. The word decoy comes from the Dutch 'eende-kooi' – literally, 'duck cage'. Decoys were curved, narrowing channels which were covered by netting supported by wooden or iron hoops. They were about 100 metres long, 20 metres wide at the mouth and gradually became narrower until they ended in a detachable net. Reed screens were built on one side of the channel and the lure worked by whistling tame ducks who would go into the decoy; meanwhile, a dog would run in and out of the screen to attract the attention of the ducks, who would go and investigate. As soon as they went into the decoy, the gamekeeper would leap up, wave his arms and scare them down to the narrow net at the end. Decoys died out in the mid to late-19th century as people's diet changed. Other decoys were built at **Sutton, Winterton, Woodbastwick, Ranworth, Westwick, Mautby, Buckenham, Reedham** and **Fritton.**

✳ Between **West Runton** and **Cromer** you may find paramoudra flints, or 'pot stones'. These are doughnut-shaped flint nodules with a core of chalk. Once the flints are exposed, the sea washes the chalk away and some of the holes left are big enough to put your arm through.

✳ At **Wiveton**, there's a cannon buried in the village green said to date from the Napoleonic Wars. Even older are the grooves in the church wall, which were made in the 16th and 17th centuries when ships used to throw their ropes over into the churchyard. Wiveton was once a thriving port but gradually the harbour silted up, leaving modern-day Wiveton about a mile from the sea.

The cannon on Wiveton Green.

The Broads

✣ The Broads National Park covers 303sq km of Norfolk and a small part of Suffolk. It's the country's largest nationally protected wetland and third-largest inland waterway. There are over 200km of navigable lock-free waterways, and the Broads are joined by the rivers Yare, Bure, Waveney, Thurne, Ant and Chet. There are 330km of paths and boardwalks within the Broads.

❊ It was once thought that the waterways were natural, but in 1952 Dr Joyce Lambert discovered that the Broads had been formed by peat diggings which were abandoned after severe flooding in the late 14th century. Most of the Broads have steep sides and are less than 3 metres in depth (Any deeper and the peat diggers would reach the water table, so the workings would be flooded).

❊ In 1960 C.T. Smith calculated that each family living in the Broads area needed to burn 8,000 peat turves a year for warmth and cooking; records show that 400,000 turves were burned every year to heat Norwich Cathedral Priory. Peat would also have been used for firing pottery and bricks at Potter Heigham, and to evaporate water in salt pans.

❊ After the peat workings flooded, the Broads were stocked with fish and water fowl. These, together with reeds, became the basis of the new industry in the Broads. Reeds were used for thatching. They were harvested with a scythe from a flat-bottomed marsh boat and, once cut, they were tied in bundles or 'shooves'. Reeds were sold by the fathom – which was equivalent to five shooves, or a bundle that was around 6ft in circumference.

❊ There are 41 broads. The largest is **Hickling** Broad, which covers 141 hectares. It's also the shallowest, with a maximum depth of 6ft, except in areas where dredging has taken place.

❊ The second-largest is **Barton** Broad, where it's said that Nelson learned to sail.

❊ There's a raptor watchpoint at Stubb Mill in **Hickling**. The best time to see the raptors (including marsh harriers and hen harries) is between October and March.

❊ A 'water frolic' (regatta) used to be held on **Hickling** Broad in Victorian times. In August 1822, thousands of fish died in the Broads from an unknown cause.

❊ Naturalist Ted Ellis called the Broads 'the breathing space for the cure of souls.' He established a nature reserve at Wheatfen, near **Surlingham**, and was also the Keeper of Natural History at the Castle Museum in **Norwich**.

❊ **Horsey** Mere is the only Norfolk Broad to be called a mere as it's surrounded by a high-level bank. The name 'mere' comes from Old Dutch, meaning 'artificial lake'. It's also the nearest broad to the sea.

✱ Arthur Ransome's novels *Coot Club* and *The Big Six* were set in the Broads; the Swan Inn at **Horning** is one of the line drawings at the beginning of *The Big Six*.

✱ The Norfolk hawker dragonfly (*Aeshna isosceles*) was thought to be extinct in the mid-1970s, but has made a comeback in the Broads. Other moths and butterflies found in the area include the leopard reed moth and white admiral butterfly, with one of the best places to see butterflies **Martham Broad. Upton** Broad is one of the UK's top 10 sites for seeing dragonflies (such as the Norfolk hawker, the hairy dragonfly and the variable damselfly), as well as the only home for the swallowtail butterfly (*Papilio machaon*), the UK's largest butterfly, which has a wingspan of up to 80mm.

✱ Some plants are only found at the Broads. There include the holly-leaved naiad at **Upton, Hickling** and **Martham**. Others, such as the intermediate stonewort and starry stonewort, are rarely found outside the Broads.

✱ Rare birds found at the Broads include the Cetti's Warbler and the Common Crane.

✱ The longest Broadland river is the River Yare, which travels 55 miles from **East Dereham** through **Norwich** to the sea.

✱ The Broads have had problems with blue-green algae in the summer, caused by nutrients entering the water. **Ormesby** Broad has been treated with biomanipulation methods to clear the water: this means the transference of fish so they don't eat the water fleas, the water fleas then eat the algae, which clears the water to allow plants to grow. Cages are also placed around growing water plants to stop the coots eating them until the plants have become established. Surveys from 2008 show that clear water is returning to the Broads, and water plants are being re-established – Crome's Broad at **How Hill** and **Hassingham** Broad have rare stonewort for the first time in decades.

A wherryman's list of the 48 reaches

✱ According to historian Walter Rye, writing in 1887, this is a wherryman's list of the reaches (or 'raches') between Breydon and Norwich:

1. Borrow [Burgh] Flats
2. Barney Arms
3. Fi' Mil' House
4. Tilekil Rache
5. Six Mil' Rond

6. Six Mil' House
7. Seven Mil' House
8. Bowlin' Alley
9. Eyht Mil' Trees
10. Reedham Town
11. Taylor's Rache
12. Reedham Ferry Rache
13. Hardley Cross
14. Cross Rache
15. Little Head
16. Darty Hole Rache
17. Devil's House Rache
18. Limpenhoe Rache
19. Cantley Red House
20. Cantley Rache
21. Under Langley
22. Langley Uppershot Rache
23. Langley Lowershot Rache
24. Hassingham Deke
25. Buckenham Rache
26. Buckenham Ferry
27. Buckenham Horseshoes
28. Ashentree Rache
29. Rockland Rache
30. Rockland Dig [Dyke]
31. Trane
32. Coldham Hall
33. Brundall Short Rache
34. Brundall Long Rache
35. Ditches Dele
36. Grace House [cart-grease factory]
37. Surlingham Ferry
38. Horse Shoe Rache
39. Six Mil' Staith Rache
40. Underhills, or Jimmy Norton's Rache
41. Bramerton's Woods End
42. Posick Rache
43. Posick Grove
44. Thorpe Short Rache
45. Whittingham Rache
46. Cave Rache
47. Thorpe
48. Cut

Other waterways

✳ The **Aylsham** Navigation, which ran for 15km between **Coltishall** and **Aylsham**, was established by an Act of Parliament in 1773. Building started the following year, and it opened in 1779. Along the route there were locks at **Horstead, Buxton** and **Burgh-next-Aylsham**. However, the competition from the railways in the 1880s meant that its use declined, and it was badly damaged by the floods of 1912.

✳ The **North Walsham** and **Dilham** Canal was set up by an Act of Parliament in 1812 to connect **North Walsham** with **Barton** Broad, but it wasn't started until 1825 after local opposition. The canal was built in a year; it was 14km long with six locks which, at 3.75 metres wide, were larger than conventional locks so that the wherries could use them. As with the Aylsham waterway, the canal was affected by the development of the railways. In 1886 it was sold to Edward Press, a miller in North Walsham, to develop for pleasure boating. However, there was a silting problem, made worse by the floods of 1912. He couldn't afford to maintain the canal, so the northern section was closed in 1892. The last commercial wherry stopped using it in 1934, and the whole canal was finally closed in 1935.

✳ **Waxham** New Cut ran for 6km from **Horsey** Mere to Lound Bridge. The cut was dug in the 1820s and had no locks. It was closed in 1953 after the drainage system in Brograve Level was changed.

✳ The New Cut was completed in 1832, and ran for 4km from **St Olaves** to **Reedham**. The idea was that Norwich merchants would have direct access to a harbour at Lowestoft. Before that, the harbour at **Great Yarmouth** was used and the cargo had to be moved from sea ships to keels and wherries which had shallow bottoms. The bill was defeated in 1826 but a revised bill was passed in 1827, and in September 1833 the mayor of Norwich welcomed the first boats from the sea through New Cut to the city. However, the cut was too narrow and as the ships grew larger the system became bankrupt by 1847. Sir Morton Peto bailed it out, but the cut was badly damaged by the 1953 floods and is now used only by pleasure boats.

✳ Ferries were set up where the river was too wide or deep for a ford or bridge. These included at **Surlingham, Buckenham, Brundall, Horning** and **Stokesby**. Although these are no longer running today, the ferries at **Reedham** and **Martham** are still going.

Floods

There have been many recorded floods on the Norfolk coast and the Broads, but some of the worst include:

✳ 12 November 1236, which chronicler Matthew Paris records 'deprived all ports of ships, tearing away their anchors, drowned a multitude of men, destroyed flocks of sheep and herds of cattle, plucked out trees by the roots, overturned dwellings [and] dispersed beaches.'

✳ 1 October 1250, when there was a major storm affecting the North Sea coastline with much flooding.

✳ 31 December 1278: according to the chroniclers Holinshed and Matthew of Westminster, the sea flowed over the land 'three or four leagues in breadth' from Yarmouth to the Humber and drowned cattle and knocked over buildings.

✳ 23 January 1362, known as 'the great drowning' or the 'grote mandrenke'. It's thought that 30,000 people died on the North Sea coast and is one of the most devastating storms recorded in England's history. The chronicler Holinshed calls it 'such a passing wind that the like had not been heard of in many years before.'

✳ 11 November 1570, where a huge storm caused much flooding at the coast.

✳ 1608, when there was a tidal flood on the Broads from Lammas to Trowse. According to historian Francis Blomefield, it took 2,000 people to mend the defences.

✳ December 1740, when a storm surge drove water many miles inland and did much damage to the cliffs.

✳ 31 January 1953 – see page 44.

✳ 12 January 1978, when there was a huge tidal surge (even larger than that of 1953). Although the sea defences held, the tides were strong enough to wash the 300-ton coaster *Function* on to the quay at Wells.

Lighthouses

✳ The original lighthouse at **Cromer** was built in 1680 by Sir John Clayton, but he couldn't afford to light fires as the ship-owners refused to pay their dues. The church tower was used as a beacon, and in the meantime the lighthouse was shown on maps as an unlit beacon or seamark. Nathaniel Life obtained a patent for the beacon from Trinity House in 1719 and charged dues of ¼ penny per ton of cargo and ½ penny per chaldron (a measure equivalent to 25 tons) of coal. Trinity House fitted a flashing light there in 1792, but there were landslips in 1799 which damaged the lighthouse and it was finally destroyed in 1866. The present lighthouse – a white octagonal tower – dates from 1833. It was converted to electric operation in 1958 and to automatic operation in June 1990. The lamp has an intensity of 294,000 candela and can be seen for 23 nautical miles.

✳ The lighthouse at **Gorleston** was built in 1878 and has two lights; there's a fixed red light, plus a white flashing light for the harbour entrance.

✳ The lighthouse at **Happisburgh** dates from 1791 and was originally one of a pair. The one still visible is the High Light. The other lighthouse, the Low Light, was on the cliff top and was taken out of service and demolished in 1883. Both were originally lit by candles,

Happisburgh lighthouse.

but in 1865 the lighthouse was converted to gas power. The gas was made on the premises from coal and stored behind the lighthouse. Paraffin replaced the gas light in 1910, and was itself replaced by electricity in 1947. The lighthouse was painted with three red bands in 1884 to distinguish it from **Winterton** lighthouse. It's the oldest working light in Norfolk and is the only independently operated lighthouse in the UK. There are 96 steps up to the light at the top, which is 134ft above sea level.

✳ The lighthouse at **Hunstanton** dates from 1844 but the first lighthouse was built there in 1666. It was decommissioned in 1921 and is now used as a holiday home.

✳ The lighthouse at **Winterton** was originally established in 1616, but the current lighthouse dates from the 1840s.

Piers

✳ The earlier recorded pier at **Cromer** was in 1390, when Richard II allowed the town to tax incoming cargo to pay for it. The first pier built in the current location was 64 metres long. It was built in 1821 and destroyed by a storm 21 years later. It was replaced by another pier, this time 73 metres long, but this was destroyed by a collision with a coal boat in 1897. The current pier, which is 136 metres long, was built in 1900, and cost £17,000. Its pavilion floor was replaced by maple in 1908 so it could be used for roller-skating. In 1923, when the lifeboat station was built, the pier extended to 151 metres. However, it was badly damaged in a series of storms in 1949, 1953, 1976 and 1978. In 1990 the amusement arcade was destroyed by a storm and has never been replaced. In 1993 a 100-ton rig collided with the pier but it was successfully repaired.

✳ **Great Yarmouth** has three piers. Jetty Pier, first built in 1560, is also known as 'Nelson's Jetty', because he landed there after his victory at the Battle of Copenhagen. Wellington Pier was opened in 1853 and was only the seventh pier to be built in the country. Britannia Pier has had a much more chequered history. It was built in 1858, but was cut in half a year later by a schooner and was replaced by a wood and steel construction 810ft long with a pavilion. The pavilion burned down in 1909; it was reopened in 1910, but burned down once again in 1914. The ballroom was opened in 1928, but that too burned down in 1932 and was rebuilt the following year. Another fire destroyed the pier in 1954; it was rebuilt and opened in 1958.

✴ **Hunstanton**'s 830ft pier was built in 1870, but was badly damaged in 1939 and in the 1950s. Most of the pier was finally swept away in 1978, and the remainder was destroyed by fire in 2002.

Fishermen's lore

✴ According to fishermen's lore, you can see the outlines of a drifter's deck on a herring's head, a picture of a fishing boat with its masts lowered on a herring's cheeks and the mesh of a fishing net in a herring's scales.

✴ In a shoal of herring there is a 'king' who leads it and has bright red fins. If it's caught, it's returned to the sea alive after it's been 'passed round the scudding-pole as any times as the fishermen desire to get lasts of herrings at their next haul.'

✴ A 'herring plaster' used to be prescribed for fever, and in the 1750s cattle suffering from murrain were fed a medicine of herring steeped in tar.

Unusual visitors

✴ On 8 June 1891 a rorqual whale was caught at **Gorleston**. It was 30ft long, with an 8ft girth. Once it was stuffed, the whale went on tour around the country.

✴ In **Blakeney** harbour, in April 1849, it was reported that four or five grampuses swam up the channel. However, when the tide ebbed they were trapped. Fortunately, once the tide rose again they were able to make their way back to the open sea.

✴ A whale was stranded at **Holme** on 6 December 1626. Eighteenth-century historian Francis Blomefield has stated that it was 57ft long and had 46 teeth in its lower jaw 'like the tusks of an elephant'. Whales have sadly also been stranded at **Ostend** in June 2002, **King's Lynn** in January 2003, **Stiffkey** in April 2003 and at **Brancaster** in February 2006.

✴ In August 1936 a group of six people, including an MP, claimed to see a sea monster at **Eccles**. The monster was 12 metres long, moved like a worm and was travelling at speeds of up to 90mph.

✴ In **Great Yarmouth**, rather than raining cats and dogs, it has been known to rain fish! On 6 August 2000 there was a shower of dead sprats – they'd been collected by a tornado from the North Sea and were then dumped on the town.

Famous mariners

Obviously the most famous naval hero from the county (and the country) is Horatio Nelson. I'm leaving him out of the Miscellany simply because so much is known about him. Instead, here are stories of other mariners from our county who have had a huge impact on navigation, as well as more humble sailors who found themselves in the middle of national events.

Thomas Allison, Arctic navigator

Thomas Allison was baptised in **Great Yarmouth** in 1647. He was employed by the Russia Company, which traded between London and the Archangel (on the White Sea). When he and his crew were blown off course in 1697 and forced to spend the winter in the Arctic, he kept a diary, which was published in 1699. It's one of the earliest English accounts of life in the Arctic.

On this particular trip, Allison left Archangel on the ship *Ann* in October 1697. The ship was damaged in a storm and they found safe anchor in Porsanger Fjord. His diary talks about the difficulty of keeping the crew of 24 healthy and cheerful. They were able to take shelter in the ship and scavenge for firewood from among the larches and willows in the fjord, but food supplies were a problem and they had to forage for scallops, shellfish and sea urchins below the ice on the sea. The temperatures were extremely cold and Allison recorded on 1 February 1698 that, as he wrote, a boy had to thaw the ink before he could put his pen back in the ink. Several of his men suffered from severe frostbite and the ship's surgeon, William Brown, had to carry out amputations.

At Christmas, Allison gave the crew extra beer and honey from his own stores so they could make a mead-like drink. In January and February there were several thaws – but before they could leave the sea froze again. In February they all had to go on reduced rations, and Allison made sure his men knew that he was joining them to keep their morale high. Finally, in March, a yawl arrived from North Cape with provisions, and on 25 March 1698 the crew of the *Ann* were able to sail back to England. They arrived on 24 April at Gravesend, having survived an arctic winter and losing only one member of the crew.

The journal is fascinating. In November Allison talks of sending men out on an expedition, where they discovered prints of deer, bears, wolves and foxes. His crew brought back three foxes to cook and eat (one of whom escaped and 'thieved' their beef stores), and as rations were short Allison tried it. He said that the cooked flesh looked black, like a hare, but he loathed the taste: 'I liked no such rank venison.' Later in the month, one of the crew complained of sore feet and the surgeon realised that the man had frostbite up to his ankles; he managed to make the man well again in only 10 days.

In December Allison saw the northern lights, which he called the northern lance: 'a stream of light enlightening all the hemisphere, so as one may read very well with it. 'Tis of a pale yellow or buff colour, like the inmost circle of the rainbow, appearing for a quarter of an hour, then vanishing and renewing itself again, by intervals during the space of five or six hours.' He believed that it was caused by frost, and also said that occasionally the lights looked like two clouds – and when they 'rushed together' it was possible to hear a sound like thunder. On 20 December he recorded that they only had four and a half hours of daylight.

The journal also gives a fascinating insight into the food they survived on. As well as the shellfish they managed to dredge with some bent iron, the crew also ate sea urchins (which Allison calls 'sea eggs') and 'dills', which Allison described as 'dark brown weeds, growing and hanging upon the rocks' and were used 'as a salad' to eat with beef. He even described the preparation: the cook boiled them first to get rid of the saltiness and then boiled them in beef broth.

Allison's will was proved in 1706, and his journal was republished in 1808. Sadly, few people today remember the Norfolk sailor who navigated the Arctic more than 300 years ago.

Henry Blogg, lifeboatman extraordinaire

Henry Blogg is the most-decorated lifeboatman ever – an extraordinarily brave man. It's been said that 'he knew what his boat could do and, as nearly as a man may, what the sea could do.'

He was born in **Cromer** in 1876 and educated at Goldsmith's School, where he was found to be a fast learner with an excellent memory and was soon top of the class. He left school at the age of 11 to join the family crab fishing business, despite the fact that he never learned to swim – which makes his career in lifeboats even more amazing.

His stepfather John was the coxswain of the Cromer lifeboat, and Blogg joined the crew in 1894 at the age of 18. He was voted second coxswain in 1902 when John retired, and unanimously elected coxswain seven years later. During his 53 years of service he launched the boat 387 times and helped save an incredible 873 lives. He was awarded the Royal National Lifeboat Institution's (RNLI) gold medal three times. The first was in 1917 for rescuing

Bust of Henry Blogg.

11 men from the steamer *Fernebo* under extremely difficult conditions: at first, the seas were so rough that the lifeboat couldn't be launched, and when it finally was it was hit by a wave which took out half the oars. Blogg refused to give up and succeeded at the third attempt – an incredible achievement, given that his crew had already rescued another vessel before the *Fernebo*, and had had to row out 350 metres through a gale (despite the average age of the crew being over 50). When the rescue ended they'd been out for almost 24 hours. His second gold medal was in 1927 for rescuing 15 men from the tanker *Georgia* on Haisboro Sands after 20 hours at sea (and his crew were each awarded a silver watch). The third was in 1941 for rescuing 88 men from a convoy of six ships. He was also awarded the British Empire Medal for his bravery in the rescue.

Blogg was also awarded four silver medals from the RNLI. The first was for rescuing 30 men and a Tyrolean sheepdog from the steamer *Monte Nevoso* in 1932 – the crew were out for a staggering 52 hours. The second was in 1933 when he rescued two men from the barge *Sepoy*, a journey which he later described as his worst in 24 years of being a coxswain; he had ended up having to drive the lifeboat over the deck of the barge to rescue the crew. The third silver medal was awarded in 1939 for rescuing 29 men from the Greek steamer *Mount Ida*. The fourth, in 1941, was one of the most dramatic: on the way to rescuing 44 men from the steamer *English Trader*, five of the lifeboatmen, including Blogg, were thrown into the water, and one later died. The Canine Defence League awarded him a silver medal for the *Monte Nevoso* rescue, and the ship's captain allowed Blogg to keep the dog, whom he called Monte. He was also awarded the Empire Gallantry Medal in 1924 and the George Cross in 1941. He finally retired in 1947 at the age of 71, 11 years after the normal age of retirement. The crew insisted on naming their new lifeboat after him in 1948.

Blogg was a reticent and kindly man who didn't boast about his incredible achievements. His crew trusted him completely – he made quick decisions, his judgement was spot on and if he was scared he never, ever showed it.

He died in 1954, and a museum dedicated to his memory was opened in Cromer in 2006. It was the first purpose-built RNLI museum to be opened in almost 70 years.

George Manby, inventor and lifesaver

George Manby was born near **Downham Market** in 1765, the son of a captain in the Royal Welsh Fusiliers. He went to school in Downham Market (where he claimed to have been friends with Nelson) and Kent, and then on to the Royal Military Academy in Woolwich.

In 1802 he moved to Bristol and wrote books on history and topography. The following year he wrote a book about the threatened invasion of England by Napoleon. When the secretary of war read it he decided to appoint him the barrack-master at **Great Yarmouth**. On 18 February 1807 Manby saw the gunship *Snipe* run aground during a storm only 60 yards off the coast of Great Yarmouth; 214 drowned, including women, children and prisoners, and he became convinced that something could be done to prevent such a disaster in the future. The event impelled him to invent the Manby Mortar, which fired a thin rope from the shore into the rigging of a ship in distress, this was then used to pull a thicker one to the ship. It was then possible to bring people safely to dry land using a 'breeches buoy'. This was a kind of canvas bucket with two holes in it, hanging from a cork float. You sat in it with your legs through the two holes and the cork float kept your head above water in rough waves.

Manby was able to get the line to move evenly without breaking under the strain or being burned by the mortar, and could fire it for 200 yards. In February 1808 the ship *Elizabeth* was stranded 150 yards from the shore at Yarmouth, and Manby was able to use his invention to save the crew of seven.

In 1814, the government planned to build 1,000 mortar stations around the country, but in practice only 45 were built and most of them were in Norfolk. By 1823 the mortar had saved 229 lives, so he petitioned the House of Commons for a reward; the committee recommended a reward of £2,000 but it never materialised. He was given a gold medal by France for the mortar in 1828, and Queen Victoria gave him the Coronation Medal after he sent her pictures of rescues using his device. However, he never got the recognition he felt he deserved. In 1842, after he retired, he built his own monument in his front garden in **Gorleston**, showing the Manby Mortar in use.

Manby invented an unsinkable ship with buoyancy tanks, but the Lowestoft boatmen feared that it would harm their living from the cargo of shipwrecks. They also disliked Manby, so during tests they rocked the ship to make sure it overturned. Manby was one of the passengers thrown into the water, and, although he couldn't swim and admitted that he was afraid of water, they left him to make his own way back to shore. In 1813 he invented the first portable pressurised fire extinguisher – the *Extincteur* – a copper vessel filled with potassium carbonate and compressed air.

He died in Gorleston in 1854 and was buried at All Saint's Church, **Hilgay**. There's an interesting tablet in the church – the last line is in a slightly different script and betrays Manby's own bitterness:

> In the churchyard near this spot
> rest the bones of
> George William Manby Capt-F.R.S.
> A name to be remembered as long as there can be
> a stranded ship
> He died Novr 18, 1854,
> aged 88 years

Out of his eight brothers and sisters
the large marble stone also recorded the deaths
of Mary Jane August 3rd 1772 aged 10 years
John May 20th 1783 aged 11
and of two infants

The public should have paid this tribute

His original mortar is in the Tide and Time Museum in Great Yarmouth, and he bequeathed his collection of Nelson memorabilia to the **King's Lynn** Museum.

Sir Cloudesley Shovell, commander-in-chief of the British fleet

Cloudesley Shovell was baptised on 25 November 1650 at **Cockthorpe**, the son of John and Anne Shovell. His unusual first name was the family name of his maternal grandmother. His father died when Shovell was four, and his mother married John Flaxman five years later. Shovell went to sea at a young age and was cabin boy and servant to Sir Christopher Myngs in the West Indies in 1663. He was incredibly brave in the face of danger and legend has it that he used to swim between ships under fire from the enemy, carrying his admiral's dispatches in his mouth. He also studied navigation, and his abilities were soon noticed. He was quickly promoted under the service of Sir John Narborough, becoming midshipman in 1672, master's mate and then second lieutenant in 1673.

At Tripoli in 1676, as lieutenant, he commanded the boats that burned four men-o'-war pirate ships. As a reward he was given 80 pieces of eight and a medal worth £100 from Charles II. In 1689 he was captain of the *Edgar* at the battle of Bantry Bay and was knighted for his part in the victory. He spent the next few years alternately fighting France and escorting William III across the Channel. In 1704 he was instrumental in capturing Gibraltar. In the same year he was named rear admiral of England and then commander-in-chief of the British fleet.

The 18th-century spy and writer John Macky wrote of Shovell:

> No man understands the Affairs of the Navy better, or is beloved of the Sailors so well as he. He loves the *Constitution* of his *Country* and serves it without *factious aim*; he… proves a very grateful Husband… hath very good Natural Parts; familiar and plain in his Conversation; dresses without affectation; is a very large, fat, fair Man.

However, in November 1707 (according to the modern calendar) Shovell was returning from an unsuccessful attempt to besiege the French at Toulon when he lost his bearings. He commanded his ships to continue in fleet formation. At 8p.m. it was dark and rainy, and when he saw the St Agnes light it was too late to do anything. His ship hit rocks off the Scilly Isles and sank quickly, as did three other ships; there was only one survivor from the 2,000 men on-board the four ships.

Shovell's body was found the next day at Porth Hellick Cove, along with the bodies of his two stepsons and his pet greyhound. It was a huge national disaster and the whole of England mourned for him. Queen Anne paid for him to be embalmed and lie in state at his home in Soho. He was buried in Westminster Abbey in December 1707, though there is also a monument to him in the church at Cockthorpe. John Molesworth wrote of him: 'He is universally regretted for his courage, capacity, and honesty, which it will be hard to parallel in another commander.'

A horrible legend of the disaster began in the 1730s when it was claimed that a woman on her deathbed had confessed that she had found Shovell alive on the beach. She had wanted his emerald ring, so had smothered him in the sand, but had then felt too guilty to sell the ring. She asked the priest to send the ring to his heirs. A ring answering that description was certainly around in 1879, but it hasn't been seen since.

It was thought that Shovell's ships perished due to an error with longitude. However, since then experts have said there was as much of a problem with his latitude co-ordinates. As a result of Shovell's death the Longitude Act was passed in 1714 and a prize was offered to anyone who could find a way of measuring longitude accurately at sea. Eventually the problem was solved by John Harrison, which led to the development of marine chronometers.

Robert Tinkler, cabin boy on the *Bounty*

Seventeen-year-old Robert Tinkler, born at **Wells**, was an able seaman on-board the HMS *Bounty*. Bligh, Captain of the ship, referred to him as 'boy', but everyone else on-board referred to him as 'Mr Tinkler'. He ate in the officer's mess, so it's likely that he was in training to be a midshipman. His brother-in-law John Fryer was the sailing master on the ship.

During the mutiny led by Fletcher Christian in 1789 – which protested against Bligh's manipulation of the food rations and tyrannical behaviour – Tinkler was turned adrift by the mutineers in the ship's 23ft-long launch, along with Bligh and 17 others. Luckily, Christian had given Bligh a quadrant and a compass. Although the food ration was meagre (one ounce of bread and a quarter of a pint of water a day) Bligh was able to navigate the 3,600 miles to the island of Timor.

Tinkler was away from England during the mutineers' trial, so he wasn't asked to give evidence. He was promoted to lieutenant on the *Isis*, he fought at Copenhagen in 1801 and was promoted to lieutenant commander after the battle. He died in **Norwich** in 1820, at the age of 46, and was buried in the churchyard at Wells.

George Vancouver, naval officer and hydrographer

George Vancouver was born in **King's Lynn** on 22 June 1757. In 1771, at the age of 14, he was a midshipman sailing with Captain Cook on the second voyage of the *Resolution* to the South Pacific, the Antarctic and the South Atlantic. The expedition's astronomer, William Wales, trained him in astronomical observation, surveying and drawing. Vancouver later named a point on the British Columbia coast after Wales and wrote in his journal that it was because of Wales that he was able 'to traverse and delineate these lonely regions.'

Vancouver was also on the third voyage of the *Resolution* to Sandwich Islands (now the Hawaiian Islands) where Cook was killed.

In 1791 he was sent to explore and survey the Sandwich Islands and the North West coast of America, leading the longest mapping expedition in history. Over the next four and a half years Vancouver and his crew in the *Discovery* and the *Chatham* sailed about 105,000 kilometres. They mapped every single inlet and outlet, mainly from small boats launched from the main ships to avoid the dangers of piloting sailing ships into uncharted waters.

Despite the danger, sickness and hardships that his voyages entailed, Vancouver followed Cook's example in taking care of his men and lost only six of his 180 crew members – one from disease, one from poison and four from drowning.

He mapped the North American west coast from northern Mexico to southern Alaska. His mapping was very accurate and his maps of British Columbia and Alaska were used well into the 19th century. He chose around 150 American and Canadian place names, many of them reflecting places in Norfolk, and they're still used today. Vancouver Island was named after him, as were the cities of Vancouver in Washington and British Columbia and the Hudson Bay Company's Fort Vancouver.

However, his achievements didn't get the recognition they deserved. He sent midshipman Thomas Pitt back to England in 1794 as he was disruptive and dangerous and Pitt never forgave him. Pitt challenged Vancouver to a duel on his return and maligned him in the papers. When Pitt accidentally met Vancouver in London he tried to assault Vancouver and was bound over to keep the peace. Even so, Pitt continued to harass Vancouver as much as he could and Vancouver's career was effectively at an end.

Vancouver fell ill and retired to Petersham, near Richmond. The Admiralty asked him to prepare his journal for publication; he did so, with the help of his brother John, but died aged only 40 and with 100 pages left to complete. (The published journal was a incredible half a million words in length). He was buried at Petersham, and each year a wreath from the mayor and council of the city of Vancouver is laid on his grave. He is remembered today with a statue in his home town of King's Lynn. The 250th anniversary of his birth was celebrated at the Vancouver Maritime Museum in 2007.

Chapter 4

Churches and Cathedrals

Norfolk is an incredibly rich county when it comes to mediaeval churches. There are 659 surviving mediaeval churches, more than any other county in England (in fact, more than anywhere else in Europe north of the Alps), so by necessity this chapter can only touch on a few of these treasures.

The *Domesday Book* was an inventory of property and so didn't catalogue all the churches: only 243 of the churches in Norfolk were listed. The Norwich Valuation of 1254 lists 818 churches, though there are some missing. H. Monro Cautley, writing in 1949, said that Norfolk has 659 churches built before 1700, 65 that are either new or complete rebuildings since then and 245 ruins, giving a total of 969 churches. He added that as well as having more churches than any other county, Norfolk also has a greater density of them: on average, there's one church per 1,850 acres.

Round-tower churches

✱ Churches with round towers are peculiar to Norfolk and Suffolk. Norfolk is particularly rich in them – there are 123 still standing, 11 in ruins and 10 that have been lost. Most are in the south and east of the county. The smallest round tower (with a diameter of 10ft) is at St Swithin's church, **Ashmanhaugh**, while the oldest is thought to be St Andrew's at **East Lexham**, dating from around AD 900. One of the most unusual is the cruciform church of St Andrew in **Great Ryburgh**.

Why are the towers round rather than square? One theory is that because there's no real source of stone in Norfolk and the churches were built from flints, it was easier to build round rather than square towers. Architects dispute this; H. Monro Cautley has said that technically neither is more difficult than the other and he believes that the round towers were originally built for defence and the church was tacked on. Another theory is that the towers were originally wells and the ground was washed away around them. Although our coast has a real problem with erosion, this rather fanciful theory doesn't explain the round towers found inland. Yet another theory is that the churches were influenced by those built in Schleswig-Holstein. The late W.J. Goode, the founder and former president of the Round Tower Churches Society, has a theory that the towers were originally bell towers, built after King Athelstan's law of 937 decreed that all thegns (local leaders) needed to have a bell tower on their land.

St Margaret's Church, Hales.

Thatched roofs

✳ H. Monro Cautley has said that in the 19th century over 300 churches in Norfolk had thatched roofs – more than any other county in England. Over the years, thatch has been replaced by other materials, so in the 21st century there are just 43 left – including **Acle, Banningham, Beachamwell, Coltishall, Drayton, Filby, Hales, Mautby, Potter Heigham, Ranworth** and **Thurgarton.**

Dedications

✳ The most common dedication within the mediaeval churches of Norfolk is to St Mary: there are 147 of them altogether. There are another 11 dedicated to the Blessed Virgin, four to her Assumption and one to her Nativity, plus several pairings. They include All Saints (**Little Melton** and **Sculthorpe**), St Andrew (**Horsham St Faith** and **Langham**), St Botolph (**Hevingham**), St Margaret (**Sprowston**), St Thomas of Canterbury (**Wymondham**) and St Walstan (**Bawburgh**).

The next most common dedication is to All Saints (133), followed by St Andrew (78), St Peter (65) and St Margaret (48). Surprisingly, local saints don't have much of a following – St Edmund has 17 churches dedicated to him, St Walstan only one (in **Bawburgh**, at the site of his well) and St Withburga likewise just one (surprisingly at **Holkham**, rather than at the site of her well in **East Dereham**).

There are also some dedications found nowhere else in England: St Wandregesilius at **Bixley** (he was a seventh-century abbot in Fontanella, Normandy); St Protase and St Gervase at **Little Plumstead**; and St Fabian and St Sebastian at **Woodbastwick**. Other dedications that appear only once in the county include St Augustine (**Norwich**), St Cecilia (**West Bilney** – and there are only three with this dedication in England), St Felix (**Babingley**), St Germaine (**Wiggenhall St Germans**), St John the Baptist's head (**Trimingham** – and apparently it really was to his head!), St Julian (**Norwich**), St Matthias (**Thorpe-next-Haddiscoe**), St Simon and St Jude (**Norwich**), St Stephen (**Norwich**), St Theobald (**Great Hautbois**) and The Holy Innocents (**Foulsham**).

Churches great and small

✳ The largest parish church in Norfolk is St Nicholas's Church, **Great Yarmouth**. At 23,000sq ft, it's also the largest parish church in the country. Its aisles, at 39ft, are the widest in England.

✳ The smallest parish church still in use in Norfolk is All Saints' Church, **Keswick**.

✳ The church with the tallest tower in the county (and also in the whole of East Anglia) is St Peter and St Paul's Church, **Cromer**, at 160ft high.

✳ The first church built in Norfolk was said to be in AD 631 at **Babingley**, dedicated to its founder St Felix. However, the church that stands on the site dates from the 14th century. The oldest surviving church is probably St Andrew's church at **East Lexham**, near **Swaffham**, built around AD 900.

✳ The church with the oldest wall paintings is St Mary's Church at **Houghton on the Hill**. The paintings are thought to date from 1090, and include the oldest depiction in Europe of Christ on the Cross before an enthroned God.

✳ What's thought to be the oldest parish chest in England, dating from Norman times, is in St Martin's church, **Hindringham**.

✳ According to ecclesiastical expert D.P. Mortlock, St Mary's Church in **Denton** has more sets of royal arms than any other church in Norfolk: Victoria's arms in stone, George III's painted on boards, plus Tudor and Stuart arms in the east window.

✻ St Mary's Church, **Kenninghall,** has a rare set of royal arms belonging to Elizabeth I, which include a spotted dragon.

✻ Even rarer is the treasure at St Catherine's Church, **Ludham:** an original rood, which had been blocked into the rood loft stairs and was rediscovered in 1879. The other side of the canvas has a set of royal arms.

✻ The most unusual church in the county has to be St Michael and All Angels' Church at **Booton.** It was designed by the Revd Whitwell Elwin and includes copies of features from many different churches, such as the west doorway from Glastonbury Abbey, as well as unusual twin towers designed by Elwin himself. The angels in the roof were carved by James Minns, who also carved the bull's head for Colman's trademark. According to John Betjeman, the carpenter usually specialised in making figureheads for boats. Given how large the angels are, that's easy to believe; and the St Michael above the door is seriously scary!

✻ The most unusual-shaped tower belongs to St Mary's Church, **Burgh St Peter,** and is a pile of telescoping brick boxes. It was the work of rector Samuel Boycott, who obtained a faculty to repair the steeple in 1793. His family gave their name to the expression 'boycott', after Samuel's grandson, Charles, became a land agent in Ireland and tried to enforce rent rises for an absentee landlord. Everyone refused to speak to him or his family, nor would they work for him or sell goods to him.

✻ St Mary's Church, **Happisburgh,** has seen one of the largest number of people baptised at the same time. The Revd Thomas Lloyd believed that so few of the local children were baptised because their parents couldn't afford to host the usual party afterwards. He offered to host the party himself, and on Whit Sunday 1793 he baptised 170 people; the story is commemorated on the village sign. St Mary's also has a very tall tower, at 110ft, which was used as a seamark. It was bombed in 1940 and repaired in 1956–58.

✻ **Norwich** Cathedral is set in one of the largest cathedral closes in England. It has the second highest spire in the country, at 315ft (as well as the tallest Norman tower), and the most complete mediaeval cloisters in the country. In the roof of the nave there are 339 stone bosses, 225 of which tell Biblical stories from the Creation to the Last Judgement; in total, the cathedral has over a thousand bosses. It also contains some of the earliest furnishings in the country, for example the bishop's throne. The timber section is made from former roof timbers and was carved in 1974, but it also includes two stone fragments from the seventh century.

✳ St Giles' Church, **Norwich,** has the tallest parish church tower in Norwich, at 120ft high (including the cupola). A beacon was installed on the top of the tower in 1549, and the original cage for the beacon fire is now on display in the church.

✳ The oldest round tower in inner **Norwich** is at the Church of St Mary Coslany. The church also contains an inscription in Norman French, dated 1298, which says, '*I Tomas de Lingcole a done a cet auter sirge e un liape e la rente de Colegate*' (Thomas de Lingcole gave a candle and a lamp to the church altar).

✳ St Helen's Church, **Norwich,** contains a ceiling boss showing a midwife at the birth of Christ. It's the only known representation in England and a picture of the boss was used on a Christmas stamp in 1974.

✳ The Church of St Peter Mancroft is the largest church in **Norwich** and is often mistakened for the cathedral by visitors. As well as its font canopy (see below), it also has a rare treasure: a Flemish tapestry dated 1573 that shows Christ as a gardener armed with his spade.

Bells

✳ All Saints' Church, **Thornham,** has a rare 12th-century sanctus bell. It also contains a ship's bell which belonged to the minesweeper HMS *Thornham*; the bell was presented to the church in 1969 and is rung each year to signal the two minutes' silence on Armistice Day.

✳ St Margaret's Church in **King's Lynn** was the first church in the county to have a ring of eight bells, in 1669. Three years later the Church of St Peter Mancroft in **Norwich** also had a ring of eight bells. (Today, it has 14). St Peter's is noted in bell-ringing history because in 1715 the 5,040 changes of Plain Bob Triples (aka the 'first true peal') were rung for the first time, in three hours and 17 minutes; this is recorded in an inscription in the tower. The first complete peals to the change of the ringing systems known as Grandsires and Stedmans were also rung in St Peter's.

✳ St Nicholas's Church in **Buckenham** once had the oldest tower bell in Norfolk, dating from 1290, but sadly it was stolen in 1973.

✳ St Peter's Church, **Great Walsingham,** has a set of three bells cast by one founder, William Silisden of **King's Lynn.** Dating from the 14th century, they're one of the oldest sets of bells cast by one founder in the country.

Bench-ends and poppy heads

Seating was introduced to churches in the 13th century, but wasn't really widespread until the 15th century. Most seating was in the form of benches placed in the church nave, which often had carved ends and poppy heads. There were also stalls in the choir, which often had misericords carved into them. The misericord or 'pity seat' was a narrow ledge on the bottom of the seat, so elderly monks could flip up the seat and rest against the misericord during long services.

One hundred and seventeen churches in Norfolk have mediaeval benches, many with gorgeous carvings. Some of the best examples are at:

✷ St John the Baptist, **Bressingham** – includes angels, lions, bears and several of the 'Seven works of Mercy'.

✷ St Agnes, **Cawston** – a wonderful dragon; plus misericords with monkeys, dogs and an antlered head.

✷ St Margaret, **Cley** – includes a monkey, a mermaid and several grotesques.

✷ St Martin, **Glandford** – the benches aren't mediaeval, but it's worth mentioning the gorgeous modern carving on the end of Sir Alfred Jodrell's pew, which is a copy of Landseer's painting *The Shepherd's Chief Mourner.*

✷ St Peter, **Great Walsingham** – has one of the most complete sets of 15th-century benches in Norfolk, with saints and grotesque animals carved on the ends.

✷ St Botolph, **Grimston** – includes a lion, a mermaid and a man wrapped in a blanket.

✷ **Norwich** Cathedral has more misericords on its stalls than anywhere else: there are over 60, including a winged lion and an ape riding a dog. There are also new misericords, commissioned to celebrate the 900th anniversary of the building, including one of a canary and one of former Norwich City Football Club goalkeeper (and its brand new manager, at the time of writing) Bryan Gunn.

✷ St Andrew, **South Lopham** – includes a wonderful elephant whose trunk is carved as a beak and whose feet have hooves!

✷ St Peter and St Paul, **Swaffham** – includes John Chapman (the Swaffham Pedlar – see page 221), his dog and a woman at work in her shop.

✷ All Saints, **Thornham** – includes several of the deadly sins, a unicorn and a ship in sail.

✳ All Saints, **Thurgarton** – includes a man playing bagpipes, an elephant and castle, two huntsmen, a gryphon holding a man's head and two dogs fighting.

✳ St Peter and St Paul's, **Tuttington** – includes St George and the Dragon, an elephant and castle (you can even see a face looking out of the castle's window), a musician with a drum, a musician with a lute, a woman making butter, a woman with a basket and a pig, a dragon eating a man, a wild man creeping up on a dragon, a fox stealing a goose and a guard dog.

✳ St Germain, **Wiggenhall St Germans** – includes most of the seven deadly sins, the seven sacraments, apostles, evangelists and animals.

✳ St Mary, **Wiggenhall St Mary** – includes various saints, Labours of the Months, animals and symbols.

✳ All Saints, **Upper Sheringham** – includes a cat with a kitten, a child in swaddling clothes and a mermaid. The carving of the mermaid reflects the legend that a mermaid once tried to attend a service here. Her face was the colour of moonstone and her hair the silvery colour of the sun on a green sea.

Mermaid bench-end at All Saints' Church, Upper Sheringham.

The church beadle saw her in the doorway, noticed her silvery tail and cried, 'Get you on out! We can't have no mermaids in here!' It was believed that mermaids had no soul and therefore shouldn't be allowed in a church, and so he slammed the door in her face. However, when he was busy with the service, the mermaid managed to creep in and sat on the pew nearest the door, which is where you'll find her wooden incarnation. (She's also on the village sign.)

Brasses

✳ The largest brasses in England are found in St Margaret's Church at **King's Lynn** and date from the mid-14th century. They're both Flemish, made of latten (an alloy of copper and zinc) and they're over two metres tall. They depict the former mayor, Adam of Walsoken (who died of the plague in 1349), and his wife, and the former mayor Robert Braunche (who died in 1364) with his two wives. Braunche's brass is known as the Peacock Brass, as it depicts a peacock placed in front of a guest; when Braunche was mayor, he entertained Edward III and presented him with a peacock feast. There used to be a third brass, to Robert Attelath, but it's said that a dishonest sexton sold it for five shillings and then hanged himself in remorse.

✳ The largest English brass is at St Mary's Church, **Elsing**, although it's not complete as many small pieces are missing. The figure of Sir Hugh Hastings (who died in 1347), measuring 5ft 6in, is shown in armour. Angels hold his pillows, St George fights the dragon, there are mourners at his side and there is an arch above him with tiny angels receiving his soul. It was originally gilded and had paste inlays, making it look enamelled. There's also a replica of the brass next to the font which is slightly more complete.

✳ The earliest brass in the county is at St Andrew's Church in **Gorleston**, to a member of the Bacon family (most likely Sir John Bacon). The figure dates from *c*.1320 and has crossed legs, which is unusual. The brass is quite big, at 4ft 8in tall.

✳ There's a rare brass at St Margaret's Church in **Felbrigg** showing Sir Simon de Felbrigg, knight of the garter. This is one of only six brasses in the country depicting a knight of the garter. (However, Sir Simon isn't buried at Felbrigg; he's actually buried in Blackfriars Hall in **Norwich**.)

Fonts

✳ Norfolk is rich in another rarity: seven sacrament fonts. According to H. Monro Cautley, there are only 40 in the whole country – and 25 of them are in Norfolk. They're octagonal and each panel depicts one of the sacraments of the church: baptism, confirmation, eucharist (or communion), penance (or confession), ordination (holy orders), holy matrimony and unction (anointing the sick/last rites). The eighth panel usually depicts the crucifixion. Some of the best seven sacrament fonts are at St Mary's, **Little Walsingham** (Pevsner states that it's the perfect Norfolk font, and a replica was displayed at the Great Exhibition in 1851); St Mary's, **Martham**; St Mary's, **Binham**; The Assumption of the Blessed Mary, **Great Witchingham** (which has retained a lot of the original colour); St Bartholomew, **Sloley** (which is beautifully preserved); and All Saints, **Gresham**.

✳ **Acle** has a wonderful octagonal font with much original colour, as well as a very rare representation of the Holy Trinity: God, holding Jesus's cross, with a dove (the Holy Ghost) on his shoulder. His face was restored in Victorian times, and you can still see the holes in the cross where the figure of Jesus used to be.

✳ The only lead font in Norfolk, dating from the 13th century, is at St Lawrence's Church, **Brundall**.

✳ There's an unusual Norman font at St Mary's Church, **Burnham Deepdale**, showing the Labours of the Months in arcading. January shows a man with a drinking horn; February a man warming his feet; March a man digging; April a man pruning a tree; May a man beating the bounds; June a man weeding; July a man scything; August a man binding a sheaf; September a hand threshing with a flail; October a man grinding corn in a quern; November a man slaughtering a pig; and December people feasting to celebrate Christmas.

✳ St Martin's Church, **Fincham**, has an unusual Norman font which came from the lost church of St Michael's in Fincham. It shows the Magi, the Nativity (with oxen lowing and an amazing star), baptism and Adam and Eve with the tree (restored): Adam is hiding his nakedness and holding his head in despair.

✳ There's a wonderful Norman font at St Peter and St Paul's Church, **Shernborne**, with plaited designs and masks.

✳ There's an unusual font cover at St Peter and St Paul's Church, **Knapton**, showing a Greek palindrome NI ON ONOMHMA MH MONAN O IN (generally translated as 'wash my sins and not my face only').

✳ **Norwich** Cathedral has a copper font, which was once a boiling pan the Nestlé chocolate factory.

✳ St Nicholas's Church, **Potter Heigham**, contains a rare brick font, dating from the 15th century.

✳ There are only four font canopies in the country and Norfolk has two of them: one at St Peter Mancroft Church, **Norwich**, and St Botolph's Church, **Trunch**. (The other two are at Durham and Luton).

✳ St Margaret's Church, **Upton,** has one of the best fonts in the county, with beautiful angels.

✳ St Nicholas's Church, **King's Lynn**, was originally a chapel to the Church of St Margaret (even though it's an incredible 200ft-long) and has a font donated by Bishop Harsant of Norwich in the 1620s. We even know who was the first to be baptised there, thanks to a brass inscription in the church: 'Here resteth Anne, daughter to Joseph and Isabel Raylie. She was the first God gave unto her parents, and the first baptised in the Funt of this Chapell and died the 10th of March 1627 aged 24 dayes.'

Glass

✳ Fifteenth-century Norwich had one of the most popular schools of glass painting in England. One of the best examples is the east window of St Peter Mancroft, **Norwich**, with 42 panels dating from 1445, followed by St Peter and St Paul's at **East Harling.** There are also stunning Annunciation panels at All Saints, **Bale**; good examples at St Margaret's, **Stratton Strawless**; and a feathered angel at St Peter's, **Ketteringham**. At St Botolph's, **Banningham**, you can see a mediaeval seraphim with purple feathers, and a cherub with feathers covering its eyes.

✳ The earliest figurative glass in Norfolk (and East Anglia) is at St Mary's, **Saxlingham Nethergate**, dating from 1250. There are also good examples of Norwich school glass and 14th-century grisaille glass, and a beautiful modern memorial window to the fallen of World War Two.

✳ Some of the earliest coloured glass in Norfolk is at St Peter and St Paul, **Mautby**, dating from the early 13th century.

✳ There is also some beautiful Victorian stained-glass in the county, some of which can be found at St Michael and All Angels, **Booton**, and work from the Morris company can be seen at St Mary's, **South Walsham**. There's also a fabulous Burne-Jones angel in **Norwich** Cathedral.

Graffiti

Norfolk churches contain some unusual markings, including:

✳ A demon and a woman with a wimple scratched into a pillar at the Saxon church of St Mary's, **Beachamwell**. Nearby, scratched into the stone, there's a record of the quantities and prices of items supplied to the masons.

✳ Graffiti dating from the civil war, including a hand inscribed with 'Roundeheade 1645' and several Nine Men's Morris boards on a tomb chest in St Mary's Church, **Hickling**.

✳ A cryptogram at All Saint's Church, **Litcham**, scratched into a pillar at eye level; it's said to be a prayer carved by a pilgrim, Wyke Bamburgh, on his way to the shrine at **Walsingham**, asking Jesus, Mary and Joseph to save his soul.

✳ Graffiti from the civil war on Bishop Goldwell's tomb in **Norwich** Cathedral. There's also a musket ball from target practice lodged in the tomb.

✳ Galleons in full sail carved into the pillars of St Mary the Virgin's Church, **Wiveton**.

Lecterns

✳ Once again, Norfolk is spoiled when it comes to lecterns: of the 42 pre-Reformation eagle lecterns in the country, 14 of them are in Norfolk. One of the most unusual of these lecterns is the pelican in **Norwich** Cathedral.

✳ There's a rare 'Peter's Pence' lectern at St John the Evangelist's Church, **Oxborough**. The lectern got its name because it had a slot in the beak to collect the annual tax of Peter's Pence for Rome.

✳ St Helen's Church, **Ranworth**, has a rare cantor's desk. One side contains the opening line of the gospel of St John ('In the Beginning was the Word...') in Latin and his symbol; the other side contains the 16th-century music *Gloria*.

✳ St Mary's Church, **Redenhall**, has a rare double-headed eagle lectern.

Monuments and Memorials

✳ Wooden effigies are quite rare; according to H. Monro Cautley, there are just 96 in the country. Again, Norfolk has more than an average share, with three. The figures were all made from oak and were originally covered in gesso (a white primer which stopped paint soaking into wood). At St George's Church in **South Acre** there is a figure with crossed legs dating from the 14th century and measuring 4ft 4in; at St Mary's Church in **Banham** there is another 14th-century example (reputedly Sir Hugh Bardolph, who founded the church – though the armour on the figure is of a later date); and at St Andrew's Church in **Fersfield** there is a figure of Sir Robert de Bois (who died in 1311, though the figure dates from 1340) which retains much of its original colouring and has a deer lying at his feet.

✳ All Saints' Church, **Ashwellthorpe,** contains the earliest alabaster monuments in Norfolk (dated to around 1417), to Sir Edmund Thorpe and his wife Joan. Both are wearing 'SS collars' (livery collars associated with John of Gaunt, the Duke of Lancaster). There are various theories about what the letters mean, including 'Seigneur-Soverrayne' (his followers supported the Duke and the King) or 'Sanctus'. There are angels bearing Joan's pillow to heaven, while Edmund rests his head on a helmet; two dogs sit at their feet.

✳ One of the more unusual churchyard memorials is the Brereton monument at St Maurice's Church, **Briningham**, which has a muzzled bear on top of a pyramid. The Breretons used the crest of a muzzled bear after one of the Breretons, who served in the king's cavalry, led his men into battle too soon; the king's response was, 'Let the bear be muzzled.'

✳ St Peter and St Paul's Church, **Carbrooke**, contains two 13th-century coffin slabs which have cross marks of the Knights Templars. Maud, the Countess of Clare, founded the only Norfolk house for the Knights Templar, near the church in the mid-12th century. The coffin slabs are believed to belong to her and her son Roger, which would make them two of the oldest memorials in East Anglia.

✳ St Mary's Church at **Haddiscoe** has an unusual ledger stone, which is inscribed in Dutch. Dated 1525, it commemorates Barbele Jans, the wife of Peter, son of Piers the dykegraaf (or 'dyke reeve'). The dykegraaf was the person responsible for draining the dykes and maintaining them.

✳ St Andrew's Church at **Hingham** contains what Pevsner calls 'one of the most impressive wall monuments of the 15th century in the whole of England' and suggests that it's based on the Erpingham gateway in Norwich Cathedral. The monument is for Thomas, Lord Morley, who died in 1435. The church also contains a bust of Abraham Lincoln, whose family left Hingham for America in the 17th century.

✳ Holy Trinity Church at **Ingham** has some interesting early monuments, including Sir Oliver de Ingham (who died in 1344) on a bed of pebbles, and Sir Roger de Bois (who died in 1300) with his wife Margaret (who died in 1315). Sir Roger's pillow is quite gruesome – the helmet contains his enemy's severed head!

✳ St John the Evangelist's Church at **Oxborough** is renowned for the terracotta monuments to the Bedingfield family. Another terracotta monument is in the Church of St George's Colegate in **Norwich**: the tomb chest is for former mayor Robert Jannys, who died in 1530. The church also contains a slate memorial stone to artist John Crome, who died in 1821.

Roofs

Norfolk is known for its wonderful hammer beam roofs with carved angels. Some of the best are at:

✳ St Michael and All Angels, **Booton.**

✳ St Agnes, **Cawston** – a single hammer beam roof.

✳ St Peter and Paul's, **Knapton** – a double hammer beam roof which is huge: over 20 metres long and almost 11 metres wide, containing a stunning 138 angels.

✳ St Catherine's, **Ludham** – although not an angel roof, the hammer beam roof is finely carved. St Catherine's wheel, the emblem of the church, is carved into the spandrels.

✳ All Saints, **Necton** – the hammer beam roof, which has figures of saints on the wall posts between the angels, still has much of its original mediaeval paint.

✳ St Mary, **South Creake** – it's believed that the roof was built to celebrate Henry V's victory at Agincourt in 1415. The angels were restored and repainted in 1958 and 1970, and it was discovered they were full of 17th-century musket balls. The churchwarden accounts talk about a problem with jackdaws in the church during the late 1600s, so it's a fair bet that the shot came from attempts to get rid of the jackdaws.

✳ St Peter and Paul, **Swaffham** – a double hammer beam roof made from chestnut wood which contains even more angels than Knapton: an amazing 192 of them!

✳ **Wymondham** Abbey – a hammer beam roof with 76 angels.

Screens

The churches of Norfolk are also known for their beautiful carved and painted wooden screens. The two major gems in the county are at St Mary's in **Attleborough**, which has a rood screen 52ft-long, and St Helen's at **Ranworth**, which Pevsner calls 'the finest screen arrangement surviving in Norfolk.' Some other churches in the county which have rare or unusual features on their screens include:

✳ St Michael and All Angels, **Barton Turf,** there's a picture of St Appolonia, who was invoked against toothache; the screen shows her holding a molar in a pair of pincers. The nine orders of angels are also shown.

✳ St Andrew, **Burlingham**, which has the latest dated rood screen in Norfolk (1536). The names of the donors are written under their name-saints (such as Cecily Blake under the picture of St Cecilia). There's also a picture of St Withburga with her does.

✳ St Agnes, **Cawston**, is a 16th-century rood screen which still has its doors, a rare survival. Pictures include Sir John Schorne (invoked against gout, because he allegedly conjured a devil into a boot), and St Matthew wearing his spectacles made of leather.

✳ St Helen, **Gateley**, has a painted panel on the screen marked as 'puella de Ridibowne.' This probably relates to Christina of Redborne, also known as Christina Markyate. Christina was the daughter of Autti, a rich guild merchant in Huntingdon. In 1112 she went to the abbey at St Albans and made a private vow of virginity. Once word got about, Ralph Flambard tried to seduce her – and failed. Her parents, who wanted her to marry a man called Burhtred, were very unhappy about the vow, particularly when Bishop Robert Bloet of Lincoln agreed that she shouldn't have to marry him. They bribed him to change his mind and Christina was bethrothed to Burhtred. She was forced to marry him, but refused to consummate the marriage and so was imprisoned for a year. The hermit Eadwin helped her to escape, and she took refuge as an anchoress, firstly at Flamstead and then at Markyate. In 1122 her marriage was annulled by the archbishop of York, as he said that her marriage was made under duress and unconsummated due to her vow of virginity. She remained at Markyate, which became a nunnery.

✳ Other pictures on the screen at **Gateley** show Etheldreda, who founded the diocese of Ely; Sir John Schorne; and Henry VI as a saint, though he was never actually canonised.

✷ St Andrew, **Hempstead,** has some rare saints painted on the dado, including St John of Bridlington holding a fish. Originally there was a rare painting of St Eligius, the patron saint of farriers, but it was stolen in 1982. (There's a painting of St Eligius on the screen at St Nicholas, **Potter Heigham**).

✷ St Mary, **Sparham,** has two very unusual Dance of Death panels. One has a shrouded skeleton pointing at a font and a Latin text from Job; the other has two fashionably dressed cadavers, with the woman giving the man a flower and the man holding a torch with the message 'sic transit Gloria mundi.' Just to make it even more gruesome, the eyes were gouged out during the Reformation.

✷ St Andrew, **Thorpe St Andrew,** contains what's believed to be the first screen built in a Norfolk church since the Reformation. In 1900 the chancel screen was commissioned as a war memorial and shows political and religious leaders from the 18th century.

✷ St Mary, **Worstead,** has a rare painting of St William of Norfolk on its screen, as well as a painting of St Wilgefortis, the bearded lady. Wilgefortis's father promised her in marriage to a pagan nobleman, but she didn't want to marry and had taken a vow of virginity. She prayed to be made repulsive and sprouted a beard overnight; furious, her father had her crucified. Women who wanted to be rid of abusive husbands used to pray to Wilgefortis to be 'disencumbered', and so she also became known as St Uncumber.

Wall paintings

According to Pevsner, there are more mediaeval wall paintings in Norfolk than anywhere else, and most have only been rediscovered since 1962. Churches were decorated from mediaeval times onwards. The earliest paintings used red and yellow ochre, along with white and lampblack. Green came from copper salts, while blue was much rarer because it was extremely expensive. Paintings included geometric designs and foliage. St Christopher, the patron saint of travellers, tended to be painted on the north wall so it was the first thing that people saw when they looked through the doorway. Other common scenes were 'doom', or the last judgement, showing what would happen to you if you didn't lead a good religious life; the 'seven works of mercy', showing what Christians were supposed to do, were also popular, as were the 'quick and the dead' (three living kings meeting three skeletons, who gave them the message 'we were once like you, and you will eventually be like us' – very like the memento mori brasses and ledger stones).

In the 16th and 17th centuries the paintings came to be considered inappropriate and were removed or covered over. In Norfolk the paintings tended to be covered with a lime wash, which has preserved the paintings. It also meant that when churches were renovated in the 19th century the builders had no idea that the wall paintings existed, so some of the paintings were damaged when windows were put through them (as at **Attleborough** and **Heydon**).

Some of the best ones in Norfolk include:

✳ St Mary's, **Attleborough** – remains above the rood screen (including a wonderful angel with feathered trousers).

✳ All Saints, **Hemblington** – a superb painting of St Christopher, with scenes from his life.

✳ St Peter and St Paul's, **Heydon** – wall paintings dating from the late-14th century were discovered in 1970, including the Three Living and the Three Dead and Salome dancing before Herod.

✳ St Faith's, **Little Witchingham** – wall paintings dating from 1360 were rediscovered in 1967, including the Passion and Resurrection scenes, St George and the Dragon and St Christopher.

✳ St Gregory's, **Norwich** – a huge wall painting of St George and the Dragon that was rediscovered in 1861; Pevsner has said that it's among the best late mediaeval wall paintings in the country.

✳ St Margaret's, **Paston** – a huge painting of St Christopher.

✳ St Nicholas's, **Potter Heigham** – a fabulous set of the Seven Works of Mercy (to feed the hungry, give water to the thirsty, clothe the naked, give shelter to the homeless, visit the sick, comfort prisoners and to bury the dead).

✳ St Edmund, **South Burlingham** – a rare scene of St Thomas of Canterbury.

✳ St Ethelbert's, **Thurton** – a faded St Christopher, with a very lifelike crayfish at his feet.

✳ St Andrew's, **Wickhampton** – the Three Living and the Three Dead (it's thought to be the best 14th-century example in Norfolk), St Christopher and the Seven Works of Mercy.

Curiosities

✳ Before churches used collecting bags and plates, they used collecting shoes. Norfolk has some interesting examples: at St Andrew's Church in **Blo Norton** there is a pair lined with green velvet (Pevsner has said that they're replicas of the originals made in 1910 and describes them as little shovels shaped like dustpans). There is also a pair at St Mary's Church, **North Tuddenham,** with an inscription: 'Let not thine hands be open when ye shouldest receive, nor shut when ye shouldest give', and three at St John the Baptist's Church, **Bressingham,** dated 1631.

✳ St Edmund's, **Acle,** has a Latin inscription on the wall referring to the outbreak of the plague; only part of it is legible as the window goes through it. The Victorian scholar and antiquary M.R. James dated it to 1349 because of the references to the hats, but the chancel wasn't actually built until 1362. However, the plague was in Norfolk in 1362 – and fashions didn't change that quickly, so it may be that the inscription was written when the chancel was very new:

> Oh lamentable death, how many dost thou cast into the pit!
> Anon the infants fade away, and of the aged death makes an end.
> Now these, now those, thou ravagest, O death on every side;
> Those that wear horns or veils, fate spareth not.
> Therefore, while in the world the brute beast plague rages hour by hour,
> With prayer and with remembrance deplore death's deadliness.

✳ There's an iron cello at All Saints' Church, **Briston,** which was made by Mr Clitheroe, the village blacksmith, in 1699. He played it for many years, and it was played again to celebrate its 300th birthday in 1999. Appropriately, its tone has been described as 'tinny'.

✳ St Agnes, **Cawston,** has an arch on the gallery with an inscription about ale-making:

> God spede the plow
> And send us ale corne enow
> oor purpose for to mak
> at crow of cok of ye plowlete of Sygate
> Be mery and glade
> wat good ale yis work mad

The Plough Inn closed in the 1960s and gave its sign to the church.

Church door, St James's Church, Castle Acre.

✳ At St James, **Castle Acre**, there's a wonderful story about a door that was made to let a knight in full armour enter the church while riding his destrier. The outline above the door is certainly tall enough, but it's nowhere near wide enough; besides which, only the priest went into the chancel until the 16th century, so the door was for the priest rather than the congregation. It's more likely that there was a window that was blocked up when the doorway was made.

✳ St Edmund, **Downham Market**, contains the only known glass chandelier lit by candles in a church. It dates from 1730 but was stored in the church and only rediscovered in the 1960s. It was restored in 1967 and rehung in its original position in the nave.

✳ According to Victorian historian C.J. Palmer, the Church of St Nicholas in **Great Yarmouth** once had a very unusual seat. When a whale was washed up on the beach in **Caister** in 1582 its skull and part of its spine were made into a seat and placed outside the guildhall, next to the church. In 1606 the churchwardens spent eight shillings on painting it. The whalebone seat became known as the 'Devil's Seat', and legend had it that you'd incur deadly disaster if you sat in it. After the guildhall was demolished, 200 years later, the seat was moved into the church by the west door. Local fishingfolk believed that whichever of the bride or groom sat in it first after their wedding would rule the home. The church was destroyed by bombing during World War Two, and it's thought that the seat was also destroyed then.

✳ St Mary, **Haddiscoe**, has one of the best Norman sculptures in Norfolk, set above the Norman doorway inside the porch. It's of a priest sitting on a throne, holding his hands high. The mouldings below it are pretty stunning too, as is the ironwork on the door.

✳ In the tower of St Margaret, **Hales,** you can still see the impress of the basketwork used to make the splays of the round windows.

✳ St Peter's, **Ickburgh,** has a beer mug and bottle in the east gable. It's said they were put there by a builder who was sacked for drinking on the job.

✳ After the Restoration in 1660, people had to attend church by law and the sermon had to last for at least an hour; priests at this time used to have an hourglass on a stand before the pulpit so they could time their sermons. St Lawrence's, **Ingworth,** still has an original hourglass stand.

✳ There's an unusual clock at St Margaret's in **King's Lynn,** which shows the tides rather than the time of day. The original clock was made by Thomas Tue in 1681, but was damaged when the spire blew down in 1741. The letters 'HIGH TIDE LYNN' mark even hours on a 24-hour system, with 'L' at the top showing noon and 'G' at the bottom showing midnight. The pointer shows the time of the flood tide and takes 29 and a half days to move round the dial; during this period it also shows the phases of the moon.

✳ St Mary's, **Long Stratton,** has a rare sexton's wheel. The only other one in the country is at Yaxley, in Suffolk. It was used to decide the day a parishioner began a fast. The wheel marked six days and a piece of string was attached to the hole by the mark. The parishioner would ask the sexton to spin the wheel and whichever string he caught would be the day the fast began.

✳ St Andrew's, **Northwold,** has a rare Easter Sepulchre made of chalk.

✳ The bishop's garden in **Norwich** Cathedral contains a hebe which was grown from a cutting from Queen Victoria's wedding bouquet.

✳ St Helen's **Ranworth,** has an antiphonary produced by the monks at Langley Abbey. It's 285-pages long, with the psalms and responses for each of the seven services held every day of year. (The name comes from the fact that the priest and the congregation speak alternately or 'antiphonally'). It was bequeathed to St Helen's in 1478 by John Cobbe. However, in 1549, as it was written in Latin and the prayer book of 1549 said that services had to be in English, it wasn't allowed to be used. It disappeared for 300 years, until it was found in a private collection and was finally returned to the church in 1912.

✳ St John the Baptist's Head, **Trimingham,** once lived up to its name as it had the head of John the Baptist as a relic. The will of Alice Cook of Horstead, from 1478, said: 'I wylle have a man to go on a pilgrimage to S. John hys hede and Trymmynham.' Obviously, it wasn't the head itself; it was one of the alabaster heads from Nottingham made in the 15th century. St John the Baptist's head is also shown on a carving on the rood screen.

✳ A niche in St Mary's, **Whissonsett**, contains the head of a Saxon cross – the only such cross known in Norfolk.

✳ The only graveside shelter remaining in Norfolk is at St Peter's, **Walpole**. It's known as a 'Hudd' (hood) and looks like a sentry box. It was used to protect the parson from getting wet during burials. Dickens refers to graveside shelters in *Sketches by Boz*. Another unusual survival is the notice, 'It is requested that all persons will take off their Pattens at the Church Door', referring to the wooden clogs once worn by farm workers.

Strange tales

✳ There was a huge row centred at St Peter's Church, **Ketteringham**, in 1853. Sir John Boileau was the squire of the estate; his wife, Lady Catherine, was an invalid, and towards the end of the year he was fretting about where she'd be buried. (Actually, it was another 10 years before she died). He believed that the squire's family should be interred in the chancel vault. The problem was that the vault was full and couldn't be enlarged. The only named coffin Sir John could see belonged to a family called Heron, dated over 150 years previously. The families had long since died out, so he formulated a plan to move the coffins and make space for his own. He asked for the bishop's permission, but the bishop said Sir John's legal right to remove them was questionable and he'd need to get the vicar's consent. The bishop added that normally you'd need a faculty to move the coffins, but as Sir John wasn't a relative or friend of the deceased, he couldn't grant a faculty. Instead, he suggested that 'the matter had better be conducted privately and quietly'.

Catherine's health had worsened, so Sir John wrote to William Andrew, the vicar of the church. Andrew knew that the vault had been used in living memory, and wasn't keen on Sir John's plan. Relations between the two men had been fraught and they had clashed for almost 20 years. However, Sir John was persuasive and got his way. The vault was emptied at night by his gardener and the village carpenter, and the bodies interred in the church graveyard. The idea was to keep things quiet, so that Catherine wasn't distressed by thinking about her own mortality, and so the village gossips didn't have the chance to spread ugly rumours.

Moving the bodies, however, had filled the church with an appalling stench and the story couldn't be hushed up. The next morning the vicar's wife – who was connected to one of the families interred in the vault – had a public row with Sir John's gardener and the carpenter in the church about their role in moving the coffins. The story spread quickly throughout the county and outraged relatives whose relatives had been moved wrote strong letters to Sir John, who immediately apologised. Sir John himself became known as 'Resurrection Jack' – the ballad-composers in the local pub had a field day – and eventually, in December, the coffins were replaced. Sir John then built a mausoleum in the churchyard for his own family, and was very careful to make sure he had all the right faculties and legal agreements to build it.

✳ St Mary's in **Martham** has some unusual entries in the parish records. In 1619 a man died from playing the fairly violent game of camping (see page 220). The records state: 'John Smyth, servant to Nicholas Cootes, brocke his legge at the footbaull, on the 6 day of ffebruary being Sunday, and was buried the eleaventh day of the same month.' Another entry states that a woman gave birth to twins 'which, through the mistake of two or three good old women, were baptised Edward and Robert when the aforesaid Edward was a daughter and Robert a son.'

✳ St Margaret of Antioch, **Upton**, has seen some very odd times, according to John Timpson. On Christmas Day 1612, two local rowdies, Will Enderton and Simon Bullock, came into the church at evening prayer with a whalebone on their shoulders and a robin and a wren tied to the bone. They fell down drunk, then knelt and prayed for the priest, his wife and his great dog. What happened to them next isn't recorded.

✳ St Mary the Virgin's, **Wiveton**, was linked with a London murder in 1779, which filled scandal sheets for weeks and was still making headlines a century later. Martha Ray, born in 1744, was the daughter of a staymaker. One of his customers was so impressed with her beauty that he mentioned her to the fourth Earl of Sandwich, John Montagu, and when Martha was 17 she became his mistress. The earl set Martha up in a house in Westminster and they had five children together. Witnesses in the murder trial referred to 'Lady Sandwich's carriage' and they were clearly married in all but name.

However, 17 years later, the earl made what turned out to be a fatal mistake: he invited a young soldier, James Hackman, to dinner. Hackman was instantly besotted with Martha and proposed to her several times. Quite apart from the fact that he was six years her junior, she was in love with the earl and refused every proposal. However, Hackman was convinced that if he could offer her a home and a more settled career she would accept. So in 1779 he left the army and became the rector of Wiveton.

On 7 April 1779, Martha had gone to the opera at Covent Garden to see a performance of *Love in a Village*. At 11.30pm, as she left, according to witness Horace Walpole, Hackman approached her from behind, and 'on her turning round, clapped [a] pistol to her forehead and shot her through the head.' He had two pistols and tried to shoot himself with the other, but only wounded himself. He was apprehended immediately, while beating himself over the head with the pistol and crying 'Oh! Kill me! For God's sake kill me!'

Sandwich, by now the First Lord of the Admiralty, was devastated. Although the papers had formerly caricatured him as a rake and claimed that he spiked Martha's champagne before seducing her at the age of 17 (he was 24 years her senior), this time they were kind to him; the *St James's Chronicle* said that in this affair the earl 'has shown a Tenderness which does the highest credit to his Heart'.

Martha was buried at Elstree in the clothes she was wearing when she was killed.

Hackman went on trial at the Old Bailey on 16 April 1779 and was found guilty; he was hanged at Tyburn. The newspapers had sympathy with him too, seeing it as a crime of passion. During the trial Hackman said 'the will to destroy her who was ever dearer to me than life, was never mine till a momentary phrensy overcame me, and induced me to commit the deed I now deplore.' Boswell reported that his last words on the scaffold were 'Dear, dear Miss Ray'.

✳ A rather happier story associated with the church is that of the **Wiveton** boy, Raulf Greneway (Ralph Greenaway). He was found by a shepherd abandoned in a 'green way', which gave him his name. The authorities at Blakeney refused to adopt him, but at Wiveton 13 old women agreed to take him for a year each and would send him to sea when he was old enough. Greneway grew up to become a grocer and alderman in London and made a fortune. He died in 1558 but never forgot Wiveton; in his will he left 200 marks to purchase land, the rents for which would give 'xiii Poore People of this Parish xiiid in money et xiii in bred' every Sunday. There was a row over the legacy in 1602, which rumbled on for 10 years when one of the trustees, John King, was accused of keeping the profits for himself and also keeping the charity archive, which had formerly been kept in the parish chest. Eventually, they got the documents back and there was enough money to improve the dole way beyond the usual parish relief. There is a brass on the church wall describing the charity, showing the Greneway arms, the grocers' arms and Greneway's merchant mark.

Chapter 5
Castles and Abbeys

Castles

Norfolk has the lowest density of castles in England. Obviously the well-known ones are at **Norwich** and **Castle Rising**; however, there are remains of several others.

The earliest castles were motte and bailey. The motte was an earth mound surrounded by a ditch and topped with a wooden tower, while the bailey was a defended area round the motte, surrounded by a wall or fence and with a ditch around it. Some of the wooden towers were eventually replaced by stone keeps.

Some of the castles were 'maisons fortes' (fortified houses, such as **Baconsthorpe** and **Oxborough**), and we know exactly when they were fortified by the date on their 'licence to crenellate'; during the mediaeval period you could only fortify your house with the king's permission. Others we know about only from documents or the earthworks that are their sole remains.

❋ There were also three Saxon shore forts built in the county: one at **Burgh** Castle, one at **Brancaster** and one at **Caister**.

❋ **Baconsthorpe** Castle is really a fortified 15th-century house with a moat; the lake was added in the 17th century. It belonged to the Heydon family, noted lawyers and bitter enemies of the Pastons (although eventually Sir William Paston married Bridget Heydon, which ended the family feud). The Heydons were quite a tumultuous family – Christopher Heydon actually took both his parents to court when they tried to break the entail on the estate! The castle was partly demolished in 1654 (although the gatehouse was inhabited until the 1920s) and the stone was used at Felbrigg Hall. It's looked after by English Heritage and is open to the public.

❋ **Brancaster** shore fort, known as Branodunum, was the most northerly of the Saxon 'shore fort' system. It was built between AD 225 and 250 to guard the entrance of Brancaster Harbour, and was garrisoned by the Dalmatian cavalry (from modern-day Bosnia/Croatia). It was thought that a road (the Jews' Way) passed through its eastern gate and connected the fort with another at **Caister**. The fort was 570sq ft (enclosing an area of 6 to 7 acres, similar to that of Burgh Castle) and the walls were 11ft thick. In 1797 the camp was pulled down and the largest malthouse in England was built on the site; it was 312ft long, 31ft wide and could wet 420 quarters of barley in a week. The malthouse was taken down in 1878. The site was excavated in 1846 and archaeologists found relics including styli, a bronze Mercury, rings and coins and an altarstone to the god Hercules. Some of the stone from the fort has been reused in the Church of St Mary the Virgin, **Brancaster**, to block up two Norman windows, and as facing stone on the east side. The fort is now in the care of the National Trust.

✳ The Saxon shore fort at **Burgh** Castle was known as Gariannonum. It was built in the late AD 200s to protect the coast against raiders. It's also the traditional location of the monastery founded by St Fursey in the early seventh century. A motte and bailey castle was built there in Norman times; traces of the motte are still visible. The fort is in the care of the Norfolk Archaeological Trust and is open to the public.

✳ **Caister** shore fort was probably built in the early AD 200s. The ditch, walls and ramparts enclose an area of 3.5 hectares. The fort fell out of use after the fourth century. It has been partially excavated, and a house within the site is the oldest domestic building you can walk around in Norfolk. The site is in the care of English Heritage and is open to the public.

✳ **Caister** Castle was the first castle in England to be built of brick, in 1432. More than 1.7 million bricks were delivered or made on the site (although some of those were destined for other houses in the area). It was built for Sir John Fastolf, who allegedly used the money he received for ransoming John II (King of France) at the Battle of Verneuil in 1429. In his will he left the castle to the Pastons. The Duke of Norfolk disputed the will and put the castle under siege in 1469; the Pastons only had a garrison of 30 men, while the Duke's forces outnumbered them a hundred times over. Unsurprisingly, the Pastons were forced to yield. However, after the Duke's death in 1476, Sir John Paston reoccupied the castle and got letters patent from the king saying that he held title to the castle. Caister Castle is in the grounds of a museum, which houses the UK's largest private collection of cars, and is open to the public.

✳ **Castle Acre** Castle was originally a country house with a bailey built by William de Warenne on the site of a Saxon hall held by the thane Toki. It was fortified with a strong keep and defences in the 12th century. The outer bailey became a planned market town, similar to New Buckenham, and the market place was at Pale's Green. The castle was derelict by the 14th century. The site is in the care of English Heritage and is open to the public.

✳ The building at **Castle Rising** began in 1138 by William d'Albini, although the castle wasn't finished or inhabited until the beginning of the 13th century. It's one of the largest and most decorated keeps in England. Queen Isabella, the mother of Edward III, lived there from her arrest in 1331 until just before her death in 1358. However, it's worth noting that her supervision there was very light; Edward gave her £3,000 a year for her expenses (equivalent to over a million pounds today), and she joined him for his birthday in Norwich 1344. The castle was left to decay in the 16th century after rabbits had severely damaged the defensive banks. The site is in the care of English Heritage and is open to the public.

✳ **Claxton** Castle was a moated maison forte, which was castellated in 1333 by William de Kerdiston (son of Roger, sheriff and MP for Norfolk and Suffolk). It was originally 40 metres long. Nowadays, five of the original six bastions remain, along with earthworks and part of the gateway. A mansion was built against the castle walls in the 16th century, but it was demolished in the 17th century and the stone used to build Claxton Manor. The site is a private home and is not open to the public.

✳ **Denton** Castle is the remains of a small motte and bailey castle which is thought to have been built by the d'Albini family between 1088 and 1254. The earthworks of the motte, horseshoe bailey and ditch are still visible, and the site has been well preserved as it's hidden within Darrow Wood. It is owned by the National Trust and is open to the public.

✳ The only remnant of **Dilham** Castle is a fragment of a 15th-century wall with a tower that may have been part of the gatehouse. It's thought to have been built by Sir Henry Inglose. The site is part of Dilham Hall, a private house, and is not open to the public.

✳ At **Great Hautbois** there are remains of a castle built by Sir Robert Baynard in 1312 and crenellated the following year. Some of the foundations of the porter's lodge survive, plus the bailey and moat.

✳ There was once a castle at **Great Yarmouth**, and an Elizabethan map shows that it had four towers. Row 99 in the town was once known as Castle Row. The site is on King Street, where a floor and foundation works were found during building work in 1965. The castle was built some time before 1208. In 1525 it was leased to the Great Yarmouth and 25 years later was given to the town. In 1554 there was a particularly bad storm and a fire-beacon was installed on top of the castle. It was later used as jail, and in 1621 it was demolished and the following year some of the material was used to repair a house in Row 76.

✳ **Gresham** Castle was built by Sir Edmund Bacon on the site of an earlier castle after he was granted a licence to fortify in 1319. The castle was 40 metres square and had four towers, each of different sizes, as well as a wet moat four metres wide. At one point it was owned by Geoffrey Chaucer's son, Thomas, who sold it to Sir William Paston. However, after Sir William's death, Lord Moleyns took the castle, saying that he had a residual claim through his wife (whose father had owned the castle jointly with Thomas Chaucer). The Pastons tried to get it back via the courts, but eventually took matters into their own hands and began collecting rents. In the end the Pastons won their case in court, but the house was no longer fit to live in and remained empty as it crumbled. The site of the castle is on private land and is not open to the public.

✳ There are the remains of a 12th-century motte and bailey castle at **Horsford**, along with a wet ditch. The castle fell out of use soon after 1431, though according to 18th-century historian Francis Blomefield the home park was still stocked with deer in the early 16th century. Unfortunately, the bailey was damaged by ploughing in the 1980s. The castle is on private land, but there is a public right of way to see it.

✳ At **Hunworth** there is the probable site of a castle which overlooks Hunworth village and the River Glaven. There's a circular enclosure with a bank and a ditch, 61 metres in diameter. It's possible that there was a motte and bailey here, and it's likely to have been a timber castle.

✳ At **Marham** there is a moat in the middle of 'Hills and Holes' plantation, enclosing an area 80 metres by 77 metres. There are four mounds, which may show the sites of the castle turrets. The manor at Marham was held in the second half of the 13th century by William Belet, who received licence to crenellate his house in 1271. However, an inquisition in 1277 found that 'the castle of Marham, raised by William Belet, is to the prejudice and nuisance of the king and country' – and so it had to be removed.

✳ There is an 11th-century motte and bailey castle at **Middleton**, which was occupied in the first half of the 12th century. The motte is 45 metres in diameter and still 10 metres tall, with a ditch 8 metres wide and 2.5 metres deep; the bailey was originally about 60 metres by 40 metres. The site is in the care of the Norfolk Archaeological Trust and is open to the public; a hedge on the site shows the outline of the castle.

✳ At **Mileham**, earthworks of the early 12th-century Norman castle are visible, along with a few fragments of flint from the once 50sq ft stone tower. The motte and bailey castle – one of the largest in Norfolk – was abandoned by the beginning of the 14th century, along with its deer park. It had two baileys, and was built across the road. Its position was probably to do with tolls on travellers and the market place. Although the castle hasn't been occupied for 700 years, the BBC actually tried to track down an unlicensed TV set among the ruins, threatening owner Richard Butler-Stoney with a £1,000 fine! According to the Department for Environment, Food and Rural Affairs, the site at Mileham is unique because the keep was built first and the motte built around it.

✳ **New Buckenham** Castle, built by William d'Albini II in around 1146, is thought to be the oldest and largest Norman circular stone keep in England. It replaced an earlier castle at Old Buckenham; d'Albini gave the old site to the Augustinian canons to build a monastery. The castle has two baileys, and at its peak the castle had a keep, two circular towers, an entrance tower, a barbican, embattled walls and a moat. Nowadays, the earthwork bailey, the keep and part of the gateway are still visible. Sir Robert de Tateshale managed to defend the castle when it was besieged by Sir Henry Hastings, an ally of Simon de Montfort, in the 13th century. The castle was besieged again in the 15th century when Sir John Knyvet didn't pay his inheritance duty to the king, but it was defended by Sir John's wife Alice. It was eventually defortified in the 1640s and was demolished in 1649. The castle is open to the public; the key is available at the garage on Castle Road during opening hours.

✳ **North Elmham** has a manor fortified by Hugh Despenser in 1388, built on the site of a pre-Conquest timber cathedral and cemetery. The site is in the care of the English Heritage and is open to the public.

✳ **Norwich** Castle is William I's only castle in East Anglia. The keep was originally wooden, but was replaced by the Norman stone square keep, 90ft by 95ft by 70ft high, by William's son, Rufus, between 1095 and 1100. The castle was originally a royal palace, but was also used as a jail from 1120. In 1193 there was a garrison of 75 knights and men-at-arms – some on foot, some on horse. The castle was falling into ruin by the 14th century, but was later patched up. The mound and bailey became pleasure gardens by 1780s, and then between 1789 and 1793 the keep was gutted and the new prison was built. The castle was refaced in Bath stone in 1835, but the Norman design was retained. In 1887 the castle became the museum for the county. The gardens were altered in the 1880s, they were made smaller to allow for road widening in the 1920s and were changed yet again when the Castle Mall was built. In its time, the castle has seen several sieges: firstly in 1075, when the first constable of Norwich, Ralph de Guader, rebelled against William the Conqueror (but left his wife to handle the siege); again in 1088, when Roger Bigod seized it to help Robert Curthose, the Duke of Normandy, against William Rufus; once more in 1136, during the civil war between Stephen and Matilda; again in 1174, when Hugh Bigod supported the rebellion of Henry II's son; and yet again in 1216, when Louis Dauphin, the heir of the king of France, seized the castle. The castle is open to the public.

✳ **Old Buckenham** Castle was built by William d'Albini in the late 11th century. The site was given to the Augustinian canons by William's son when his castle at New Buckenham was completed in 1146. Only the moat remains, though some of the stone in the wall of Abbey Farm came from the priory.

✳ **Oxburgh** Hall is a 15th-century fortified manor house, founded by Edmund Bedingfield in 1482 when he was given a licence to crenellate. (The licence can still be seen in the King's Room in the hall). The spiral brick staircase is a tour de force, but it was for show rather than defensive, as the way the spiral turns would block your sword arm. The original Great Hall with its 54ft-long hammer beam roof was demolished in 1775, and the house was extensively remodelled in the mid-19th century. Oxburgh Hall is famed for the embroidered wall hangings completed by Mary, Queen of Scots, during her captivity at Tutbury Castle with Elizabeth, Countess of Shrewsbury ('Bess of Hardwick'); the creatures shown include a stoat and a rhinoceros. The hall is in the care of the National Trust and is open to the public.

✳ At **Quidenham** there is a mound which has also been known as the Viking Mound and The Bubberies. At one point it was thought to be either the site of Boudicca's burial or a Bronze Age barrow. However, now it's believed that the motte belongs to a small motte and bailey castle built by the d'Albinis' in the 12th century.

✳ At **Raveningham** there is a motte but no bailey; it's most likely to have been a moated mediaeval manor house. A wet moat remains around the motte and there is a bridge across it.

✳ **Thetford** has the remains of two castles. The earlier one, **Red Castle**, was built at the end of the 11th century and was rediscovered in 1867. It's an earthwork with a bank and ditch, 120 metres in diameter, which was also part of the Saxon town ditch. The other castle is built right in the middle of an Iron Age fort. The motte is 25 metres high and 90 metres in diameter, and it's reputedly the second-tallest mediaeval earthwork in the country, next to Silbury. It's likely that there was a wooden fence and a castle at the

Thetford castle mound, in the middle of the hillfort ditches.

top. Part of the bailey includes a house and inn from the 16th century, and a jail dating from 1816. The site is in the care of English Heritage and is open to the public.

✳ **Weeting Castle** was a mediaeval manor house built by Ralph de Plaiz in the late 12th century. It's unusual because instead of being a motte and bailey castle there is a small moat and a hall with a three-storey tower at one end – practically a century before such buildings were fashionable. The moat was added in the 14th century, but by the end of the 14th century the building was abandoned. There is also an 18th-century ice house on the site, which belonged to a hall built in the same period as the ice house but since demolished. The remaining building is 20 metres by 14 metres and is surrounded by a dry moat that's 10 metres wide and 2 metres deep. The site is in the care of English Heritage and is open to the public.

✳ There was probably a castle at **Wood Norton** as there are remains of a moat with a 2-metre-high bank. The building was founded in the reign of Henry III and a licence to crenellate was given to Sir John de Norwyc in 1343. The building was known as **Lyng** Hall in 1359.

Weeting Castle.

✴ **Wormegay** Castle was a timber castle on a small motte and bailey site that was once an island in the peat fens. It was fortified in the 11th century by Hermer de Ferrers. In the 12th century Reginald de Warenne modified the fortification and founded the earthworks for the motte and bailey – the motte is 5 metres high and the bailey measures 77 metres by 62 metres. You can still see the remains of ramparts and ditches.

✴ It's thought that the d'Albinis built a castle in **Wymondham** between 1088 and 1139 in the area known as Moot Hill. There's a large ring motte measuring 160 metres by 120 metres.

Abbeys, monasteries and nunneries

More than 150 religious houses were founded in Norfolk, and remains can still be seen in around 50 sites.

✴ Some of the houses were founded as hospitals. Hospitals gave shelter to pilgrims, homes to the poor and care for the sick. Some were specifically set up as leper (or lazar) houses; there were six in **Norwich**, five in **Lynn**, four in **Thetford** and two in **Yarmouth**. One hospital which still survives is the Great Hospital of St Giles in **Norwich**, founded in 1249.

❊ The first Benedictine monastery founded after the Viking raids was at St Benet at Holme, between **Horning** and **Ludham**, which was established around 1016 by King Cnut on what may have been an earlier foundation. Nowadays, the main survivor is the gatehouse, with the remains of a windmill in the middle.

❊ The west front of the church at **Binham** Priory has a stunning window, which Pevsner has claimed to be the earliest surviving example of bar tracery in the country. In 1212 the monks there were besieged by Robert Fitzwalter after his friend, the prior, was removed from office. The monks were forced to eat bran and drink water from drainpipes until King John sent his forces to drive Fitzwalter's men away.

❊ **Bromholm** Priory (**Bacton** Abbey) was famous for owning a piece of the True Cross. According to the 15th-century chronicler John Capgrave, many miracles resulted, including people being cured of leprosy and blindness, and 30 people being brought back from the dead. John Paston was buried at the priory with a very lavish funeral in 1446: the list of victuals includes 13 barrels of beer, 27 barrels of ale, 15 gallons of wine, 41 pigs, 49 calves, 1,300 eggs, 20 gallons of milk and 8 gallons of cream. The Pastons also spent the equivalent of over £5,000 on candles in today's money, so it's not

Binham Priory.

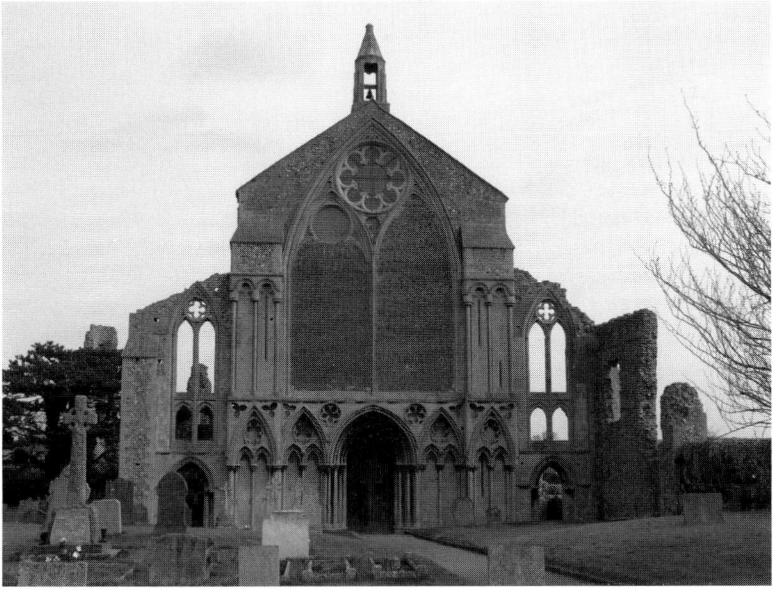

surprising that the Pastons also paid a glazier 20 shillings to take out two of the windows in the church (to stop the congregation suffocating from the smoke) and then put the windows back again.

✳ **Carrow** Priory in Norwich was founded by King Stephen in 1146. A huge row erupted in 1416 when William Koc of Trowse was set upon by seven men armed with spades and sticks and was beaten to death. Koc's widow Margery knew their names and accused Edith, the prioress of Carrow, of harbouring them. Edith and another nun were arrested and charged with murder, but were eventually acquitted.

✳ Archbishop Peckham visited **Coxford** Priory in 1281, and later wrote to the prior to reprimand him as his canons went coursing with hounds, played chess and chatted with girls!

✳ Greyfriars Tower in **King's Lynn** was a finalist in the first series of the BBC2 programme *Restoration*, beating a windmill in Lincolnshire and a fort in Essex in the regional heat. The tower was used as a seamark and was referred to as the 'leaning tower of Lynn'. At its worst, the lean was 67.5 centimetres, which, given its height of more than 28 metres, is just over 1 degree. (This compares to the 5.5-degree lean on the tower at Pisa). The 14th-century chronicle of the Greyfriars contains one of the earliest references to the plague: 'In this year, 1348, in Melcombe in the county of Dorset, a little before the feast of St John the Baptist, two ships, one of them from Bristol, came alongside. One of the sailors had brought from them from Gascony the seeds of the terrible pestilence, and through him the men of that town of Melcombe were the first in England to be infected.'

✳ **Hickling** Priory was badly affected by floods in 1207 and the plague in 1349. Only two people were left alive after the plague, so a novice was allowed to become the prior.

✳ The refectory wing of the priory at **Horsham St Faith's** is now part of a private house, which is occasionally open to the public. It contains an amazing series of wall paintings telling the story of the priory's foundation: Robert Fitzwalter, the lord of the manor at Horsham and Horstead, went on pilgrimage to Rome with his wife Sybilla. On their return they were robbed and imprisoned by pirates. They prayed for help from St Faith and she appeared to them in a vision and freed them. At her shrine in Conques, they vowed to found a monastery – which they did at Horsham, bringing two monks from Conques back with them.

✳ **Ingham** Priory was part of the Order of the Holy Trinity and St Victor for the Redemption of Captives (Trinitarian), which was founded in 1198.

Only 12 houses of this order were found in England. Ingham, although it was the last to be founded, became the head of the order in England. It's the only Trinitarian house in England with any surviving buildings.

✳ Isabel, the widow of Hugh Albini, Earl of Arundel, founded a Cistercian house at **Marham** in 1249 for the good of the souls of her father, mother and late husband. It was the only Cistercian female house in England to have the status of an abbey, rather than a priory.

✳ **Shouldham** Priory was the only Gilbertine house in Norfolk. There were two monastic communities contained within one church, with a wall down the middle of the church so they could share service, but not see each other. There was a tragic accident at the priory in 1321 during a football game when a man ran against William de Spalding and was stabbed by his knife. William was stricken with guilt and remorse, but the Pope ruled that it had been an accident.

✳ The only remains in England of a house belonging to the canons of the Holy Sepulchre is in **Thetford**. The canons of the Holy Sepulchre were set up to assist pilgrims visiting the shrine built on the site of Christ's burial chamber in Jerusalem.

✳ The Cluniac priory at **Thetford** was founded by Roger Bigod. Many local worthies were buried there, including Thomas Howard, the seventh Duke of Norfolk. His funeral in 1524 cost the equivalent of nearly £600,000 in today's money – and that didn't include the massive stone tomb which covered the grave! However, Henry VIII didn't spare the priory during the Reformation, despite the fact that his illegitimate son and his aunt were buried there; he simply had their bodies moved and reinterred. The priory's history includes some very violent episodes. In 1248, Prior Stephen had a huge disagreement with a Welsh monk who'd just arrived from Cluny; the monk drew his knife and killed Stephen at the church door. The monks weren't too unhappy about it as Stephen had been a poor prior. He and his two greedy brothers, Bernard the knight and Guiscard the clerk, would stay up all night, drinking and carousing, and eating all the rations while the poor starved. However, justice had to be seen to be done and the monk died in the dungeons at Norwich Castle. There was also a riot in 1313, when a mob broke into the priory and murdered some of the monks.

✳ **Walsingham** – which was never an abbey, though it liked to call itself that – was the richest priory in Norfolk, apart from Norwich, by the 15th century. It was also the second most famous place of pilgrimage in England, after Canterbury, even Henry VIII, who eventually dissolved the priory, walked barefoot to Walsingham and offered a very expensive necklace to the Virgin Mary. The Pilgrim's Path, which went from Cambridge to Walsingham via Newmarket and Fakenham, was known as the Pilgrim's Way. It was also known as the Milky Way, because one of the relics at Walsingham was a vial of the Virgin's milk. The priory was built after Richeldis, the foundress, had a dream in 1061 telling her to build an exact replica in Walsingham of the house in Nazareth where the Annunciation had taken place. Many miracles were ascribed to the place. According to the 18th-century historian Francis Blomefield, for many years a copper plate engraved with a picture of a knight on horseback was nailed to the priory door, in memory of the miraculous deliverance of Sir Raaf Boutetort. In 1314 the knight was being chased by an enemy towards a wicket door in the priory gates. He said a prayer and found himself on the other side of the door, still on horseback, although the door was small enough for people to have trouble getting through it on foot!

✳ **Wymondham** Abbey was founded by William d'Albini, the chief butler to Henry I and lord of the manor at Wymondham. He and his wife Maud were buried before the high altar. On Christmas Eve 1833, while the churchyard was being enlarged, two lead coffins were found. They contained a woman and a prematurely born child, both embalmed, and archaeologists of the time believed them to be Maud, who'd died in childbirth. Archaeologists also found a lead ingot weighing a ton, with the royal stamp on it.

Chapter 6

Epitaphs

If you wander through any Norfolk churchyard (or a church containing wall tablets, ledger stones or brasses), there's a fair bet you'll come across an interesting tale. Along the coast you may find tales of shipwrecks and skulduggery (see chapter 10); inland, you may discover monuments to strong characters, clever epitaphs reflecting someone's name or occupation or strange and unusual stories.

Lost epitaphs

✳ Sadly, I wasn't able to verify some of the more interesting epitaphs I found in ancient books. Given that gravestones are exposed to the elements and many inscriptions have worn badly, it's possible that the epitaphs were there at the time but have simply eroded since then. I particularly regret not being able to find the epitaph for the 'gossiping woman' at St Andrew's, **Colton**, which is especially appropriate as the church has a wonderful wall painting of the warning to gossips:

> Her husband prays, if e'er you walk this path
> Tread softly, if she stirs she'll talk.

✳ Other lost epitaphs include one on the cook of the corporation of **King's Lynn**, which was once in St Margaret's churchyard, but had been lost by the end of the 19th century:

> Alas! Alas! Will Scrivener's dead, who, by his art,
> Could make Death's skeleton edible in each part –
> Mourn, squeamish stomachs, and ye curious palates,
> You've lost your dainty dishes and your sallets;
> Mourn for yourselves, but not for him i' th' least –
> He's gone to taste of a more heavenly feast.

✳ And a wonderful rhyming one at St Peter and St Paul, **Salle**:

> Against his will
> Here lies George Hill,
> Who from a cliff
> Fell down quite stiff

✳ John Chambers, in his *General History of the County of Norfolk, 1829*, talks of an epitaph to Thomas Jackson, an actor in the Norwich Company who was buried at St Peter Mancroft, **Norwich**, but whose fellow professionals set up a memorial stone in St Mary's, **Gillingham**:

> Sacred to the memory of Thomas Jackson, comedian, who was engaged, December 21, 1741, to play a comic cast of characters in this great theatre, The World, for many of which he was prompted by nature to excel. The season being ended – his benefit over – the charges all paid, and his account closed – he made his exit in the tragedy of *Death* on the 17th of March, 1798, in full assurance of being called once more to rehearsal; when he hopes to find his forfeits all cleared – his cast of parts bettered – and his situation made agreeable by Him who paid the great stock debt for the love he bore to performers in general.

✳ Eighteenth-century historian Francis Blomefield mentions two other epitaphs for players at St Peter Mancroft, **Norwich**:

> Anne Roberts 1743, age 30
> The World's a Stage, at Birth our Play's begun,
> And all find Exits when their Parts are done.

> Henrietta Maria Bray 1737, age 60
> Here Reader you may plainly see,
> That Wit nor Humour here could be
> A Proof against Mortality.

✳ Silvester Tissington, writing in 1857, spoke of the epitaph of Matthew Mud at St Mary's, **West Walton**:

> Here lies Matthew Mud
> Death did him no hurt
> When alive he was mud
> And now dead he's but dirt.

✳ Henry James Loaring, writing in 1880, mentions the epitaph of a Mr None at **Wymondham** Abbey, with a witty play on his name:

> Here lyes None, one worse than None for ever thought
> And because None of None to thee, O Christ gives nought.

✳ William Andrews, writing in 1899, talks of an epitaph at All Saints, **Walcott**, which has a very modern feel to it:

William Wiseman
who died 5th of August, 1834, aged 72 years.
Under this marble, or under this sill,
Or under this turf, or e'en what you will,
Whatever an heir, or a friend in his stead,
Or any good creature, shall lay o'er my head,
Lies one who ne'er cared, and still cares not a pin
What they said, or may say, of the mortal within,
But who, living and dying, serene, still, and free,
Trusts in God that as well as he was he shall be.

The sea, the sea

✳ At St Nicholas, **Blakeney**, there is a gravestone for John Easter, who died on 9 February 1861. It reflects a fate that awaited many on the Norfolk coast:

I with seven others went
Our fellow men to save
A heavy wave upset our boat
We met a watery grave

✳ At St John the Baptist's Head, **Trimingham**, there's a beautifully carved ship at the top of a gravestone with an epitaph to the crew of a Dutch ship:

October 1881 the cruel sea took the
De Vrouw Arendje
of Katwyk
along with her ten crew
Willem Schaap captain
Jacob Schaap
Willem Schaap
Jacob van Duyn
Huig van Duyn
Pieter Kuyt
Cornelis de Best
Arie van der Plas
Floris van der Plas
Pleunis Pronk

Over the sea, the calm blue sea
There came upturned and silently
Beneath our cliffs on our lonely shore
The little bark that shall sail no more.

Strong personalities

✳ Ursula Hewyt's gravestone at St Margaret, **Breckles** is very unusual: it's small and oval-shaped rather than long and rectangular. This is because she asked to be buried standing up (like Ben Jonson was in the north aisle of the nave of Westminster Abbey). Her Latin epitaph reflects this: *Stat ut vixit erecta* ('As upright in death as she was in life').

✳ Also at **Breckles**, inside the tower, is a memorial to John Stubing, who died in 1806 at the age of 107 – so living in three different centuries:

> The remains of John Stubing lie in the middle of this steeple, aged one hundred & seven years & eight months. Lived in this parish sixty-seven years, & died with the character of an honest industrious man.

✳ At St Margaret, **Clenchwarton**, a tablet on the south wall commemorates the bravery of Francis Forster, who died in 1741:

> When the terrible inundation Feb 16 1735
> Threatening the destruction of this whole Level,
> He with unshaken resolution when all around him droop'd under their Misery,
> Opposed the Flood, repaired the broken Ramparts, and sav'd the Land from that fatal ruin which the next assault must have overwhelm'd it.

✳ Johnson Jex of **Letheringsett** was a remarkable man. He died in 1852 at the age of 73, and his obituary in the *Gentleman's Magazine* makes fascinating reading. He taught himself to read and write; at the age of 12 he saw a watchmaker take his mother's watch apart and clean it – so when it was returned he promptly tried doing the same, and was successful. The first watch he made was for the Revd T. Munnings, who lived near **Dereham**; more remarkably, he'd made all the horological tools himself. He also built a gold chronometer. He taught himself French when he was 60, so he would be able to read a book of horology in French, but was disappointed to discover that he knew all the information in the book already. He invented a lathe where he could cut the teeth of wheels – amazingly, he could cut up to 2,000 teeth per wheel and they would all be mathematically correct. He could tell the time by the stars and made telescopes. However, he was also a 'timid' man, and, although he was desperately afraid of infections, he refused to let any woman enter his house and lived in squalor. In St Andrew's Church, his death mask is on display along with a handwritten epitaph:

Born in obscurity
He passed his days at Letheringsett as
A Village Blacksmith.
By the force of an original and inventive genius
Combined with indomitable perseverance
He mastered some of the greatest difficulties of science;
Advancing from the forge to the crucible
And from the horse-shoe to the chronometer
Acquiring, by mental labour
And Philosophic research
A vast and varied amount of
Mechanical skill
And general knowledge.
He was a man of scrupulous integrity and moral worth;
But, regardless of wealth
And insensible to the voice of fame
He lived and died a scientific anchorite.

✳ One of the earliest examples of spin is to be found at St Mary's, **Rougham**. If you believe the ledger stone, Sir John Bladwell was a wonderful man, caring for his neighbours and doing all kinds of good deeds:

Here lyes interred Sr John Bladwell
The eldest son of William Bladwell
of Wanington Esq. Of that ancient family
He was a loiall subject a faithfull freind [sic]
a good neighbour Truly just & wisely
charitable He loved the church & her
well composed liturgy & was a constant
receiver of the Holy comunions [sic]
he endowed
the vicaridg of this towne with a good
house & son land adioning to it he left
this word the 14th day of October in ye
Yeare of his age 64 & in the year
of our lord god 1680

What the stone doesn't tell is that Sir John was actually a bit of a charmer. He persuaded the lord of the manor, Sir Thomas Peyton, that he should go and live abroad while Sir John would take care of the estate – and also of Sir Thomas's wife, Eliza Yelverton. Despite what it says on the ledger stone, Sir John never actually gave the 'vicaridg' to the village. And when Sir Thomas returned to Rougham he discovered that his house was in a bad state of repair and his estate was in such debt that he had to sell it! What happened to Eliza (or what she thought about being left in the care of Sir John) isn't recorded.

✳ Of a rather better character was the servant Will Gilman, whose memorial is at St Andrew's, **Burlingham:**

> Will Gilman heere lies buried in dust
> Who thirty-two yeares was a servant just
> To masters twow, the second whereof came
> First in his armes to church to get a name
> And least his name should with his body dye
> His master heere has placed his memorye.

✳ At All Saints, **Thurgarton,** there's a memorial to William Spurrell (who died in 1761) and his wife Elizabeth (who died in 1732):

> He was a Father to the Fatherless
> He helped the Widows in their Distress
> He never was given to Wordly Pride
> He lived an honest man and so he dy'd
> They was tender parents our Loss was great
> We hope that both eternal joys will meet.

✳ However, someone who really wasn't sure at all was Sarah Bear, who died at the age of 85 in 1757. Her epitaph at All Saints, **Marsham,** reads:

> To die I must
> To stay I'd rather
> To go I must
> I know not whither.

Medical matters

✳ In the early days of preventive medicine inoculation was viewed with much distrust. A tablet in St Andrew's Church, **Buxton,** shows exactly why:

> In memory
> of Mary Anne Kent
> the daughter of
> Mr & Mrs Kent of Fulham, Middlesex
> Who died under Inoculation

on the 16th day of March 1773
In the fourth Year of her Age
This much lamented Child
was in the highest State of Health
and her mental Powers began to open
and promise fairest fruit
when her fond Parents deluded by
prevalent Custom suffered the rough
officious hand of Art, to wound
the flourishing Root of Nature,
and rob the little Innocent of
the gracious Gift of Life
Let this unhappy event teach
distrustful Mortals that there is no safety
but in the hand of ALMIGHTY GOD.

✻ Epidemic illnesses took their toll on several parishes in Victorian times. A memorial at St Peter's, **Upwell,** to parishioners who died of cholera directly addresses those who read the epitaph:

In memory of sixty seven individuals of various age and either sex who in the short period from June 21st to August 13th 1832 died in this rectory of Asiatic Cholera, a frightful and previously unknown disease in this country – Reader, why hast thou been spared? To what purpose hast thou been left until now?

Wordplay

✻ Epitaphs in the late 17th to 18th centuries were often full of wordplay, either on the deceased's name or occupation.

✻ An epitaph at St Margaret, **Cantley,** to huntsman Robert Gilbert, who died in 1714, includes some very clever wordplay on his occupation:

That subtile FOX DEATH
Earth'd him here at last
And left a Fragrant Scent, so sweet behind,
That ough to be persu'd by all Mankind.

✻ At St Mary's, **Old Hunstanton,** there's an epitaph to Roger le Strange, who died in 1654:

In Heaven at home, O blessed change!
Who while I was on earth was strange.

✳ At St Peter Mancroft, **Norwich**, there was reputedly an epitaph to a Mr
Knott:

Here lies a man who was Knott born
His father was Knott before him.
He lives Knott, and he did Knott die,
Yet underneath this stone Doth lie.
Knott christened, Knott befot.
And here lies, and yet was Knott.

✳ At St Giles, **Norwich,** there is a brass to an Elizabetha Bedingfold with
wonderful wordplay on her name:

My name speakes what I was and am and have
A Bedding Field a peece of earth a grave
Where I expect vntill my sovle shall bring
Vnto the field an everlasting spring
For rayse and rayse ovt of the earth & slime
God did the first and will the second time
Obiit Die Maii 1637

✳ At St Mary's, **Haddiscoe**, there's an epitaph to the Yarmouth stagecoach
man, William Salter, who died at the age of 59 on 9 October 1776. The
wordplay on his occupation is particularly nice:

Here lies Will Salter honest man
Deny it Envy if you can
Trust to his business and his trust
Always punctual always just
His horses could they speak would tell
They loved their good old master well
His up hill work is chiefly done
His Stage is ended Race is Run
One journey is remaining still
To climb up Sions holy hill
And now his faults are all forgiv'n
Elija like drive up to Heaven
Take the Reward of all his Pains
And leave to other hands the Reins.

Families

✳ At All Saints, **Cockthorpe**, there is a testament to an enormous family:

> In assured hope resteth here the bodies of Sir James Calthorpe, Knight and Dame Barbara his wife, daughter of John Bacon Esq of Hesset. By her he had 8 sons and 6 daughters, in whose severel [sic] marriages and issues the ancient glory of the name of the family (resting them chiefly and almost solely in himself), did reflourish and is dilated into many of the best houses in the country, He was buried the 16th day of June AD 1615 and of his age 57. The said Barbara, surviving him, and much comforted with the sight of 193 of their children and their offspring, at the age of 86 years exchanged this life for a better, upon the 3rd of November AD 1639.

✳ There's a similar tribute to Richard and Clemens Stone at St Mary, **Holme-next-the-sea**: he died in 1607, aged 87, after 64 years of marriage, which produced 13 children and 72 grandchildren.

✳ Another couple who were married a long time were the Parmenters, commemorated at St Margaret's, **Witton-by-Walsham**. The epitaph is especially interesting because it uses the word 'Hollymus' for Christmas:

> Here lyeth buried the boddyis of Thomas Parmenter and Francis his wife who weare married 47 year together, and Thomas Paramenter died 12 days before Hollimvs 1631. His wife died on St Stevens day 1627.

✳ Infant mortality was very high before the middle of the 20th century. One heartbreaking epitaph which encapsulates the misery of the loss is that of Susan Browne in St Peter Mancroft, **Norwich**:

> Susan Browne, the last deceased of eleven children
> (the first ten interr'd before the northern porch) from their
> surviving parents, John and Susan his wife. She sought a
> city to come, and upon the 30th of August departed hence
> and found it.
> A M. 19. Dm. 1686.
> Here lies a single Flower scarcely blowne,
> Ten more, before the Northern Door are strowne,
> Pluckt from the self-same Stalke, only to be
> Transplanted to a better Nursery

✳ There's a similar ledger slab in St Michael's, **Braydeston**:

> Here lyeth the body of Ann, daughter of
> John & Eliz. Cotton, who died Aug
> 13. 1727, aged 2 years and 6 months,
> adjacent lie nine more of their children.

✳ And another to an even younger child in St Margaret's, **Starston**:

> Philip, the sonne of Francis Bacon Esq., and Dorothy his Wife, who
> died unweaned at Nurse, and was buried the 21st day of Nov. 1657.
> Death is the Sentence of the Lord over all flesh.

✳ A much stranger tale unfolds in St Mary's, **Martham**, where a slab declares:

> Here Lyeth The Body of Christo Burraway, who departed this Life
> ye 18 day of October, Anno Domini 1730. Aged 59 years. And there
> Lyes Alice who by hir Life Was my Sister, my mistres, my mother and
> my wife. Dyed Feb. ye 12. 1729. Aged 76 years.

This grew into a most salacious story about a modern-day Oedipus. The story went as follows: Christopher was the result of an affair between father and daughter and was placed in a foundling hospital. When he grew up he was apprenticed to a farmer. He was hired by Alice Burraway of Martham as her steward – neither of them knew it at the time, but she was his mother. She was pleased with his work and, although she was 17 years his senior, made him an offer of marriage. He accepted – which made Alice his sister (as they shared a father), his mistress (he worked for her), his mother and his wife. She allegedly discovered a birthmark on his shoulder, realised that he was her long-lost son and died of shock; he died 'scarcely four months' later. (Actually, it was more than a year).

However, historian Barbara Cornford, in an article in *Norfolk Fair*, provides the true explanation: Christopher was born in 1671 and his father died two years later. His mother, Mary, remarried the following year and the family moved to Martham in 1691. When Mary died, Christopher's stepfather, Gregory, married Alice Ryall. After Gregory had died in 1700, Christopher married Alice. It isn't clear how Alice could be called Christopher's 'sister' (possibly meaning his sister in the church community, if they were particularly religious?), but if he managed her farm that would make her his mistress; she was his stepfather's widow, so could be called his mother; and she was his wife for nearly 30 years.

Love and loss

✳ In St Margaret's, **Hempnall**, there's a poignant epitaph to 24-year-old Susanna Stone, who died in 1784:

> No sculptur'd Tomb, or storied urn,
> Decks the lone, simple, Village Grave;
> Yet here unseen, soft Virtues mourn
> Her, whom not Art, nor Vows could save.
> 'Farewell!' a weeping Husband cries,
> 'All cold my Love, thy gentle Heart;
> Farewell! Till Hev'n shall bid thee rise,
> Then: Once more given: no more to part.'

✳ Elizabeth Alec, who died in 1641, was clearly greatly missed, judging by her epitaph in St Peter's, **Great Walsingham**:

> Heaven hath her soule, this earth her earth,
> Her love her husband keepes,
> The ods twixt him and her is breth
> Which gon all flesh thus sleeps.

✳ At St Mary Magdalene, **Mulbarton**, there's an epitaph to Sarah Scargill, wife of Daniel, the rector, written on one page of a copper 'book'. It describes her as 'most Religious' and says that 'death Divorced them upon the 22th day of August 1680 in the 30th yeare of her Age'. On the page opposite there's a beckoning hand and the inscription:

> Deare Love, one Feather'd minute and I come
> To lye down in thy darke Retireing Roome
> And mingle Dust with thine...
> ...More Swift than Wind
> Or Flying Hind
> I come, I come away.

However, rector Daniel Scargill's 'one minute' lasted 41 years; he was able to remarry and bury his second wife during that period!

✳ William Ruddock died on 12 January 1812 at the age of 35, leaving his wife Sarah and five children to mourn him at St Mary's, **Bridgham**:

> Time swept by his o'erwhelming tide,
> My faithful partner from my side

And you of yours depriv'd maybe
As unexpectedly as me.
Set then your heart on things above,
Death soon will end all mortal love.

Accidents

✳ At St Michael's, **Barton Turf**, there's a tablet on the outside of the church referring to a tragic accident:

In
Memory of four Sons
of John and Elizh
Doyley
who were unfortunately
Drowned in Barton Broad
the 26 of Decr 1786
John Aged 23 Robt 20
Willm 16 James 10 Years

✳ At St Andrew's, **Colney**, there is a tablet warning of the dangers of road accidents:

Sacred to the Memory of John Fox who on the 20 of Dec 1806 in the 79th Year of his Age was unfortunately kill'd near this spot having been thrust down & trampled on by the Horses of a Waggon. Tho his Life was humble yet is it deserving of imitation. He was a useful and deserving Member of Society an honest & industrious labourer. READER If thou drivest a team be careful & endanger not the Life of another or thine own.

✳ At St Peter, **Riddlesworth**, a memorial records a major storm in 1703; two women in the village were killed when a chimney stack fell on them. One was Lady Elinor Drury and the other was her niece, Mary Fisher. The ledger slab at the east end of the nave declares:

Here lyeth the Body of Dame Elinor Drury, 2d daughter of Sam: Harsnet of Great Fransham in Norfolk, Esq; the Relict of Will: Marsham of Stratton-Strawley, Gent. the second wife of Sir Robert Drury of Ridlesworth in the county of Norf, Bart, who was unfortunately kill'd in the fatal Hurricane, Nov. the 27th in the Year of our Lord, 1703.

The Pious and Virtuous Mrs Mary Fisher
Whose Soul tooke her Flight to Heaven in the Furious hurricane on

November thee 27th 1703. This Monument is Dedicated by her true & Faithfull lover Anthony Drury of Mendham in Norfolk, Gent.

Sad tales

✳ In the churchyard of St Nicholas, **East Dereham**, there is a stone placed in tribute to Jean de Narde, who was a prisoner of war during the Napoleonic Wars and was kept in the church tower at Dereham:

> In memory of Jean de Narde, son of a Notary Public of St. Malo. A French prisoner of war, who, having escaped from the Bell tower of this church, was pursued and shot by a soldier. October 6th, 1799, aged 28 years.

✳ In the church of All Saints, **Dickleburgh**, there's a monument to rector Christopher Barnard, who died in 1680. A staunch royalist, he refused to take the covenant in 1643, so the Earl of Manchester threw him out of his living. His house was looted and Cromwell's soldiers arrested him – but he'd been the rector of Dickleburgh for 21 years at this point and his flock had no intention of losing him. The story is recounted on his epitaph. He was:

> well beloved by his parishioners who thought it a Judgement upon them when ye souldyers drag'd him away to carry him to Norwich Castle; but his beloved flock follow'd him and resqued him and hid him a long time after.

They also looked after his wife and nine children, and when his house was ransacked again, the parishioners – including women and children, according to Francis Blomefield's account – went to his house to take whatever they could find and hide it from the soldiers. Barnard was one of the first ministers restored to his living after the Restoration, on 22 September 1662, and remained the rector of Dickleburgh until his death at the age of 84.

✳ Another sad tale is told in the churchyard at St Mary's, **Brancaster**:

> Sacred to the memory of Susanna Roche aged 32 years and also to her nephew Alexander David Roche aged 4 years, who were unfortunately drowned with many others in the cabin of the Earl of Wemyss, Leith Packet, which was stranded on this coast during the dreadful gale on September 1st 1833 on its passage from London. Which melancholy affair has been doubly afflicting for the relatives of the deceased from the fact that no attempt was ever made to

rescue them from their situation, and in continuation of such inhuman conduct their persons were stripped of every valuable and their property plundered.

✳ Six women, a man and four children drowned on the *Earl of Wemyss*. The inquiry at the Hare Arms in **Docking**, later that month, revealed a tale of negligence and tragedy, along with accusations that no attempt was made to rescue them and that the bodies were looted. Newman Reeve – the son-in-law of the lord of the manor – was accused of taking things from the bodies 'for security' and then refusing to give them back, on the grounds that they were wreckage and therefore property of the lord of the manor. After a spell in **Norwich** Castle prison, Reeve was acquitted at the assizes, despite the fact that a second trial of others who were also accused of theft included some very damning evidence. The families of the dead, however, were unconvinced of Reeve's innocence and put their own testament in stone.

✳ A light-hearted stunt by a circus clown ended in disaster and much loss of life. The story of the suspension bridge and how it broke is carved at the top of nine-year-old George Beloe's grave in St Nicholas's churchyard, **Great Yarmouth**. On 2 May 1845, Nelson the clown from Mr Cook's circus had been advertised as travelling from a drawbridge on the quay to the suspension bridge in a bath drawn by four geese. Even though it was raining, thousands of people stood on the sides of the banks to watch. People thronged the bridges too, and when Nelson was spotted, people rushed to the side of the bridge to see him. One or two rods were seen to give way and people shouted a warning, but it was too late. The chains snapped and the bridge went down. *The Times* reported that between 300 and 600 people went into the water – many of them children. Most were saved, but the final death toll stood at 79.

Memento mori

✳ A memento mori tends to show the deceased as a cadaver or decayed corpse. The idea was that – like the mediaeval wall paintings of the 'quick and the dead' – they would remind passers-by of their own mortality: as I am, so you will be. There are verses on this subject in many churches, but a particularly nicely done epitaph is that of Thomas Gooding in **Norwich** Cathedral.

Like Ursula Hewyt (see page 104), Gooding was reputedly buried standing up. The inscription reads:

> All you that do this place pass bye
> Remember death for you must dye
> As you are now then so was I
> And as I am so that you be

Thomas Gooding here do staye
Waiting for God's judgement daye.

✳ Similar sentiments can be seen at St Peter and St Paul's Church, **Salle**, on the ledger stone to John Brigge from 1454:

Here lyth John Brigge undir this marbil ston,
Whos sowle our lorde Ihu have mercy upon,
For in this world worthyly he lived many a day,
And here his body is berried and cowched undir clay,
So, friendis free whatever ye be pray for me I you pray,
As ye me see in soche degree so schall ye be another day.

✳ There's an even stranger version of this at St Andrew's Church, **Little Barningham**: a box pew which contains a carved skeleton in a shroud with an hourglass in one corner. Sadly, the carving is a modern copy as the original was stolen in 1995. There are two inscriptions dated 1640 explaining this:

For couples joynd in wedlock and my friends that stranger is, this seat
did I intend, built at the cost and charge of Steven Crosbee.

All you that doe this place pass by
As you are nowe even so was I
Remember death, for you must dye
And as I am soe shall you be.
Prepare therefore to follow me.

Murder most horrid

✳ Some epitaphs record unpleasant deaths – and their consequences – such as Edward Allen's memorial at St Mary's, **Wroxham**:

In memory of Edward Allen
of this place limeburner
who was attacked and
murdered the 3rd Feb 1799
in the 34th year of his age
Justice soon overtook the
perpetrator of the atrocious
deed and the next
morning he was apprehended

and soon afterwards he was
condemned and executed
and his body given to the
surgeons for dissection

✳ The tablet to former rector William Whitear at St Margaret's, **Starston**, is vague about the actual circumstances of his death in 1826. After hearing that a group of poachers were going to be at the woods at Gawdy Hall on 27 November, he went out with an armed committee who intended to catch them. However, it was too dark to see properly, and when a shot was fired both William Whitear and Thomas Pallont (who was also in the armed committee) fell to the ground. Pallont lost a finger and thumb and Whitear was wounded in the chest, so severely that he died just under a fortnight later. Thomas Pallont was charged with manslaughter at Thetford Assizes in 1827, but was acquitted.

More than an epitaph

Many gravestones and memorials are beautifully carved. Often there are cherubs, or reminders of death (such as the wonderful monument to Susanna Kinges at All Saints, **Morston**, where you can see the gravedigger's tools of a coffin, a skull and bones, an hourglass and a bell; or the charnel house you can see on Sir Edward Barkham's memorial at St George's, **South Acre**). However, sometimes you'll see carvings or memorials that are very specific to the deceased, to do with their interests or their occupations. Good examples are:

✳ The unknown blacksmith at St Botolph, **Grimston**, whose headstone is simply a plain black iron anvil.

✳ The memorial to Revd Thomas Havers (1659–1719) at The Holy Cross, **Stoke Holy Cross**. As well as being a vicar, he was also a surgeon, so there's a set of 18th-century lithotomy instruments carved on his memorial. The Latin inscription praises his skill in 'theology, medicine, surgery and especially cutting for the stone' (that is, removing bladder stones by surgery) – he charged five shillings for the operation.

✳ The memorial to Thomas Keppel North (who died of the flu in 1918) at St Mary's, **Rougham**, showing the biplane he designed for Allcock and Brown.

✳ The grave of millwright Thomas Smith (who died in 1725) at St Mary's, **Wiveton**, showing a millstone and the tools of his trade.

✳ The graves of farmers George and Anne Basey at St Mary, **Ashby St Mary**, with their turkeys and geese.

Memorial to Sarah Hare.

✳ However, perhaps the memorial with the most shock value (particularly if you're not expecting to see anything like it when you open the plain mahogany door to the cabinet) has to be Sarah Hare's life-size wax monument at Holy Trinity, **Stow Bardolph**. It's the only wax monument known in the country outside Westminster Abbey, and is also the one with the latest date. There is a legend which states that she died after pricking her finger while sewing on a Sunday, but this isn't actually true. She gave very detailed instructions in her will about the monument, instructing her executors to have her 'face and hands made in wax with a piece of crimson satin thrown like a garment in a picture.' The effigy was untouched for nearly 250 years, but had been damaged by mice and damp, and so in 1984 it was restored by Jean Fraser, a former studio manager at Madam Tussaud's, and textile conservator Judith Dore.

The inscription over the top of the effigy reads:

Here lyeth the body of Sarah Hare, youngest daughter of Sr Thos Hare Bart and Dame Elizabh his wife and sister to the preset Sr Thos Hare who departed this life the IX day of Apr MDCCXLIV and ordered this effigies to be placed here.

Chapter 7
Norfolk Folk

Charlotte Atkyns, the Norfolk Scarlet Pimpernel

In St Peter's Church, **Ketteringham**, there's a monument to Norfolk's version of the Scarlet Pimpernel, Charlotte Atkyns. Born in Ireland in 1758, Charlotte Walpole became an actress and made her debut on Drury Lane in 1777. The *Bristol Journal* praised her work: 'She is a good Singer, an excellent Actress, and it is a matter of dispute with the young Londoners in which characters she appears to most advantage, male or female.' She fell in love with Edward Atkyns of Ketteringham Hall and married him in Piccadilly in 1779 before retiring from the stage. They moved to France in 1784, where she became friendly with the Versailles set, including Marie Antoinette, but moved back to Ketteringham in 1791 as life in Revolutionary France grew more dangerous.

Charlotte continued to stay in touch with various French émigrés. She went back to France in 1793 and met Marie Antoinette in secret; the queen asked her to save the Dauphin, Louis Charles (the future Louis XVII). After her husband's death in 1794, Charlotte went back to France and teamed up with her friends to rescue the Dauphin, who'd been separated from his mother and kept in seclusion in the Temple.

In May 1795 the Dauphin was said to be seriously ill. His doctor, P.J. Lesault, died suddenly on 1 June; new doctors weren't called for several days and the Dauphin himself died on 8 June. An autopsy the next day referred to the 10-year-old son of Louis Capet dying from 'a scrofulous affection of longstanding' (tuberculosis). He was buried on 10 June in an unmarked grave in the cemetery of St Marguerite.

As soon as the news was announced rumours arose that the Dauphin had actually escaped. Nobody could prove it, but, interestingly, the Dauphin's sister Marie Thérèse wasn't asked to identify the body. The people who'd supposedly inspected the Dauphin were different each time, and the Dauphin was seriously ill for a month – hardly long-standing.

When Louis XVIII was restored to the throne in 1814, rumours were still circulating that the Dauphin had escaped from the Temple and another child had been substituted for him. According to papers Charlotte gave to her notary (which disappeared shortly after they were given to author Frédéric Barbey for his book, published in 1905), the rescue attempt in 1795 was successful. There seems to have been a complicated fraud involved, but what really happened has never been proved. A deaf mute child was delivered to Charlotte Atkyns's agents, but it's unknown who he was. Forty people subsequently tried to claim that they were the real Louis XVII. The Comte de Richemonte claimed in 1828 that he was smuggled out in a basket by an earlier attendant, Madame Simon. Karl William Naundorff was the other major claimant, and the most likely. His explanation of his disappearance from the Temple was that he was substituted for a wooden figure, which was in turn exchanged for a deaf mute child, who was then substituted for a child with scrofula. Naundorff said he left the Temple in a coffin and was smuggled out en route to the funeral. The Dutch authorities certainly believed him, because the name they put on his death certificate in 1845 was 'Charles Louis de Bourbon, duc de Normandie (Louis XVII)'; his children took the name de Bourbon.

But was he really Louis XVII?

Charlotte Atkyns couldn't explain what had happened to the Dauphin, the child she believed she'd rescued. In 1814, when she asked the Bourbon government for £30,000 to cover her expenses in her work supporting the émigrés, they refused to pay her anything because she'd included costs for rescuing the Dauphin. Charlotte had already mortgaged Ketteringham Hall in 1799 and was desperate for money. She made over the house to her sister-in-law Mary Atkyns in 1824 in return for an annuity, and died in Paris in 1836, heavily in debt but still believing that she had rescued the Dauphin.

The story of Louis XVII has an unusual postscript: the doctor who performed the autopsy on the 10-year-old boy secretly cut out his heart, in the tradition of keeping royal hearts separate from their bodies, and smuggled it away in a handkerchief. He kept the heart in a vase of alcohol, but it was stolen by one of his students. On his deathbed, the student repented of his crime and asked his wife to return it. The heart was eventually kept by the Spanish branch of the Bourbon family, who brought it back to Paris in 1975. The heart was kept in the basilica of Saint-Denis, and tests were carried out by Ernst Brinkmann of Münster University and Jean-Jacques Cassiman, a Belgian professor of genetics. Academics compared DNA from the heart to DNA taken from Marie Antoinette's hair in 2000, confirming that the heart belonged to a close relative of hers. Finally, on 8 June 2004, the heart was buried in the basilica of Saint-Denis, near the graves of Marie Antoinette and Louis XVI.

Henry Cable – from convict to colonial settler

Henry Cable (originally Kabel or Kable) was born in Suffolk in 1766 and became a labourer like his father. However, he joined a gang of burglars and was caught in 1783; he was sentenced to death, along with his father and an accomplice. He was the only one reprieved, his sentence commuted to transportation.

While Cable was imprisoned in **Norwich** Castle in 1786, he had a son with Susannah Holmes, who was also awaiting transportation. Susannah was ordered to be sent out on the first fleet from Plymouth. She was not allowed to take the baby with her and Cable was refused permission to marry her. When this was reported in the press, the sympathetic public subscribed £20 (the equivalent of just over £2,000 today) to help them. Lord Sydney intervened and ordered that they should all go to Australia together. They arrived at Sydney Cove in 1788, and Henry married Susannah at the first religious service performed by the colony chaplain on 10 February.

In July 1788 Cable issued a writ against the master of the *Alexander* for withholding the goods that he and Susannah had bought from England. This was the first case heard in the colony's court of civil jurisdiction. They won and the master was ordered to make restitution. Susannah and Cable went on to have 10 more children. Cable also became a pillar of the new colony: in 1789 he set up a night watch, becoming its overseer two years later. In 1794 he became the chief constable. He also set up merchant trading, having ships built in the colony which would then take passengers and cargo to England. However, in 1805 he clashed with Governor William Bligh, who refused permission for goods to be moved between two of Cable's ships. Bligh put Cable and his business partners in jail for a month and also fined them £100 each (the equivalent of just over £6,000 today) for addressing him 'improperly'. Bligh was deposed in 1808 and Cable supported the rebels, eventually helping them to petition the prince regent for civil rights.

Susannah died in 1825; Henry lived with his son John until his death just over 20 years later and was buried beside her.

Howard Carter and the discovery of Tutankhamun

Howard Carter was born in Kensington in 1874, the youngest of eight children, but spent most of his childhood in **Swaffham**. His father Samuel was a staff illustrator at the *Illustrated London News* and Carter inherited his artistic ability.

In 1891, at the age of 17, he went to Egypt to work alongside the archaeologists and trace the tomb scenes. While working with William Flinders Petrie, he drew the painted reliefs in the temple of Queen Hatshepsut at Thebes, which are thought to be among the best records of Egyptian monuments. It was Petrie who inspired him to learn how to excavate.

In 1899 Carter was appointed as the first inspector general of monuments for Upper Egypt, which meant that he supervised and controlled archaeology along the Upper Nile Valley. During this period he discovered the tomb of

King Tuthmosis IV in the Valley of the Kings. He also installed the first electric lights at Abu Simbel and in various tombs in the Valley of the Kings. His career was marred, however, by a row in 1904 following a fight between some French tourists and the Egyptian antiquities guards. The tourists went to Lord Cromer, the Egyptian consul, and demanded an apology; Carter refused as the drunken tourists had started the fight and the guards had merely defended themselves. He was transferred to Tanta, where he had very little involvement in archaeology and was pushed into resigning in 1905.

The next four years were spent painting watercolours and showing foreign tourists around. However, in 1909, he started working for the Earl of Carnarvon as his supervisor of excavations. It was while working for him that on 4 November 1922 he finally uncovered the stairway to Tutankhamun's tomb.

On 26 November he made a tiny hole in the top left-hand corner of the doorway and peered in with a candle. When Carnarvon asked if he could see anything, he replied, 'Yes, I see wonderful things.' He still didn't know if he'd found a cache of treasure, or a completely undisturbed tomb, but he'd been able to see a sealed doorway – and things were looking promising.

The discovery stunned the world. Over the next few months the contents were conserved and recorded with care. Carter was very much ahead of his time in that respect, making sure everything was recorded rather than just shipping everything out. The antechamber alone took seven weeks to clear: each item was recorded with photographs from different angles, along with a numbered record card and a written description, as well as its position being marked on a ground plan of the tomb.

It was in February 1923 that they discovered the untouched body and funeral goods of the Egyptian king, Tutankhamun. Carnarvon died of pneumonia in the April, and the media soon latched onto the idea of the curse of the mummy's tomb. It's said that by 1929 11 people connected with the discovery had died. However, the media frenzy was the least of Carter's troubles; local politics were turbulent and Carnarvon had signed an exclusive media deal with *The Times* which upset both the Egyptian and worldwide media. Carter was no diplomat and couldn't see that he needed more Egyptian involvement in the excavation. The row deepened to the point where, on the day that the sarcophagus lid was lifted, Carter closed the tomb and posted a notice saying, 'Owing to the impossible restrictions and discourtesies of the Egyptian Public Works Department and its antiquity service, all my collaborators, as a protest, have refused to work any further upon their scientific investigations in the tomb.'

Pierre Lacau, the Director General of the Antiquities Service, said that Carter had violated the terms of the Carnarvon concession in the excavation and that the Egyptians would finish the work. Carter left Egypt and rather naively printed a pamphlet which he thought would explain the politics, but which instead lost him much support. However, when Sir Lee Stack, the British Governor General of Sudan and Egyptian army commander, was murdered in Cairo in November 1925, and the British disbanded the Nationalist Government, Carter returned to work on the excavation. Work on recording the tomb continued for the next seven years.

When the work was finally finished, Carter retired. Sadly, he became ill with Hodgkin's disease and died in London on 2 March 1939, aged 65.

Joseph Clover, the father of modern anaesthetics

Joseph Clover was born in **Aylsham** in 1825, above his father's draper's shop. He went to school in Norwich, and at the age of 16 became a dresser at the Norfolk and Norwich Hospital. In 1844 he went to University College Hospital in London, and was present at the operation where Robert Lister amputated a leg under the first general anaesthetic given in England, in December 1846. After he qualified, he worked at University College Hospital, operating and teaching anaesthetics. He moved to Mortimer Street (later renamed Cavendish Place) with his parents and lived there for the rest of his life.

He produced several inventions, including a bladder syringe to remove crushed fragments of stone; the Clover crutch, which held the patient in position for a lithotomy operation; and a gas cautery. However, one of his most important inventions came in 1862 when he developed the first apparatus to regulate the amount of chloroform breathed in by the patient without the problems of cooling the anaesthetic. It consisted of a bag filled with a known concentration of chloroform, plus a facepiece which diluted the chloroform with air. He exhibited it at the International Exhibition of 1862 to much praise, although the apparatus was cumbersome and he had to hang it on his back.

It's thought that he was instrumental in the recommendations of the Royal Medical and Chirurgical Society's report into chloroform deaths in 1864, including recommending that the anaesthetist should monitor a patient's pulse continuously. He also did much private work in dental anaesthetics, and was very much in demand as an anaesthetist because he was so calm and accurate.

In 1869 he married Mary Ann Hall and they had five children. The Clovers were friends with many notable people in London, including the artist Burne-Jones, the poet Tennyson and the engineer Brunel. Unlike many of the medical specialists of his era, he didn't publish textbooks, instead, he wrote articles, lectured and taught by example. He continued to work on improving anaesthetic apparatus and developed a 'portable regulating ether inhaler' in 1877.

He died of tuberculosis in 1882, but his work hasn't been forgotten; even today he's depicted on the coat of arms of the Royal College of Anaesthetists.

John Coan, the 'Norfolk Pigmy'

John Coan was born at **Tivetshall** in 1728. As a small child he stopped growing, and in 1750 he was measured by the **Norwich** doctor William Arderon, who said that he weighed 38lb fully clothed and was 38 inches high including his hat and shoes – the same size as a normal three-year-old child.

Coan worked at fairgrounds and toured as an exhibit. In July 1744 he was exhibited at the Lower Half Moon in the Market Place at Norwich. Midgets and dwarfs were very popular with royalty, so it's not surprising that he was presented to the Prince of Wales in 1751 and George II the following year. He was received very well by them amd they made him a 'handsome present', according to the *Illustrated News*.

Despite the fact that Thomas Frost describes his appearance at the Swan in Smithfield during Bartholomew Fair in 1751 as 'the principal show [which] seems to have been one containing two dwarfs, a remarkable negro, a female one-horned rhinoceros, and a crocodile', Coan was more than just a freak show. He was bright, with a sharp wit, was fond of bright clothes and was very good at imitating people. He did song and dance routines; contemporary reports describe his voice as 'a little hollow, but not disagreeable.'

His health started to fail in 1762. By then he was working 12-hour shifts at The Dwarf's Tavern, an inn in Chelsea Fields owned by the showman John Pinchbeck, singing and dancing on the table tops every night. After his death on 16 March 1764, rather gruesomely, Pinchbeck exhibited his corpse for as long as possible. When he was finally forced to bury Coan, he had a waxwork model made of the dwarf and exhibited that instead.

Sir Astley Cooper – surgeon, anatomist and bodysnatcher

Astley Paston Cooper was born on 23 August 1768 at **Brooke** Hall, the sixth child of Reverend Samuel Cooper and his wife Maria, a novelist. All five of his sisters and one of his brothers died from consumption, and Cooper's own post-mortem showed evidence that he'd had tuberculosis. In early life he was a practical joker and a lazy scholar, but when one of his brothers bled to death after an accident Cooper decided to become a doctor. His grandfather and one of his uncles were surgeons in London, so Cooper became a medical student at St Thomas's in London and studied under Henry Cline and John Hunter. This sparked his lifelong interest in dissection and experiments.

In 1789 he became Cline's anatomy demonstrator and two years later he started lecturing with him on anatomy and surgery. He married Anna Cock in December 1791 – and spent the evening of his wedding giving his usual anatomy lecture! The marriage was, however, happy, and although Anna Maria, their only child, died at the age of 16 months, they went on to adopt two children.

During the 1790s Cooper taught at St Thomas's and worked on dissections. Rather than publishing textbooks, he published collections of his lectures. These were included in the very first issue of *The Lancet* in 1823, and were published in America and Germany as well as in England. He once dissected an elephant in his front garden – hiding it from public view by putting a carpet over the railings.

George IV created him a baronet in 1821 after Cooper removed an infected sebaceous cyst from his scalp, and agreed to Cooper's request that the baronetcy would pass to his adopted son. Cooper became sergeant surgeon to George IV, then to William IV and Victoria. He was a popular and respected doctor and won the Royal Society's Copley Medal in 1800 for his work on problems with the Eustachian tubes (in the ears) and treatment via myringotomy (putting a tiny cut into the eardrum to relieve pressure). He was particularly interested in circulation and aneurysms, and performed a famous operation in 1817 where he tied an abdominal aorta for an aneurysm (the patient lived for another 13 years after the operation).

His treatises on anatomy were important and influential, particularly those on hernias, the thymus gland and the breast. Several anatomical structures have been named after him, as he was the first to describe them. These include Cooper's fascia (which covers the spermatic cord), Cooper's stripes (in the ulnar ligaments) and Cooper's ligaments (the suspensory ligaments in the breast). He also discovered several diseases, including Cooper's disease (benign cysts in the breast), Cooper's neuralgia (neuralgia of the breast) and Cooper's hernia (a femoral hernia in the thigh).

He was elected professor of comparative anatomy at the Royal College of Surgeons in 1813 and was also one of their examiners. He was also president of the college twice, and a fellow and vice-president of the Royal Society of Medicine.

Before the Anatomy Act of 1832 was passed it was difficult for surgeons to work on anatomy as few bodies were available for dissection. Cooper had helped build up the anatomy and surgical museum at St Thomas's and had helped to establish a similar museum at Guy's Hospital. Many of the specimens from his dissections had been supplied by bodysnatchers. At the House of Commons select committee on anatomy in 1828, Cooper said that no dead person was safe from the activities of the resurrectionists: 'There is no person, let his station in life be what it may, whom, if I were disposed to dissect, I could not obtain...The law only enhances the price, it does not prevent the exhumation.'

After his wife's death in 1827 Cooper retired to the country, but soon grew bored with farming. He remarried the following year, and began treating animals, before later reopening his surgical practice in London. He used to do two or three hours of dissection before breakfast, as well as a full day's surgical work.

He died in 1841 after developing congestive heart failure and was buried in the chapel of Guy's Hospital.

Harold Davidson, the Prostitutes' Padre

Harold Davidson was born in Southampton in 1875. Originally he wanted to perform on the stage, but his father persuaded him to become a clergyman instead. He studied at Oxford, but did the occasional acting job during his studies. In May 1906 he was appointed as the vicar of **Stiffkey**, and married Moyra Saurin in November of that year. It was a turbulent marriage, not helped by his habit of filling the vicarage with what she called 'waifs and strays'. It was also not helped by the fact that he was conned by a man called Arthur Gordon and ended up filing for bankruptcy in 1925.

He spent much time in London and had permission from the bishop to be a chaplain around London's West End theatres. He rescued teenage girls who were being drawn into prostitution, including saving a girl from throwing herself into the Thames. He would take them for a cup of tea, listen to their problems and help them find a job and somewhere to live. He even paid for one of them, Rose Ellis, to be treated for syphilis.

Despite the fact that he only spent one day a week in Stiffkey, he was still popular in the parish. However, when he wasn't at Stiffkey on Remembrance Day 1930 he was reported to the bishop. The bishop hired a private detective to follow Davidson and then pressed charges, stating that the vicar had offended against public morality through adultery and accosting women in London. Davidson supported by his family, fought the case. He said, 'For years I have been known as the Prostitute's Padre', and that it was 'the proudest title that a true priest of Christ can hold.'

The trial opened in March 1932 and immediately hit the headlines. Public support was with Davidson, until the prosecution produced a photograph of him with a young girl standing with her back to the camera, naked but for a shawl. Davidson protested that it had been a honey trap, but the damage was done. He was found guilty on five counts of immoral conduct and thrown out of the church. Although he tried to protest his innocence at an assembly in 1936, the archbishop of Canterbury told him that he had no right to speak.

Without a job and deeply in debt, Davidson joined the circus to raise money for an appeal. He was exhibited in a barrel on Blackpool's Golden Mile. The following year he signed up with a menagerie in Skegness, as 'a modern Daniel in a lion's den'. The idea was that he would preach from a cage containing two lions – but unfortunately he trod on one of the lion's tails and was badly mauled. He died on 30 July 1937 at Skegness and was buried at Stiffkey.

Pablo Fanque, the first black circus proprietor in Britain

Pablo Fanque was born in **Norwich** in 1796, the son of a butler; his original name was William Darby. His first professional appearance, as 'Young

Darby', was at William Batty's circus in Norwich, on 26 December 1821. His circus acts included horsemanship, rope-walking, leaping and rope-vaulting. He spent some time with Andrew Ducrow's troupe, but then returned to Batty's circus in 1834. Two years later, he was described as the 'loftiest jumper in England' – his acts included jumping through a military drum and leaping the length of a post-chaise with two horses in the shafts.

In 1841 Fanque founded his own circus, the Circus Royal, and toured Yorkshire and Lancashire. He married Susannah Marlaw, the daughter of a button maker, and she too joined in the circus. At his 1847 debut in London, the *London Illustrated News* said: 'Mr Pablo Fanque is an artiste of colour, and his steed...we have not only never seen surpassed, but never equalled.' Fanque had trained the horse, Beda, himself.

Fanque later established a base in Manchester. However, Susannah died in March 1848 in a freak accident when part of the gallery collapsed and several planks hit her on the head, killing her instantly. (To top it all, someone stole that night's takings of £30 – the equivalent of £2,269 today.)

In the summer of 1848 Fanque married Elizabeth Corker, a circus equestrian performer 30 years his junior. Later that year, Fanque returned to Norwich and 'Fanque's Amphitheatre' opened in the Victoria Gardens for the winter season. The show was a huge success: his clown, Tom Matthews, was presented with a silver snuff-box and the acrobat Arthur Barns managed to do 50 consecutive somersaults.

Fanque died in Stockport in May 1871 and was buried in the private Woodhouse Cemetery in Leeds, next to Susannah. At his funeral a band played the *Dead March* before the hearse and Fanque's favourite horse, Wallet, followed begind. The Reverend Thomas Horne, chaplain of the Showman's Guild, said at his funeral: 'In the great brotherhood of the equestrian world there is no colour bar, for, although Pablo Fanque was of African extraction, he speedily made his way to the top of his profession. The camaraderie of the Ring has but one test: ability.'

The Beatles track *For the Benefit of Mr Kite* on the Sergeant Pepper album was inspired by a poster from Fanque's circus, which appeared in Rochdale on 14 February 1843. The poster states that the show was for the benefit of Mr Kite, one of the circus's star performers, who was to perform a tightrope walk and introduce the horse Zanthus. John Lennon saw the poster in an antique shop in Sevenoaks while making the promotional film for *Strawberry Fields Forever*, he bought it and the rest is musical history.

Robert Hales, the Norfolk Giant

Robert Hales was born in **West Somerton** in 1813. He wanted to be a sailor, but by the time he was 17 he was too tall to fit below deck. He reached an incredible 7ft 8in and weighed 33 stone (210 kg), with a chest measurement of 62 inches and a waist measurement of 64 inches. According to a letter written by him in 1851, his father was 6ft 6in tall, his mother was 6ft, his five sisters averaged out at 6ft 3in and his three brothers 6ft 5in. He travelled round fairgrounds with his sister Mary – who was 7ft 2in – in a yellow van, until her death from pneumonia in 1842. They were exhibited at Tombland Fair in **Norwich** and also at Britannia Pier in **Great Yarmouth**.

In 1840 Hales was presented to Queen Victoria at Epsom Races and she said that he reminded her of her uncle, George IV.

In 1849 P.T. Barnum paid Hales £800 (the equivalent of just over £63,000 today) to appear in the US. On the outward journey, Hales jumped overboard to save a boy's life; he was swept out to sea and it was six hours before he was rescued. He was hailed as a hero for his actions.

He was a huge draw, with 28,000 people coming to see him in the space of 10 days. While he was there he married Irishwoman Elizabeth Simpson, who was 7ft 6in tall. However, it's thought that this was a Barnum publicity stunt as Hales returned without his bride in 1850. Certainly, when Barnum heard that a rival showman had brought a Quaker giant from England, he immediately stated that Hales had always been a Quaker and made him wear Quaker clothes.

He was one of the curiosities at the Great Exhibition in London and was presented to the queen once again in April 1851; she gave him a gold watch and chain.

Hales became a pub landlord and kept the Craven Head tavern in Drury Lane, London, from 1851–55. He then moved back to live in a caravan in Norfolk. He died of bronchitis at **Great Yarmouth** in 1863, and was buried at West Somerton.

Robert Hearne, comedy legend 'Mr Pastry'

Robert Hearne was born in Lady Lane in **Norwich** in 1908, the son of an acrobat and an actress. He made his stage debut aged only six weeks at Norwich Theatre Royal, playing the baby in his mother's arms in *For the Sake of a Child*. He attended Crook's Place School (nowadays known as Bignold First), and later worked in the circus, where he went on tour developing a 'dumb' act. His first appearance in the West End was in a pantomime; when the flu wiped out half the cast of the show, he was persuaded to speak the lines of half a dozen different characters. Leslie Henson, who was also in the pantomime, was so impressed that he offered Hearne a part in his show *Nice Goings On*, and Hearne continued to play in musicals up to the war.

In 1936 he appeared at the Alexandra Palace. His sketches included a cookery demonstration, *Take Two Eggs*, plus *Shifting the Piano* and *The Handyman*. He starred with Fred Emney in a stage show, *Big Boy*, and developed his act as the bungling clown Mr Pastry, with a walrus moustache and flappy coat tails. In 1937 he became one of the earliest stars of children's TV. In the 1950s and 1960s he had his own TV series, with a signature tune of *Pop Goes the Weasel*. When he was offered the chance to star in an ice show, as long as he was able to skate, he assured the producer that it was fine... and then promptly booked skating lessons!

One of his sketches, *The Lancers*, was borrowed from Tom D. Newall, where he danced round a ballroom with imaginary partners completely out of step. This act brought him to the attention of Ed Sullivan in America, and he was invited onto *The Ed Sullivan Show* in 1954, which was followed by another 16 appearances on the show. At one point he made a TV show with the famous American silent movie comedian, Buster Keaton, called *The Adventures of Mr Pastry*, where Mr Pastry took method acting lessons from a fake American 'professor'. It was meant to be a series but Keaton fell ill and returned to America and the series was never completed.

Despite his success in slapstick comedy, Hearne was also an accomplished actor and was offered several Shakespeare parts at the Old Vic. He was considered as the next Dr Who to replace John Pertwee, but as he wanted to play the role as Mr Pastry the idea was rejected. He also made his own props, including a bicycle with collapsible handlebars, folding pedals and wheels that fell off. He rarely sat still and was full of practical jokes: once, when he was chatting with his neighbours on the way to London the train went into a tunnel...when it came out he'd disappeared. Eventually, his neighbours discovered him lying on the luggage rack above their heads.

Hearne was awarded the OBE in 1970 for his charity work – he raised a lot of money for therapy pools and was president of the Lord's Taverners charity in 1963 – and retired in 1971. Musician Harvey Andrews wrote a song about him. He died in 1979 from a heart attack, aged 70, and was buried in St Mary's Platt, near Borough Green, in Kent.

Margery Kempe, visionary

Margery Kempe was born about 1373 at **King's Lynn** (then known as Bishop's Lynn), the daughter of the merchant and MP John Brunham. She was very much a larger than life character, reminiscent of Chaucer's Wife of Bath. She married a burgess, John Kempe, in 1394 and suffered from severe post-natal depression after their first child was born, but was 'cured' when she had a vision of Jesus sitting on her bed. She ran a brewery, but when the business collapsed she thought that she was being punished for her sins, so she began going on pilgrimages for penance.

She had had 14 children before she persuaded her husband that they should live chastely. He countered that if he couldn't enjoy his conjugal rites with her he'd be forced to commit adultery, which in those days was a serious sin. In her biography Margery talks of responding to his advances while clutching a cross and praying! Eventually, by 1413, she had persuaded him to live chastely – in return for settling his debts. She visited Julian of **Norwich** that year, and then went from **Great Yarmouth** to Jerusalem via Venice, living on alms. She visited Calvary and started crying uncontrollably and noisily, a form of devotion that was to become her trademark. It made her very unpopular in Assisi and Rome on her way home; and when she returned to Lynn later that year, wearing white and weeping noisily, she was treated as a scandal.

In 1417 Margery went on pilgrimage to Santiago de Compostela. On the return journey she visited various cathedrals around the country and was accused of being a heretic and a Lollard (a crime punishable by burning at the stake) because of the way she dressed and her noisy weeping. She was imprisoned at Leicester and at York and was forced to obtain letters from several bishops to prove that she was orthodox.

When Margery returned to Lynn in 1418 she lived apart from her husband; however, when he was injured in an accident, she nursed him until his death in 1431, saying that it was penance for enjoying his body when she was younger. At the age of 60 she accompanied her daughter-in-law back to Danzig. It was then that she decided to compile an account of her pilgrimages. She couldn't write, so she hired someone to write it for her. *The Book of Margery Kempe*, which was begun in 1436, was the first biography of a woman written in English. It's not known when Margery died, but the book was completed in 1438, the same year that Margeria Kempe was admitted to the Trinity Guild in Lynn (her father had been an alderman in the guild). The last mention of her in the guild records is from the following year.

Her manuscript then faded from view. Parts of it were published in a pamphlet by Wynkyn de Worde (mainly the devout parts, so people thought she was a mystic like Julian of Norwich – 15th-century readers certainly didn't know the earthy housewife and businesswoman!), but the manuscript found its way to the priory of Mount Grace in Yorkshire. After the Reformation it disappeared and was lost until 1934, when it was found in a private collection in Lancashire. The book was finally published in a modern edition in 1936, 500 years after it was begun.

Mary Mann, the Norfolk Thomas Hardy

Mary Mann was born in **Norwich** in August 1848, the daughter of merchant William Rackham. She married farmer Fairman Joseph Mann when she was 23 and moved to **Shropham**. Moving from the city to a backwater was a real shock, especially when the depression started; cheap grain imports meant that local farmers couldn't compete and suffered greatly.

She started writing in the 1880s, influenced by her nephew Thomas Fairman Ordish. Her first novel, *The Parish of Hilby*, was published in 1883. During her lifetime she wrote 35 novels and several collections of short stories set in 'Dulditch' (Shropham). Most of them are from the viewpoint of a yeoman or tenant farmer, but she's also sympathetic to agricultural workers. Her own husband had financial problems, and she said of him in 1902 in an unpublished foreword to a collection of stories, *The Fields of Dulditch*: 'a man well-to-do, kind and generous once; an excellent husband, father, master, farmer: getting now poorer in pocket, shorter in temper, year by year, a man who has struggled in a dogged, quiet fashion, but who is beaten and knows it, finding the knowledge bitter to a degree.'

She saw the squalor of the countryside, rather than the rural charm that Flora Thompson chronicled, and parallels have been drawn between her work and that of Thomas Hardy's. One particularly painful tale is *Little Brother*, where the children play with their stillborn brother because they don't have any toys – the mother merely comments that they weren't doing any harm and it kept them quiet for a few hours. A.S. Byatt said of the story that it's 'plain, and brief, and clear and terrible...she is recording, not judging, but her telling is spiky with morals and the inadequacy of morals.'

When Fairman Mann died in 1913, Mary moved to **Sheringham**. She died there, aged 70, in 1929, but was buried in Shropham. Her epitaph is very fitting for a writer: 'We bring our years to an end as it were a tale that is told.'

Harriet Martineau, writer and political thinker

Harriet Martineau was born in **Norwich** in June 1802, the sixth of eight children born to the cloth manufacturer Thomas Martineau. Martineau was incredibly bright, but – as she admits in her autobiography – a difficult child. She had no sense of taste or smell; she also had poor eyesight, but nobody picked up on it, thinking at first that she was a slow-witted child. She realised that her hearing was poor when she was 12; it deteriorated until she was 20, when doctors confirmed that she was deaf. This added to her sense of isolation and was perhaps one of the reasons why she was such a prickly character. She was, however, a very confident speaker, and the writer and clergyman Sydney Smith once claimed he had a nightmare in which he was chained to a rock and was being talked to death by Harriet Martineau!

In 1821 she began writing anonymously for a Unitarian magazine, *The Monthly Repository*. It was soon after that disaster struck. Her oldest and favourite brother, Thomas, died of tuberculosis in 1824; her father's business fell into difficulties in 1825 and he died the following year; and then in 1827 her fiancé, John Hugh Worthington, died. The family business finally collapsed in 1829 and Martineau had to earn her own living. She couldn't teach because of her deafness, so she wrote instead. Before this period her writing work had been unpaid, but W.J. Fox started to pay her £15 a year; she wrote for other publishers as well. In 1831 her *Illustrations of Political Economy* were published by Charles Fox. It was greatly successful and her future was secure.

She moved to London the following year and became friends with George Eliot, John Stuart Mill and Henry Hallam. In 1834 she published *Poor Laws and Paupers*, supporting the Poor Law Reforms. Not surprisingly, she was unpopular with the Tories and the Radicals but the Whigs loved her. Darwin's sisters recommended that he read her work.

When she visited America in 1834 she supported the Abolitionists, who wanted to end slavery, which at the time was a controversial choice. Darwin's brother, Erasmus, was sweet on her, but their father loathed her. Darwin visited her and decided 'she was very agreeable, and managed to talk on a most wonderful number of subjects, considering the limited time', but added, 'I was astonished to find how ugly she is' and 'she is overwhelmed with her own projects, her own thoughts and abilities.'

It was those abilities that were her strength. She wrote about mining and public health, fought unjust laws and taxes, the prison system and press gangs and the treatment of the insane, bringing the facts to full public notice.

In 1839 she collapsed while she was in Venice: she had a prolapsed uterus, caused by an ovarian cyst. She moved to Newcastle so that her brother-in-law, the surgeon Thomas Michael Greenhow, could treat her, then to Tynemouth, where she spent the next five years. She was confined to her couch and wrote *Life in the Sickroom*, which, as always with her work, divided critics between strong admiration and equally strong hostility. She refused a civil list pension to help her financially through her illness, and demanded the return of all her letters, forbidding her friends to publish them.

In 1844 she took a course of mesmerism and was restored to health. This led to friction with her sister and brother-in-law, particularly when Greenhow published a pamphlet about her condition, as a consequence of which she moved to Lake District. She also fell out badly with her brother James, who had criticised the book she'd written on mesmerism.

She travelled to Egypt and Syria in 1846, then settled at Ambleside, having 'The Knoll' built for her. She was the main writer of leading articles for the *Daily News* (having written more than 1,600 pieces by the time she retired in 1866 – missing only one deadline, when her niece forgot to post the copy) and wrote many articles for the *Westminster Review*, the *Edinburgh Review* and *Household Words*.

In 1855 she fell ill again, which prompted her to write her autobiography. She lived for another 20 years and died in 1876 from a combination of an ovarian tumour and fatty degeneration of the heart. She was buried in Birmingham.

She said of herself: 'Her original power was nothing more than was due to earnestness and intellectual clearness within a certain range. With small imaginative and suggestive powers, and therefore nothing approaching to genius, she could see clearly what she did see, and give a dear expression to what she had to say. In short, she could popularise while she could neither discover nor invent.' However, she sold herself short – her 'certain range' was huge. George Eliot was nearer the mark when she said that Martineau was the only Englishwoman to thoroughly possess the art of writing.

Robert Marsham, the father of phenology

Robert Marsham was born in January 1708, and was the owner of an estate at Stratton Strawless. In 1736 he started to record his *Indications of Spring*: these were records of 27 natural events, including when 13 different types of tree came into leaf and when the first snowdrops appeared. He researched birds and insects too; he recorded the arrival or first song he heard from migrant birds, signs of when rooks were breeding, when the first swallows and butterflies arrived and when frogs and toads were active.

He maintained the records for 60 years and after his death at the age of 89 his family continued his tradition for a further 161 years. This provided the longest British record of phenology (the study of the times of recurring natural phenomena, especially in relation to climate) recorded in one place.

Marsham is known as the father of British phenology because, although there are older records, his collection of data was systematic. The main reason Marsham kept the records was to improve the timber production on his estate, but his work inspired phenological recording in the centuries after his death. He was one of the first to carry out repeated experiments on root cutting, trenching and bark scrubbing.

When he was 10 he collected and planted acorns, and he was still measuring one particular oak 70 years later. He kept records of the growth of more than 93 individual trees, and the Royal Society elected him as a fellow in 1780 because of his interest in trees. One of the trees he planted still survives today – the Stratton Cedar – which was planted as an 18-inch sapling in 1747. When it was measured in 2007 the circumference of its trunk was found to be a massive 7.2 metres. The tree is also featured on the village sign.

Thomas Paine, author and revolutionary

Thomas Paine was born in **Thetford** in 1738, the son of a Quaker staymaker. He added the 'e' to his surname when he moved to America. He enlisted on a privateer ship, *The Terrible* (which he claimed had a Captain Death,

The Stratton Cedar on the village sign.

Lieutenant Devil and surgeon Mr Ghost), but his father persuaded him not to go to sea. However, the wanderlust was too strong and he enlisted on another privateer.

In 1758 Paine worked for a staymaker in Dover and then set up his own business in Sandwich. He married in 1759, but when his business fell into difficulties he and his wife moved to Margate, where his wife, Mary, died in childbirth in 1760. Paine decided to become an exciseman, like his father-in-law, but was sacked for 'stamping' (that is, saying he'd examined something when he hadn't). He was forgiven and eventually settled in Lewes, where he spent much time debating at the Headstrong Club. He married the daughter of a fellow exciseman, writing his first political pamphlet, *The Case of the Officers of Excise*, in 1772; however, he failed to get the cause brought before parliament.

Life became very difficult for him over the next couple of years: his business collapsed, he was sacked for deserting his duty as an exciseman without permission and his wife divorced him. In 1774 he left England for America, sailing to Philadelphia and becoming the editor of the *Pennsylvania Magazine*. His pamphlet on the case for American independence, *Common Sense*, had a plain, simple style that made it original as well as popular, and Paine was the first to use the term 'United States of America'. Although it became the most widely distributed pamphlet of the American War of Independence (he later claimed that he'd sold 150,000 copies in America alone), he made no money from it and lived mainly on handouts from political sympathisers. He continued writing propaganda leaflets to encourage the American army and George Washington would read them aloud to his troops.

During the French Revolution Paine began writing the *Rights of Man*, in response to Edmund Burke's attack on the Revolution, *Reflections on the Revolution in France*. Paine advocated votes for all, the abolition of monarchy, religious toleration and an end to war. More than 50,000 copies were circulated, but his publisher was indicted for publishing seditious material and then Paine himself was indicted on a charge of seditious libel. His reply was, 'If, to expose the fraud and imposition of monarchy... to promote universal peace, civilization, and commerce, and to break the chains of political superstition, and raise degraded man to his proper rank; if these things be libellous... let the name of libeller be engraved on my tomb.'

In 1792 Paine was given honorary French citizenship. He travelled to France and, even though he couldn't speak French, was elected to the National Convention. He misjudged the politics slightly, however, as although he supported the Revolution, he was against the execution of Louis XVI. The following year Robespierre passed a decree saying that non-French nationals couldn't have a place on the Convention and Paine was arrested and imprisoned. He protested that he was an American citizen, not a British one, but the American ambassador didn't press the claim. Paine narrowly missed being guillotined: each day a chalk mark was made on the door of those destined for the guillotine, but when his door was chalked it was open and the mark couldn't be seen when the door was closed. He kept his head and was released in 1794 with the help of the new American minister to France, James Monroe.

He then wrote *The Age of Reason*, calling for religious freedom. Although he stayed in France he loathed Napoleon. Eventually, he returned to America in 1802 at the invitation of Thomas Jefferson, but he'd become very unpopular there. He'd upset the devout with *The Age of Reason*, while the Federalists disliked him for his association with the French Revolution. He'd also upset many people by his scathing letter to George Washington saying: 'the world will be puzzled to decide whether you are an apostate or an impostor; whether you have abandoned good principles or whether you ever had any.'

When he died in 1809, only six people attended his funeral. His obituary in the *New York Citizen* said, 'He had lived long, did some good and much harm.' He was buried at New Rochelle in New York. Ten years later William Cobbett had his bones dug up and brought back to England, but they disappeared and their whereabouts remain unknown.

Over the years his reputation has been restored. Tony Benn described him as 'one of the very greatest figures in the history of popular struggle', and the *Rights of Man* was the first book placed on the shelves of the new Millennium Library in **Norwich** on 8 October 2001. Readers of the *Eastern Daily Press* had voted for the book they wanted to be placed on the shelves first and Paine's book took 44 per cent of the vote.

Humphrey Repton, landscaper

Landscape designer Humphrey Repton was born in Bury St Edmunds in April 1752. When he was 10 his family moved to **Norwich**; his father then sent him to the Netherlands to learn a commercially useful language. He returned to Norwich in 1768 and became an apprentice in the textile industry. After he married in 1773, his father gave him money to set up a business, but Repton preferred drawing to trade. He lost money in speculating and also had expensive tastes.

In 1776, after both his parents had died, Repton decided to retire from trade and became a tenant at **Sustead** on the **Felbrigg** estate. He spent his time sketching and improving his farm. Within five years he was running out of money again. He became William Windham's private secretary, but wasn't paid for his work. He then invested money with John Palmer in Bath in reforming the mail coach system, but gained nothing from it, despite the fact that the government adopted their scheme. In 1786 he moved his family to Essex and tried his hand at being a writer. Finally, in 1788, he decided to be a landscape gardener, as he enjoyed high society, sketching and improving scenery. His first commission was in **Catton**, for the textile merchant Jeremiah Ives, quickly followed by another commission at Thomas Coke's estate in **Holkham**.

Repton made his reports in the Red Books that were to become his trademark. The Red Books showed his suggested improvements through a combination of maps, sketches and writing. Clever paper engineering had an overlay of the present scene, which, when removed, showed Repton's proposed scene. He claimed that he made over 400 of these books during his career. He charged five guineas a day (the equivalent of just under £500 a day today), plus expenses and the cost of his Red Books.

However, Repton said that he was a consultant, not a contractor. As he didn't do any physical organisation of the work, such as the planting or building, his plans were often ignored. He realised that he would have to publish a treatise on the principles and practice of landscape gardening to educate his clients. *Sketches and Hints on Landscape Gardening* was published in 1795 and was incredibly popular, as were his later books. However, taxation and inflation during the Napoleonic Wars meant that fewer people could afford to employ him. Business declined, and then in January 1811 his carriage overturned on the way home from a ball and he suffered a spinal injury from which he never fully recovered.

In 1812 he was commissioned to work at **Sheringham** Park. Although it was his favourite work it was never finished. As it became harder to get commissions, he gradually retreated from public life. Jane Austen satirised him in *Mansfield Park* (1814) as a generic name: 'Repton, or any body of that sort' for the fashion-conscious to commission; and Thomas Love Peacock slated him in *Headlong Hall* (1816) as the obsequious advocate of 'picturesque gardening'.

He died suddenly in March 1818 at his home in Hare Street, Essex – but he'd already designed where he wanted to be buried, in a rose garden in the churchyard at **Aylsham**. He had also composed his own memorial:

> Not like Egyptian tyrants consecrate
> Unmixed with others shall my dust remain;
> But mold'ring, blending, melting into Earth,
> Mine shall give form and colour to the Rose,
> And while its vivid blossoms cheer Mankind
> Its perfumed odours shall ascend to Heaven.

Although his star faded during the 19th century, he influenced American landscape gardeners. He was rediscovered in England by Christopher Hussey in 1927, and championed by Nikolaus Pevsner in 1948. Now Humphrey Repton has his rightful place as an influential English landscaper, whose style was flexible enough to fit small gardens or large parks.

Amy Robsart, the queen's rival

Amy Robsart was the woman who stood between Elizabeth I and the alleged love of her life, Robert Dudley. There's mystery surrounding her death that to this day still has people asking questions.

She was born in 1532, in **Stanfield**, Norfolk, the only legitimate child of Sir John Robsart. They were neighbours to the Dudleys and it's possible she met Robert Dudley when Warwick came to put Kett's forces down in 1549. At 18 years of age she married Dudley at the royal palace of Sheen in Richmond on 4 June 1550, and Edward VI attended the wedding. As both families were wealthy it was seen as a very good match and their marriage contract said they could only marry if they did 'condescend and agree' to the match.

However, they spent much of their marriage apart. Dudley was the MP for Norfolk in 1547, 1553 and 1559 (despite the fact that he never lived in the county). In 1553, because he was implicated in the plot to crown Lady Jane Grey, he was put in the Tower until October 1554 and his properties confiscated. His fortunes were finally restored in 1558 when he fought at Picardy and was Master of Ordnance to the army.

Dudley was very ambitious and spent most of his time at court. Amy wasn't there because courtiers' wives didn't usually go to court – and besides, her presence would have reminded Elizabeth that Dudley was married. It was rumoured that Dudley was having a love affair with the queen. She certainly showed him great favour, giving him a position as Master of the Queen's Horse at court and making him Knight of the Garter.

Between 1557 and 1559, Amy lived at William Hyde's house in Throcking, near Bishop's Stortford. In September 1559 she moved to Sir Richard Verney's house in Warwickshire, and by December had moved to Cumnor Place near Abingdon, owned by some of Dudley's friends. It wasn't far from Dudley himself, who was Lieutenant of Windsor Castle in November 1559.

On Sunday 8 September 1560 Amy gave her servants permission to go to 'Our Lady's Fair'. Her companion Mrs Oddingsell and the mother of the house's former owner, Mrs Owens, stayed behind. When the servants returned from the fair they found Amy at the bottom of the stairs with her neck broken. It was claimed that she'd been playing at tables, left the room suddenly and fell down the stairs. (Though that raises the question: why didn't Mrs Oddingsell and Mrs Owens check on her earlier, and why didn't they raise the alarm?)

Amy's servant, Bowes, rode to the court at Windsor to tell Dudley of the news. On the way he met Dudley's household officer Thomas Blount and told him what had happened. When Dudley heard the news he sent a note after Blount asking him to find out the exact circumstances. On 9 September Dudley wrote to Blount, 'The greatness and suddeness of the misfortune so perplexes me... how this evil doth light upon me, considering what the malicious world will bruit as I can take no rest.' He told Blount to make sure that the coroner chose the 'discreetist and most substantial men' for the jury. The jury had already been chosen by the time Blount got there, but Blount reassured Dudley that they were 'wise men'.

Rumours spread saying that Amy had been poisoned, though the inquest said it was an accident. The records were later lost in a fire; we know of the verdict because John Appleyard, her half-brother, tried to reopen the case in 1567. He saw the records and stated that he was satisfied it had been an accident.

Amy was buried in the Church of St Mary the Virgin in Oxford on 22 September. The funeral was lavish, costing £500 (the equivalent of £100,000 today), but people noticed that Dudley didn't attend and he failed to raise a memorial to her.

Even though Dudley was cleared of any misdeed, the mud stuck. His reputation was ruined and in 1566 Lord Cecil told the Privy Council that the queen would not marry him because 'he is infamed by the death of his wife'. However, Elizabeth made him the Earl of Leicester in 1572.

In 1584 *Leicester's Commonwealth* was published, claiming that Dudley tried to poison his wife, failed and so got Sir Richard Verney to murder her, disguising it as a fall. Contemporary correspondence of the Spanish ambassadors suggests that Amy was ill and Dudley was trying to poison or divorce her. However, there is absolutely no proof connecting Verney with Amy's death.

Stories evolved that Amy's ghost haunted Cumnor Place. In 1850 it was said that nine clergymen had come from Oxford to lay her ghost in a pond that ever after would never freeze. The owners didn't live at Cumnor Place after the exorcism and the house became a ruin. It was eventually pulled down in 1810.

However, the story didn't die. Sir Walter Scott used the tale as the basis of his novel *Kenilworth* in 1821. Stories of Amy's ghost (both at Cumnor and in her childhood home at Norfolk) seem to have been more prevalent after the novel was published, so the tales were probably pandering to the tourists. Scott's theory was that because of the scandal Elizabeth made Dudley the Earl of Leicester instead of marrying him.

So did Amy fall, or was she pushed?

To put the event into context we need to take into account the fact that Amy may have had breast cancer. The pain of the disease, combined with the misery of her marriage, may have led her to want to kill herself, and that would explain why she was so insistent that the servants should go to the fair.

Tragic accident, murder or suicide: we will never know the truth.

Anna Sewell, author of *Black Beauty*

Anna Sewell was born in **Great Yarmouth** on 30 March 1820, the first child of Quakers Isaac and Mary Sewell. Her father was a draper and her mother a writer. The family moved to London soon after Sewell's birth, but shortly after her brother Philip was born in 1822 her father's business failed. The family moved around a lot as Isaac pursued a career in Nottingham lace and in banking. Sewell was good at drawing and very interested in natural history, but an accident at the age of 14 put paid to any academic plans. She was running home from school in the rain when she slipped and fell, injuring both ankles. The doctors may not have given her the right treatment and afterwards Sewell was lame. She found it hard to stand or walk for long periods, and also suffered from chest pains, a sore back and what she termed a 'weakness' in her head. She visited several spas for treatment, both in England and abroad, but nobody was able to help.

She went to stay with her family at their farm in Norfolk, where she learned to ride and drive horses. Partly because of her dependence on the horses for transport and partly because of her caring nature, she became very vocal about cruelty to animals.

Sewell moved back to Norfolk permanently in 1867 and lived in the White House in **Old Catton**. Her health soon deteriorated: when she began writing *Black Beauty* in 1871, she dictated the book to her mother from the sofa, but by 1876 she was able to write on slips of paper and her mother then copied them into the manuscript. She finished it in 1877 and her mother's publishers, Jarrold & Sons, bought it for £40, publishing it as *Black Beauty: his grooms and companions; the autobiography of a horse, 'Translated from the Original Equine, by Anna Sewell'*. Although it's seen as a children's book, Sewell wrote it for people who worked with horses, to make them treat the animals more kindly. The book was a runaway success and at one point was said to be the sixth best-seller in the English language.

Although Anna Sewell lived long enough to see the early indications of success of her book, she died in 1878, just five months after it was published. She's buried in the Quaker burial-ground at **Lamas**.

'Turnip' Townshend, politician and agriculturalist

Charles, the second Viscount Townshend, was born at **Raynham** in April 1674 and was baptised in London. After being educated at Eton and King's College, Cambridge, he went travelling for three years. He married Elizabeth Pelham and together they had nine children. He gave his maiden speech as a Whig in 1701, and, although he was a poor orator, he was judged to be a good man. He was appointed as a diplomat to the Hague in 1709 and managed to conclude a treaty with the Dutch, but it wasn't well thought out and there were many rows afterwards.

In 1711 Townshend's newborn daughter Elizabeth died, followed by his wife and then his eldest son, Horatio: he was utterly grief-stricken. He married again in 1713; his new wife, Dorothy, was the sister of his close friend Robert Walpole. They had 11 children together, but whether the marriage was a success is open to debate, as Dorothy is believed to haunt Raynham Hall in the guise of a 'brown lady'. After Dorothy's death from smallpox (which has as many legends about it as Amy Robsart's, with some saying that she was pushed down the stairs), relations between Townshend and Walpole soured. For several parliamentary sessions between 1714 and 1730 Townshend was the Secretary of State, but after falling out with Walpole over foreign policy he resigned in 1730 to concentrate on his farm at Raynham.

Townshend's championship of the value of turnips and crop rotation gave him his nickname 'Turnip' Townshend. Alexander Pope made him a figure of fun in *Imitations of Horace,* Epistle II, calling him a 'turnip obsessed person' and adding in a note that Townshend's favorite topic of conversation was 'that kind of rural improvement which arises from turnips.'

Townshend wasn't actually the first person to introduce the four-crop rotation system – it had already been in use for years. However, he brought it to prominence through his enthusiasm. The four-crop method involved growing turnips in a particular piece of land one year, barley or oats the next, then clover or rye and, finally, wheat the next, before starting again with turnips. This meant he didn't have to let the land lie fallow for one year out of four, and could feed his cattle and sheep with the extra turnips over the winter instead of slaughtering them all in November. With the help of agriculturalist Jethro Tull, he used a seed drill which allowed him to sow seeds in well-spaced rows at specific depths. This made sowing more economical and yielded a greater amount of crops. He also gave his tenants long leases to encourage them to improve their land.

He died at Raynham in June 1738 and was buried there.

Saint Walstan

The life of St Walstan was first published in Wynkyn de Worde's *Novea Legenda Anglie*. Walstan was born to royal parents, but renounced all rights of royal succession so he could devote himself to prayer. He became a farm labourer in Taverham, and, despite being poor himself, he looked out for the sick and needy and shared his meals with them, as well as giving them his clothes and shoes. The farmer's wife, hearing of his behaviour, urged her husband to get rid of him. However, one day she found Walstan trimming a thorny hedge and walking among the cuttings barefoot – without sustaining so much as a scratch. She asked his fellow labourers what had happened to his shoes and they told her he'd given them to a neighbour who needed them more.

Seeing this as a sign that Walstan was under divine protection, she fell to her knees and begged his forgiveness. She and her husband had no children and so decided to adopt Walstan and leave their farm to him. Walstan gently refused, saying that he was happy as he was, and besides, an angel had visited him the previous evening telling him the exact hour of his death. Instead, he asked that when he died the farmer would put his body on a wagon, harness two bullocks to it and let them wander wherever they wanted; wherever they stopped would be where he should be buried.

Just as he foretold, he died soon after, on 30 May 1016. His wishes were followed to the letter. The bullocks walked in the direction of Costessey; one version of the legend says that there was a pool of deep water in the wood and the cart travelled over the water as if it were solid ground; the marks of the wheels were apparently visible on the surface of the pool. Where the bullocks stopped for a rest in Costessey, a spring welled up. As the bullocks headed for Bawburgh, and settled at the top of a hill, a second spring emerged; this was where Walstan's body was buried. According to the legend, the water could restore sight and hearing, cure paralysis and demonic possession and cure animals from any complaint.

The spring next to the church at Bawburgh still exists, and it's said that it has never run dry.

Chapter 8

Why is it called that?

If you've ever wondered how places got their names, or where dialects come from, this is where you might find the answer.

Place names

✳ Some place names come from the Old English name for the geographical features. According to expert James Rye, **Barton Bendish**, near Devil's Ditch, comes from the Old English 'barley farm' (*beretun*) 'inside the ditch' (*be innan dic*). Similarly, **Fersfield** means open land (*feld*) covered with furze (*fyrs*), and **Hethel** is a 'hill overgrown with heather (*hæth* and *hyll*). Several places that were formerly heavily wooded (or still are, in the case of **Foxley**) take their name from the type of tree or creatures found in the wood: **Salle** means 'sallow wood', from *salh* (sallow willow) and *leah* (wood). So it's easy to guess that Foxley means 'fox wood'. **Acle** means 'in the lea of the oaks' (a clearing) – and in Tudor times hundreds of oaks were felled there for use in building Elizabeth I's warships. **Woodton** is a settlement (*tun*) in the woods (*wudu*), and **Woodbastwick** is a settlement in a lime grove. **Taverham** is a 'homestead with red soil' (the Old English *teafor* means 'red pigment' or vermilion – though the soil in Taverham isn't particularly red).

Interestingly, **Tivetshall** means 'lapwings' nook', from the Old English lapwing (*tewhit*) and nook (*halh*). **Hautbois** is an unusual one – anyone who knows a little French might look at it and think that it means 'high wood'. However, when you remember that it's pronounced 'hobbis', you might not be surprised to learn that it too comes from Old English: *hobb* and *wisce*, meaning 'meadow with tussocks'.

For those settlements built near water: we have **Reedham**, the meadow by the reeds (*hreod* or reed, and *hamm* or meadow). **Horsford** means exactly what it sounds like: a ford crossing the River Hor. (Next door is **Horsham**, the meadow next to the river Hor). **Narford** is another ford, this time from a 'narrow place' (*nearu*), while **Upwell** is a settlement higher (*upp*) the stream (*well*). **Loddon** has a slightly more unusual derivation became it comes from the Celtic *lutna*, meaning mud – in other words, a settlement by the river. Interestingly, the River Chet used to be called the River Loddon.

Some place names arise from the occupation of people who once lived there. **Lexham** is from the Old English for leech's (or doctor's) settlement (*læce*), and Swanton means 'herdsman's settlement', from the Old English *swana* (which came down as 'swain' in mediaeval times). **Carleton** means the 'settlement of free peasants' (from the Old English *ceorl*, meaning peasant). The **Rode** comes from Robert de Rode, who was lord of the manor in 1346; and the **Forehoe** is an interesting mixture with a bit of Norse added, meaning 'four mounds' (Norse *haugr* meaning 'hill' or 'mound'). We see other 'hoe' names in the county, too – **Hoe** itself, and **Greenhoe** (using the Old English *grene*), or 'green hill'.

Place name scholars Karl Sandred and Bengt Lindström have some interesting definitions from the coastal and Broadland areas of the county. **Somerton** is a 'farm or dwelling used in summer', (at Domesday, 95 acres of grazing area were recorded). Unsurprisingly, **Winterton** is a 'farm or dwelling used in winter.' There are some surprises: **Ashmanhaugh** is 'the enclosure of the aesc-mann', a pirate's settlement; and **Smallburgh** isn't just a small hill – it's a hill on the River Smale (which was the name for the River Ant, recorded back in 1363). **Horning** means 'shaped like a horn' and refers to the (horn-shaped) bend of the River Bure around which the settlement grew up.

Naturally the areas where the Danes settled have a concentration of '-by' endings, such as **Mautby** (meaning Malti's farm). There used to be a gerry there, and Mautby Swim gets its name because it was the spot where cattle used to swim across the river to and from the marshes. **Ormesby** has an even more interesting origin: it's likely to be from 'Orms' bei', meaning 'bay of ships'. Why? Because the Norsemen used to call ships 'orms', after the serpent shape at the front. *Orm* is similar to the Old English *wyrm*, also meaning serpent. Another Danish-derived placename is **Lound** (from *lundr*, meaning 'grove of trees'). **Fritton** derives from Freyr, the Scandinavian god of weather and agriculture; interestingly, Fritton Lake was once called Gunhilde's Mere, after one of Canute's aunts.

There are also Icelandic names in the county: **West Carr**, near **Attleborough**, comes from the Icelandic *kjarr* meaning copse or spinney.

What about **Potter Heigham**? Potter is easily accounted for because pots used to be made there (and it was also a centre of brickmaking – which is why the church has a rare brick font). As for the Heigham: in Norfolk, it's pronounced 'ham' – which is simply the Old English for 'settlement'. It's thought that **Swaffham** derives from the name of the Swaefas tribe, who were among the Saxon invaders of East Anglia after the Romans left.

Dilham got its name because the herb dill was grown there. **Cromer** was originally known as 'Crowsmere', meaning 'pond of crows'; when **Shipden** fell into the sea in the 1390s, its residents were granted land at nearby Cromer.

Honeypot Wood is a Norfolk Wildlife Trust reserve. It might be thought that its name comes from bees, but actually it's a euphemism. The wood is a remnant of the ancient woodlands dating back to the retreat of the last ice age, and the name is because it's very near a 'honey pit' – a mediaeval sewage dump.

Pigg's Grave

✱ The second highest point in Norfolk is Pigg's Grave, which is just north-east of **Swanton Novers**. It's marked by an Ordnance Survey triangulation pillar in the middle of the trees, and is 101 metres above sea level. It's believed that Mr Pigg (possibly Thomas Pigge, a gentleman of Swanton Novers whose will was proved in August 1737) was waylaid by a highwayman, at what is now the junction of the Holt-Dereham and Thursford-Aylsham roads, and killed. The highwayman, when caught, was probably hanged at Gallowhill Lane, on the edge of Melton Park.

Stewkey Blues

✱ The village of **Stiffkey** is renowned for its cockles, known as 'Stewkey Blues', as they have a dark grey-blue shell. Stiffkey is actually pronounced 'Stewkey'; the name means 'island of stumps' and refers to the tree stumps that are found in the marshes. There was once a harbour at Stiffkey, but it's now silted up.

Grimes Graves

✱ Grimes Graves is a series of Neolithic flint mines and pits (see page 27). It was given the name in Saxon times, as people believed that the holes in the ground were made by Grim (aka Woden), the chief of the gods; the Old English *grave* simply means a hole, rather than the more specific modern meaning. Early archaeologists thought that the pits were tombs, but Canon Greenwell had worked on an excavation at the Cissbury mine in Sussex and believed that this was another mine. He excavated a shaft and explored some of the galleries between 1868 and 1870. Further excavations were made between 1920 and 1939, and in the early 1970s radio carbon dating showed that work began on the site in the early Neolithic period.

Lothingland and King Edmund

✱ Lothingland is the area on the Norfolk/Suffolk border bounded by the sea on the east, Lake Lothing (Oulton Broad) to the south, the River Waveney to the west and Breydon Water to the north. It's thought that the name comes from Ragnar Lothbrog, a Danish raider from the mid-ninth century. Lothbrog was fond of hawking and when his favourite bird fell into the sea he rushed to the rescue. His boat was swept away by a storm and he landed near **Reedham**, where King Edmund received him kindly. Lothbrog asked permission to stay and learn more about Saxon ways, and Edmund was pleased to grant it. He ordered Bern, his falconer, to accompany Lothbrog on hunting trips. However, Bern was jealous of Lothbrog and murdered him. When Edmund asked where the Danish king was, Bern claimed that Lothbrog had tarried behind in the wood. At that moment, Lothbrog's greyhound appeared; Edmund, thinking that Lothbrog would be nearby, made a fuss of the dog. However, when the dog kept disappearing, only returning to be fed, he had the dog followed and Lothbrog's body was discovered. Edmund soon discovered the truth and commanded that Bern should be put into Lothbrog's boat and cast adrift without any oars or sails, so that God could decide his fate.

Somehow the boat made its way to Denmark where Lothbrog's sons. Ubbe, Ivar and Halfdan, recognised it, seized Bern and questioned him. Wanting revenge on Edmund, he told them that Edmund had murdered Lothbrog. They immediately raised troops and sailed for England to avenge their father's death.

Edmund, hearing about the invasion, raised his own army. He was captured at Haegelisdun (Hoxne in Suffolk, although some associate the place with **Hellesdon**) and bound to a tree, where the Viking archers used him as target practice before beheading him and leaving his body to rot in a field. When the Danes eventually retired, Edmund's followers found his body and his head being guarded by a wolf. He was buried nearby, but his body was later moved to a shrine at Bedricsworth (Bury St Edmunds).

Edmund – struck with arrows – appears on many church screens in Norfolk; 17 churches in the county are dedicated to him, and he also appears on the oldest figurative glass in Norfolk, a 12th-century roundel in **Saxlingham Nethergate**.

A Viking burial ship was found in **Ashby** (formerly Haskeby) near Fritton in 1830. The ship was 54ft long and 8ft wide, and so well preserved that the estate carpenter was able to make a detailed drawing of its construction. There were no signs of a masthole in the thwarts (rowers' seats) or any stepping in the keel, so it was thought that it was powered by oars alone. There were seven locks on each side and a seat next to each fastened with pins and lashing.

King's Lynn

✳ King's Lynn was originally called Bishop's Lynn as it was one of the planned new towns built under episcopal lordship between the 11th and 13th centuries. Herbert de Losinga, the Bishop of Norwich, began building it in 1101 between the Purfleet and the Millfleet. He built the Church of St Margaret and authorised the market, and the town became known as

Bishop's Lynn (*Lenne Episcopi*) when the new bishop of Norwich, John Grey, gave it a charter in 1204. After the Dissolution of the Monasteries, Henry VIII renamed the town King's Lynn. The 'Lynn' part of the name is Celtic and means 'pool'; this is because it's next to an estuary lake where various rivers join the Wash.

Seven Burnhams by the Sea

✴ In *Urn Burial*, Thomas Browne says that Burnham was a town of seven parishes. There is **Burnham Market, Burnham Overy, Burnham Norton, Burnham Deepdale, Burnham Thorpe, Burnham Ulph** and **Burnham Sutton**. There's an old rhyme which references it:

> London, Bristol and Coventree,
> And the Seven Burnhams by the sea.

Interestingly, according to William Dutt in 1906, on the parish map of Burnham Deepdale, dated 1780, one field is called 'Thieves' Hole' and three more are marked 'Robb's Occupation'. He quoted the *Norfolk Chronicle*: 'We hear from Burnham Deepdale that one Robb, a noted smuggler, who has resided there some years, was this month apprehended.' Apparently, Robb had a price on his head of several hundred pounds – a huge sum in those days, so he must have been fairly notorious – and he had broken out of Edinburgh Castle in 1772. He was eventually caught by men who'd arrived from Edinburgh.

Salthouse

✴ As the village name suggests, Salthouse was named after a 'house for storing salt', and was recorded in the *Domesday Book*. Sarbury Hill, to the west of the village, was known as Salt Hill in 1649 and may have been where the salt-makers worked. They would boil sea water in clay pans until it evaporated, leaving the salt behind, and then make the salt into blocks. In Essex, the salt-making sites along the Thames estuary are known as 'red hills'; the hills are partly made of earth and partly from the remains of the clay troughs, supports and moulds, they're 'red' because of the fire. It's possible that the low hills around Salthouse are from salt-making rather than being formed naturally.

Diss and its mere

✴ The name **Diss** comes from the Old English *dic*, meaning 'ditch of standing water': in other words, the six-acre mere at its centre of the town. According to the folklorist W.B. Gerish, the mere was once thought to be the crater of an extinct volcano and was bottomless – and, worse, it was said to 'purge itself' once a year and smelled disgusting!

Modern measurements have shown that the deepest water is only about 20ft down, although there may once have been a stream running across the bottom of the mere. It was formerly used as a reservoir and drain for the inhabitants of the town, but nowadays is used by anglers fishing for carp and tench.

There's a floating fountain on the centre of the mere, which was presented by Diss and District Rotary Club in June 2005 to celebrate 100 years of the Rotary Club.

Feltwell Anchor Corkway

✳ Corkway is probably a corruption from the original spelling, 'Caukway'. 'Cauk' is an old East Anglian word for limestone; and there are limestone pits close by, which would give the area its name.

California and the gold rush

✳ In the mid-19th century a new hamlet was built near **Scratby**, but its name hadn't been decided until a cache of 16th-century gold coins were found on the beach at Scratby. At the time, the California Gold Rush was in the news and so **California** got its name.

Buildings

✳ Magazine Cottage on Docking Road, **Sedgeford**, was built as a powder magazine for Sir Harmon L'Estrange of **Hunstanton** in 1643, when he held **King's Lynn** for the royalists. There are few surviving magazines in the country and most of them are either part of a fort or part of the Royal Gunpowder Factory at Waltham Abbey (which closed after being damaged during World War Two). Nowadays the building is a private house and is used as a landmark for the **Peddars Way**.

✳ Martyr's Cottage in **East Bilney** is said to be where the martyr Thomas Bilney was brought up.

✳ Dutch Row (now Church Row) in **Horsham St Faith** was originally built as housing for Dutch refugee weavers; the top floor of the cottages was once a large shared work-room. When the demand for hand-woven yarn declined, the inhabitants wove horsehair instead.

✳ According to *Harrod's Directory* of 1878, Gate Farm in **Bressingham** got its name from the fact that three gates hang from one post at the farm, 'and is considered by the parties living in the neighbourhood to be one of the greatest curiosities in Norfolk.'

Syleham lights and lantern men

✳ According to William Dutt, writing in 1906, the will-o'-the-wisp seen over the marshes by the River Waveney was known as 'Syleham lights', after the village of Syleham, which is just over the Suffolk border. The area around the village is marshy, so the dancing ghostly lights seen at night were probably due to marsh gases.

The lights were also known as 'lantern men', and a sober tale about the will-o'-the-wisp is mentioned on wherryman Joseph Bexfield's grave at **Thurlton**. On 11 August 1809, Bexfield had been drinking with his colleagues in the White Horse pub at Thurlton Staithe when he remembered that he'd left a parcel for his wife on the wherry. His friends warned him not to cross the marsh to the wherry because the lantern man was out on the marshland. The lantern man would show a light to attract his victim and then drown him in mud. Holding a lantern yourself didn't help, because the lantern man would come straight to the light.

Bexfield retorted scornfully, 'I know the marshes too well to be led astray by any Jack O'Lantern,' and off he went. He was never seen alive again: his drowned body was washed up near Reedham. He was buried in the churchyard of All Saints, aged only 38, leaving a widow and two children. His headstone reads:

> O cruel Death that would not spare
> A Father kind and Husband dear
> Great is ye loss to ye three he left behind
> But he they hope will greater comfort find.

Sporting names

✳ The Barclay End at **Norwich** City Football Club's ground at Carrow Road is named after former captain Evelyn Barclay, a vice-president of the club, who donated the cost of the roof.

✳ Yarmouth Town Football Club is known as 'The Bloaters', after a type of cured herring for which **Great Yarmouth** was famous. The nickname was also used for Yarmouth's speedway team from 1948 to 1962.

Markets and spaces

✳ Despite being right next to the cathedral, Tombland in **Norwich** has nothing to do with tombs. It's simply the Anglo-Saxon for 'empty space' as it was the site of the original Saxon market.

✳ Fish Hill in **Holt** got its name because it was originally the site of the fish market. It was burned down in 1708.

Yarmouth Rows

The old town in Great Yarmouth was built in what Dickens has called the 'Gridiron of Norfolk' – long alleys running back from the quay. As the town grew, houses were built on to and conditions became crowded and insanitary. A mixture of slum clearances in the 1930s, bombing during World War Two and demolition for rebuilding in the 1950s has cleared many of the rows.

The names of the rows changed frequently over the years; eventually they were numbered in 1804, from north to south, and there were officially 145 rows (excluding the half rows, Broad Row and Market Row). Most of the names came from pubs or inhabitants – or in some cases, from events. These included:

✳ Rampart Row (Row 1) – named after the rampart or town wall.

✳ Snatchbody Row (Row 6) – named from an incident with the 'resurrection men' (see page 184).

✳ Ferry Boat Row (Row 8) – because immediately opposite it was the ferry across the Bure, used until the suspension bridge was built.

✳ Deneside Austin Row (Row 60) – named because the Augustine Friars had a house there in the 13th century. It later became known as Quakers Row as the Quaker Meeting House was built on the site.

✳ Old Hannah's Back (Row 89) – took its name because it backed on to Old Hannah's Row (Row 90). John Hannah was accused of strangling his wife in 1813, and, as he was over 70, he was known as 'Old Hannah'. He was found guilty of murder, hanged on the Denes and his body given to the surgeons for dissection. He was the last person to be hanged in Yarmouth.

✳ Kittywitches (Row 95) – there are several theories as to where the name came from. One is that witches lived there (although there are records of witches being tried in Yarmouth, they're not actually connected with the row); another that the name came from baker Christopher Witchingham, who lived there in the 17th century. It's also the narrowest row (27 inches wide, at its west end), and one of the names for a crab on Breydon water is 'kittywitch'. There's a theory that because many people had to enter the row sideways, in a crab-like fashion, the name came from there.

✳ Prison Row (Row 110) – during the 18th century it was used as a prison for Frenchmen. Apparently, the prisoners were given bones to carve to relieve the boredom.

✳ Gun Row (Row 125) – this is the widest row, at 9ft wide in places. There are several suggestions for the name: one is that two cannons were once placed at the east entrance, to protect the walls from the wheels of the Harry Carriers (see page 195). Another was that there was a foundry there and that a large gun was once carried through it. More prosaically, it might well have been named after a nearby tavern.

Paths, roads and tracks

✳ Marriott's Way is a 21-mile foot and cycle path between **Whitwell** (and from there to **Reepham** and **Aylsham**) and **Hellesdon**. It follows the trackbed of a railway line which was closed in 1985. It's named after William Marriott, who was chief engineer and manager of the Midland and Great Northern Railway (M&GN) for 41 years, and who had a 'mobile office' in the form of a railway car.

The waymarkers on the route are all painted in the same brown and cream as the M&GN's livery. Between Whitwell and Reepham is the Themelthorpe Curve, which was the sharpest bend in the British Rail network when it was built in 1960. It was the last section of railway track to be built in Norfolk.

Marriott's Way is one of the longest disused railway paths in the country and is part of Route One in the National Cycle Network. At Hellesdon it joins up with the **Norwich** Riverside Walk, which runs to the boom towers by Carrow Bridge, and at Aylsham it joins up with the Bure Valley Walk to **Hoveton**.

✳ Peddars Way runs from just over the county border at Knettishall Heath Country Park in Suffolk through to **Holme-next-the-Sea** and along the route of a Roman road constructed in about AD 61. It was first shown on a map in 1587, and it's thought that the name comes from the Latin *pedestere* (to go on foot). At Holme it joins the Norfolk Coast Path, which runs from **Hunstanton** to **Cromer**. The two routes were officially joined in 1986 and Prince Charles officiated at the ceremony. The road is also part of the Icknield Way, which runs from Hunstanton to Lyme Regis in Dorset.

✳ Beech Avenue in **Taverham** is now the site of Taverham High School, but a row of beeches were planted there in 1805 to commemorate the Battle of Trafalgar, thereby giving the road its name. The beeches existed until the 1960s and are commemorated on the village sign.

Little Switzerland

✳ There were major chalk extraction pits at **Horstead**. The quarries, spoil heaps and canals are known as 'Little Switzerland', and an area to the north is called 'Hills and Holes'. Much of the chalk was transported on wherries along the River Bure. The pit closed in about 1875, and as the fir trees planted on the slopes began to reach maturity, the scenery really began to fit the name.

Hellfiregate and Wicked Hampton

✳ There's a quaint tale about how the villages of Halvergate and Wickhampton got their names. According to Victorian folklorist John Glyde, the story goes that two brothers argued over the boundary between their lands and tore out each other's heart. God turned their bodies to stone and placed them in the church (with their heart in their hand). From them on one parish was called Wicked Hampton (Wickhampton) and the other called Hell Fire Gate (Halvergate). In the church at Wickhampton there is indeed an effigy holding a heart-shaped piece of stone in his hand. However, this is actually the figure of Sir William Gerbygge, who refounded the church during the reign of Edward I and dates from about 1280. The reason Sir William holds a heart is possibly because he died abroad and his heart was returned home for burial.

Sir William Gerbygge at Wickhampton.

Heartsease

✳ The Heartsease estate in **Norwich** was once part of Mousehold Heath. The development was named after the heartsease, a type of violet native to the county, which grew in the area before the estate was built.

St Edmund's Point

✳ The cliffs at **Hunstanton** used to be known as St Edmund's Point. The story goes that when Edmund arrived from Germany to be crowned King of East Anglia, he landed at Hunstanton and built a tower there. He'd made a vow to memorise the Book of Psalms if he landed safely and so he lived in the tower until he'd completed his vow. However, the name is more likely to be linked with the old chapel on the cliff, which Edmund allegedly built in thanksgiving for being saved from drowning.

Chapter 9

Notable buildings

Norfolk has 532 Grade I, 817 Grade II* and 9,098 Grade II listed buildings, as well as more than 350 scheduled monuments. These range from castles, henges and stately homes to more unusual buildings such as a concrete toilet and an AA box. Around a third of the listed buildings are in the market towns, and 10 per cent of them are in **Norwich**. According to Pevsner, **Little Walsingham** has more 17th-century buildings than any other village of its size in Norfolk.

There are around 400 moated sites in the county; there were originally double that number, but they have been ploughed in over the years.

The earliest town houses in Norfolk are both in **Norwich**: these are the stone house remains under the magistrates' court (which date from around 1170 and include the remains of a latrine arch, showing that the building had indoor toilets, which were flushed by the river) and Wensum Lodge in King Street. The oldest standing civic building in the county is the Tolhouse in **Great Yarmouth**, dating from the 12th century. Originally a private dwelling, it was used as a public building from the following century. In its time it has been used as a warehouse, a court, municipal offices, a gaol, the police station and a library, and is now a museum. The building was gutted during World War Two and was restored in 1959–60.

✳ **Attleborough** has one of the few memorials in the country commemorating the end of the Crimean War in 1856.

✳ **Blakeney** Guildhall is the remains of a mediaeval merchant's house, complete with a 15th-century brick-vaulted undercroft. It was later used as the guildhall of the fish merchants in the village.

✳ Pevsner describes **Blickling** Hall as one of the major Jacobean houses in England. It measured 120ft by 220ft, and was rebuilt by Sir Henry Hobart between 1618 and 1629 on the site of a moated house from the 1390s. It has a stunning gallery 123ft long, and the plasterwork for the ceiling cost £95 19s (the equivalent of £14,000 today). The ceiling has panels containing Hobart's arms and motto, plus emblems from Henry Peacham's *Minerva Britannica*, which was published in 1612. In the gardens there is a pyramid with a base 45ft square, commemorating John Hobart, the second Earl of Buckinghamshire, who died in 1793. It was commissioned by his second wife, Caroline, and was based on the Roman tomb of

Cestius, designed by Joseph Bonomi. (It isn't the only memorial pyramid in Norfolk: there's also a six-foot white limestone pyramid in the cemetery at **Attleborough**, to Melancthon William Henry Lombe Brooke, a solicitor who died in 1929.

The house topped a National Trust poll in 2007 as the Trust's most haunted building. Not only does it have Anne Boleyn, who is said to appear every year on 19 May, the anniversary of her execution, it also has her father, Thomas, who was allegedly cursed for not trying to save his daughter. Each year his ghost has to cross 12 bridges before the cock crows. It's also believed that the ghost of Sir John Fastolfe, who sold the hall to Sir Thomas (and also owned **Caister** Castle), visits the hall.

✳ The AA 'sentry' telephone box at **Brancaster** was installed before the 1950s and is the oldest one in East Anglia. There are few such boxes left in the country. The box, painted black and yellow, was restored in 2001.

✳ **Bradenham** Hall has over 850 varieties of tree in its arboretum, all of which are named. Allegedly, Lady Hamilton was once a tenant of the hall and entertained Nelson there. The house was also the inspiration for Brandham Hall in L.P. Hartley's *The Go-Between*.

✳ Willow Farm at **Cranworth** has a rare sign saying 'cheese room'. Back in the years of the window tax, cheese rooms were exempt from the tax. Most of these signs are found in the northern counties and this is the only known example in Norfolk.

✳ **East Walton** has a brick-built wheelwright's oven on the village green dating from the middle of the 19th century. It was used in the manufacture of iron tyres for carts and carriages until 1940, and was restored in 1977. Remains of Roman metal working have also been found at East Walton.

✳ **Fakenham** has a gasworks dating from 1846 and is said to be the only surviving example of a hand-fired horizontal retort in England. The gasworks produced gas from heating coal, but closed in 1965 following the discovery of natural gas in the North Sea. It is now a museum (and a scheduled monument), complete with all the equipment used for the manufacture of gas from coal: retorts, a condenser, purifiers, a meter and the gasholder.

✳ **Felbrigg** Hall was mentioned in the Paston letters (see page 35), but the mediaeval house was destroyed; the only remains are part of the cellars. The present house was built for Thomas Windham in 1621 and is unusual as it has the words 'Gloria Deo In Excelsis' cut across the front of the house. According to Pevsner, this is only seen in three other places in

England: Skipton Castle in Yorkshire, Temple Newsam in Leeds and Castle Ashby in Northamptonshire. The garden at Felbrigg has a national collection of colchicums (crocuses).

✳ Denton Lodge at **Feltwell** (which takes its name from former owner Captain Denton) is an extremely unusual building: it has a huge sundial instead of a porch window on the first floor. Feltwell used to be a port until the Fens were drained in 1632, and the face of the sundial has the names of various ports inscribed upon it: Bantam, Surat, Diu, Bagdat, Constantinople, Rome, Amsterdam, Lisbon, Teneril (Tenerife), Corvo, Cape Raz and Barmudus (Bermuda). At noon, you can tell what the time is in these ports.

✳ At Phillipo's Farmhouse in **Fulmodestone** is a barn with inscriptions by William Skinner Philippo (the family's original spelling of the name – unlike the name of the house) against the game laws. They're dated 1847 and say:

> Who can believe it blest with common sense that
> Taking game in Lent gave God offence
> Or that untested pheasants have the charm
> Th'Almighty's fierced pleasure to disarm
> In majesty enthroned supreme – divine
> Does he regard on what we chance to dine

Opposite is another inscription:

> This memorial is erected to transmit to posterity
> The fact that in the middle of the 19th century
> The owner of this estate was committed for 14 days
> Imprisonment in a Felon's jail by two clerical
> Justices for having taken and eaten his own game
> Out of season as decreed by English Statute law

✳ **Great Yarmouth** has the longest mediaeval town wall still standing. Henry III gave permission to build a wall and ditch in 1261. Work on the 23ft-high wall started in 1285 and was completed in 1393. There were 10 gates and 18 towers. The oldest tower, King Henry's, was also the only octagonal one. The south-east tower has fish-curing works dating from the early 1800s built against it and is one of the oldest surviving such works.

✳ The Hippodrome Circus in **Great Yarmouth** is Britain's only surviving purpose-built circus building, and is one of only three circuses in the world to have a sunken ring, which allows the circus to put on spectacular water shows (the other two are at Blackpool and Moscow). The Hippodrome was opened in 1903. Escapologist Harry Houdini once performed there; other famous performers who appeared there were singer Lily Langtry, Little Titch the clown and comedian Max Miller. It's said that the building is haunted by the ghost of its founder, George Gilbert.

❋ Number 20 South Quay in **Great Yarmouth** was built in 1720 for John Andrews, who was said to be the greatest herring merchant in Europe. He died in 1747 at the age of 72 and left his estate to his clerk, Thomas Martin. The house was bought by the government in 1802 and turned into the customs house. Today, it's the office of Great Yarmouth Port Authority.

❋ Nelson's Monument in **Great Yarmouth** was built between 1817 and 1819. Originally it stood in the middle of a racecourse (the racecourse was later moved) and was used as a seamark. It was designed by William Wilkins Jnr and is 144ft tall – that's a mere 12 inches shorter than Nelson's Column in Trafalgar Square. It was meant to be 20ft taller, but the foundations had to be dug more deeply than expected because of the sand. The figure of Victory at the top was originally made of Coade stone, but it was replaced by a fibreglass replica during restoration work in 1982. The monument was looked after by James Sharman, one of Nelson's men from the *Victory* (and, legend has it, the man who carried him below decks when he was fatally injured), until he died in 1867 at the age of 81.

❋ The Windmill Theatre at **Great Yarmouth** was originally called the Gem Cinema, and was built in 1908, five years after the first cinema was built in Victoria, London. At first it was intended to be a wild animal theatre but was instead opened as a cinema. Men and women had to sit on opposite sides of the auditorium, but could stay all day for a payment of between 2 and 6d. The Regent Cinema, on the south side of Regent Road, was built in 1914 and was the most luxurious cinema outside London. It still has a stage (which was used for live stage entertainment), dressing rooms and original mouldings.

❋ **Great Yarmouth** may also have had the earliest documented purpose-built theatre in the country. The 'Game Place House' is mentioned in 1539 when it was leased to Robert Coppyng – 38 years before Burbage's theatre in London was established.

❋ The village of **Glandford** is a model village built by Alfred Jodrell in the 1890s. Jodrell also built a museum to contain his collection of shells; it's the oldest purpose-built museum in Norfolk. He collected the shells over the space of 60 years from all over the world. The museum also contains other items, such as a piece of Pompeii, a tapestry by the fisherman-artist John Craske, fossils and a sugar bowl used by Elizabeth I.

✱ **Hales** Hall has a national collection of citrus, vitis (indoor) and ficus trees.

✱ Also at **Hales** is a brick barn, built in 1480 by Sir James Hobart, who was Henry VII's Attorney-General. It's thought to be the oldest brick barn in England. The walls are two and a half feet thick and 180ft long, making it one of the longest barns in the country. **Waxham** Great Barn was built almost 100 years later, in 1570, and at 180ft long and 35ft wide it's one of the biggest in the country. Only a little shorter is the 174ft-long Grove Farm Barn at **Booton**, which was re-thatched in 2008 using 6,500 bundles of reed. Hall Farm Barn at **Hemsby**, built around 1300, is Norfolk's oldest known timber-framed building.

✱ Sir Arthur Conan Doyle once stayed at Hill House in **Happisburgh**, and it's said that it was during his stay that he first got the idea for *The Hound of the Baskervilles* after hearing the legend of Black Shuck. The name of Baskerville was also inspired on his Norfolk trip – it was the name of the coachman who took him to **Cromer** Hall.

✱ **Heydon** Hall was built in 1581 for Henry Dynne, who was the auditor of the Exchequer. It has an ice house and a lookout tower. The hall and the village have been used as the setting for various television programmes and films. (See Chapter 12.)

✱ **Holkham** Hall became the second stately home in England to open to the public when it threw open its gates in 1777. It has a 9-mile wall around the deer park, which took six years to build and contains an estimated 10 million bricks. It also has a huge obelisk as a memorial to Thomas Coke. There are angled podiums similar to those of the lions in Trafalgar Square, but instead there are four different sculptures. One is a cow with the podium inscribed 'breeding in all its branches'; another is a wheeled implement, inscribed 'the improvement of agriculture'; one is a plough, inscribed 'live and let live'; and the final one is a sheep, inscribed 'small in size and great in value.'

✱ **Houghton** Hall was built by Sir Robert Walpole, and contains a unique collection of 20,000 model soldiers.

✱ **King's Lynn** has two guildhalls. St George's Guildhall in King Street, built in 1410, is the largest surviving mediaeval guildhall in England and has a

Great Hall that measures 100ft in length. It's now in the care of the National Trust and is used as a theatre and cinema. The theatrical tradition goes back a long way, and there are records of the mayor, aldermen and their guests attending a nativity play there followed by a great feast in Christmas 1442. Although he isn't recorded by name, Shakespeare is reputed to have acted there as he was connected with the Admiral's Men, who played in Norwich in 1593. In 1756, Thomas Sharpe built a playhouse there, with the last performance in 1814; a new playhouse was built in St James's Street in 1815. Trinity Guildhall, opposite St Margaret's Church, is used as the town hall. Its gables have flint chequerwork, and it was built after the previous guildhouse on the site was damaged by fire in 1421. The eastern half of the undercroft was used as a prison in 1571 after the Trinity Guild was disbanded. Nearly 50 years later, in 1618, the western part of the guildhall was used as the Bridewell House of Correction. The hall has also been used as a magistrates' court and an assembly room. Its contents include the 700-year-old silver and enamel King John Cup, one of the oldest paper books in existence and the King John Sword.

✳ The Red Mount Chapel in **King's Lynn** (also known as the Chapel of St Mary-on-the-Hill) was built in 1485 by Robert Currraunce as a wayside chapel for pilgrims visiting **Walsingham**. It's a red-brick octagonal tower with a cruciform stone chapel. It measures 18ft east to west, 14ft north to south and is 13ft tall. The roof is almost identical to that of King's College, Cambridge. The lower part of the chapel was used as a conduit and then as a stable; in 1638 it was used as a powder magazine, and during the siege of 1643 it was known as Mount Fort.

✳ **King's Lynn** has England's only surviving Hanseatic warehouse, built in 1475 after the Treaty of Utrecht allowed the Hansa merchants to establish a trading centre in the town. It was used as a warehouse until 1751 when it was then sold to merchant Edward Everard and he added a townhouse on the side. Part of the building is currently used as the town's register office.

✳ No. 38B High Street, **Little Walsingham**, has extremely rare wall paintings that were discovered in 1994. The 15th-century paintings show a huntsman blowing his horn and following some stags. It's very unusual to find wall paintings such as these, that are secular rather than religious. There are also wall paintings in the Old Vicarage, **Methwold**, which have floral motifs from the early and late 16th century. Abbey Farmhouse in **Old Buckenham** has 16th-century distemper floral and leaf patterns over the fire surround; and at Spiny Den in **Shipdham** there's a house containing wall paintings dating from 1680 that depict a hunting scene and include some Hebrew text.

Langham dome trainer.

✱ The anti-aircraft dome trainer at **Langham** is one of only three in the country; 40 of the domes were built during World War Two. This particular dome was built in 1942 from concrete and mesh and is 12 metres in diameter. It was used as a simulator to train anti-aircraft gunners. The gunner would sit in the middle of the dome with the controls round him; a film of aircraft flying would then be projected onto the white painted ceiling of the dome and the gunner would use his controls to aim at the projected aircraft. It was unused after 1946 and fell into disrepair.

✱ **Mundford** has a site that was formerly used by the Royal Observers Corps to detect, track and report aircraft over Britain. They were set up in 1925 and disbanded in the 1990s. From the mid-1950s onwards they operated from bunkers. Those at Mundford are unusual because the officers built a second one for their wives and children – without authorisation! The bunkers at Mundford were closed in 1991.

✱ The first large, purpose-built tuberculosis sanatorium in Britain was constructed in **Mundesley** in 1899. It was a timber-framed prefabricated hospital with a brick chimney and an iron roof. It had movable wooden huts, so the patients could spend all day in the fresh air but would be protected from the wind. The treatment was developed by Claude Lillingstone after he received similar treatment in Norway when he suffered from tuberculosis. It became a hospital in 1957, closed in 1992 and was refurbished in 1997 to become The Diana, Princess of Wales Treatment Centre for drug and alcohol problems.

✳ **Mannington** Hall has some very misogynistic black-letter inscriptions in the hall, written by Horatio William Walpole, the fourth Earl of Orford, who died in 1894: 'Trust your bark to the winds do not trust your heart to girls. For the wave is safer than a woman's faith. There is no good woman, and if one attains to any good I know not how an ill-made thing becomes good.' On the other side of the door he's added: 'A tiger is something worse than a snake, a demon than a tiger, a woman than a demon, and nothing worse than a woman.' However, women weren't the only ones to upset him; he built a monument in the church to himself, with an inscription saying that he didn't trust his successors to do it. They had the last laugh though; burying him quietly at **Itteringham**.

✳ One of the more unusual buildings in the county is Templewood in **Northrepps**, which was built as a shooting box in 1938 for Sir Samuel Hoare, Lord Templewood. It contains two sphinxes, which originally came from Nuthall Temple, near Nottingham (which was demolished in 1929) and columns from the Bank of England (which was rebuilt in the 1930s).

✳ Dragon Hall in **Norwich** is the only mediaeval merchant's hall known to have survived in Europe. It was built in about 1430 by Robert Toppes, Mayor of Norwich, and its name comes from the beautifully carved dragon in one of the spandrels. After Toppes died in 1467, the hall was sold and divided into tenements and cramped, cheap housing was built into the yard. There were at least three pubs on the site: the Black Horse, the Three Merry Wherrymen and the Old Barge. Most of the slums were cleared away in 1937. In 1970 the hall was rediscovered, restored and developed as a heritage site.

✳ The Assembly House in **Norwich** was built on the site of the college of St Mary-in-the-Fields. The house contains fragments of the college in its west wing, as well as the original brick-vaulted cellar. After the Dissolution of the Monasteries, the house was built by Sir Henry Hobart, who leased it to the city as an assembly house in 1753. It remained so until 1856, when dancing master Frank Noverre had a ballroom built there. The ballroom was converted to the Noverre Cinema in 1950 by Rowland Pierce (who also designed the city hall); the cinema was opened in 1950 and closed in 1992. Shoe manufacturer Henry Sexton bought Chapelfield House in the Assembly House and restored it at a cost of £70,000 in 1950, after which he presented it to the city. Pevsner states that 'no other town of its size in England has anything like it except of course for a spa like Bath.'

✳ The Briton's Arms in Elm Hill, **Norwich,** is the only surviving building in the area from the severe fires of 1507. There are only four other buildings within the city that were originally thatched. It was known as Le Godes House at one point, and has also been a surgeon's house. It was then used for weaving, cordwaining and saddlemaking and as a béguinage (a place where women live as nuns but don't take formal vows). Norwich is the only English city known to have supported béguinages.

✳ Stranger's Hall in **Norwich** has a squint in the undercroft. It was used by the porter to keep an eye on visitors and is said to be longer than a sword's length to prevent any harm being done to the porter.

✳ The 10-sided concrete urinal on St Crispin's Road, **Norwich,** was built in 1919 and is the oldest concrete urinal in Britain. It was Grade II listed in 1998.

✳ The balcony of City Hall in **Norwich,** at 365ft, is the longest in the UK.

✳ The Forum in Millennium Plain, **Norwich,** was given an Urban Design Award in the Civic Trusts Awards 2003.

✳ Two of the most thermally efficient buildings in Europe are at the University of East Anglia in **Norwich**: the ZICER and Elizabeth Fry buildings. The UEA also has a number of low energy buildings which contribute to their carbon reduction policy.

✳ One of the most unusual houses must be the 'Dutch Tutch' in **Potter Heigham,** situated on the banks of the River Thurne. The two-storey house is the middle section of a helter-skelter that was sited on the Britannia Pier at Great Yarmouth before the fire of 1914. The shed behind it is made from the top part of the helter-skelter. It was the first residential building put up on that stretch of the river, though nobody knows who rescued the helter-skelter from the pier or who turned it into a house.

✳ **Rougham** Hall had a line of lime trees leading from the hall in the 1690s that was nearly a mile long; the diarist John Evelyn recorded the trees being planted.

✴ The firehouse in **Stalham** is the oldest in Norfolk and is thought to be the second oldest in the country. It was built in 1833 and remained in use until 1962, but then became derelict. It was restored in November 2002.

✴ At **Tharston** there is a brick kiln. According to Pevsner, two million bricks were made there for use on the railways.

Follies

Follies are buildings made for fun, as decoration, rather than as conventional housing. Often the designs have some very eccentric elements. There was a fashion in the 18th and 19th centuries for building fake ruins (as at **Crimplesham**). Although not all the buildings below are strictly follies, their unusual elements are worth a look!

✴ At **Briningham** there is the Belle Vue Tower. Originally built in 1721 by Sir Jacob Astley as a smock windmill, his great-grandson Sir Edward Astley had the wooden upper sections rebuilt in brick between 1771 and 1780 and added a cupola roof. It has the oldest smock-mill base in the county, and it's said that you can see for 25 miles from the top. It was restored in 1980 and is now a private house.

✴ There's an 18th-century building in **Cley** called Whalebone House which was formerly the post office. What makes it unusual is that its cornice is made from cattle vertebrae (not, as to be expected from the name, whalebone). There's also a band of flint at the front outlined by cattle vertebrae.

✴ **Crimplesham** Hall has a folly with an underground boathouse. It also has a turreted balcony with a flagpole, the first of which has an unusual mosaic made from black pebbles and horses' teeth.

✴ Denton House in **Denton** has a grotto made of flint, which Pevsner has said to be the best in the county. It dates from 1770, but also contains a later circular room, which was decorated by Stockhouse Thompson with shells and coral from the Great Barrier Reef.

✴ Castle Cave in **Didlington** isn't actually a cave, despite its name: it's a turret on a mound. The building is derelict and contains graffiti from soldiers billeted there in World War Two.

✴ **Merton** Park has a folly called the Shell House, which was built in the 19th century. All the internal walls are covered in shells – many of which came from a grotto at Fawley in Hampshire – and at one time it also contained a shell model of the church.

✳ There's a derelict folly by Morton Hall in **Morton on the Hill**. During its heydey water was pumped into it to make artificial waterfalls inside the folly.

✳ At **Salthouse** there was once a castle-like structure called Randall's Folly. It was built in about 1860 by Onesiphorous Randall, who was born in **Cley** in 1798; it's said that he used the place for 'entertaining ladies'. The folly had double carriage doors at the back and the front, so one could drive straight through the building and turn the horse and carriage round, ready to return through the house and over the bridge to Beach Road. When Onesiphorous died in London in 1873, the government bought the folly and used it as a coastguard station; it was later used as a holiday home. It was badly damaged in the 1953 floods and had to be demolished.

Ice houses

✳ Ice houses were introduced to the UK in 1660 by King Charles when he had one built in St James's Park, London. The buildings are usually partly underground, to help with insulation, and are lined with brick. They're often built close to a lake or stream for a ready source of ice, although ice was sometimes imported. The ice was stored in the ice house in winter and insulated with straw or sawdust. The store would last for the whole of the summer.

Examples in Norfolk are at **Boyland** Hall, **Brinton**, **Crimplesham** Hall (which is unusual as its roof is made out of pipes), **Heydon** Hall, **Hoveton** (although it's situated in Ice Well Wood, it's definitely a house rather than a well), **Narborough, Ryston, Sandringham, Stratton Strawless** Hall (which the Norfolk Industrial Archaeology Society has said to be the most perfect example in the county), **Thursford** and **Wroxham** Hall. There's also a huge ice house in **Great Yarmouth** with a capacity of 42,588 cubic feet. It was built in 1840 and used for storing ice from South Walsham Broad and Norway. The last recorded wherry load of ice was brought there between 1898 and 1899. It was restored in 1980 and is thought to be the only one of its type left in the country.

Water pumps

When you consider that it hasn't been many years since water had to be pumped by hand instead of through a mains supply, it's surprising that so few water pumps remain.

✳ The water pump on Queen's Square in **Attleborough** was set up in 1897 to celebrate Victoria's 60th jubilee. It was restored in the 1970s and again in 2002. Interestingly, the plaque describes it as a tree pump:

1837–1897
Victoria
To
Commemorate
the
60th year
of
Her Majesty's
reign.
Queen & Empress
enclosed
June 1897.
This tree pump
was renovated
to commemorate
the Queen's
Golden Jubilee
June 2002.

✳ The water pump at **Cringleford** is made of cast iron. It was originally sited over a bore but was moved in 1974. The pump was one of six built for the Norwich and Thetford Turnpike Trust in 1835; another for the same association is located at Hethersett and was moved in 1985.

✳ At **Downham Market** the stone remains of the old town pump can be seen on the Howdale; it was moved there by stonemasons J. Long and Sons in 1935. Nelson allegedly used to sail paper boats on the gully containing the waste water from the pump, and the water was still meant to be drinkable in the early 1930s.

✳ There's an unusual pump on the **Holkham** estate which has a pagoda-like roof that contains holes for birds to build their nests.

✳ The pump house at the centre of **Little Walsingham** houses the remains of the village pump. The structure was built just after the Dissolution, using stones and bricks from the priory, and supplied most of the village with water. There was a pinnacle on the pump house, but apparently it was broken off during village celebrations of the relief of Mafeking in the Boer War in May 1900.

✳ **Norwich** has several remaining water pumps, though some are easier to find than others. There's a wooden pump in Websdale's Court (just off Bedford Street); another in a courtyard off Elm Hill; and one by the old coachouses in Ferry Lane in the close. Probably the easiest to find is the enormous cast iron pump just by the graveyard of St John Maddermarket – the water from the pump was said to go through the churchyard first! Another is Gibson's Conduit, which was also known as Gibson's Pump, just off Westwick Street. It was built by Robert Gybson in 1578 and is particularly interesting because it may be the oldest dated pump in England. It's been moved from its original position and unfortunately most of the workings have been lost. The inscription reads:

> This water here caught
> In sorte as yowe see
> From a spring is broughte
> Thre-skore foot and thre
>
> Gybson hath it sowghte
> From Saynt Lawren's Wel
> And his charg this wrowghte
> Who now here doe dwel
>
> Thy ease was his coste not smal
> Vouchsafied wel of those
> Which thankful be his work to se
> And there to be no foes

Gybson was a brewer, and although he paid for the parish well he definitely profited from it! He's an interesting character, particularly during his feud with the mayor in 1603. During an outbreak of the plague the mayor asked everyone to remove their drapes; Gybson refused. The mayor commanded him to remove them. Gybson retorted, 'I would see who dare pull them down.' The mayor's reply was, 'That dare I.' He did so and, following their row, Gybson was no longer allowed to be an alderman or have the freedom of the city.

The conduit was converted into a drinking fountain in the 19th century by brewer Harry Bullard and moved to the wall of his brewery in Westwick Street. When the Anchor Quay development was built the conduit was moved to the other side of the wall, away from the road.

✳ **Swannington** has a water pump under a thatched canopy, dating from 1888. It was built in memory of Hastings Parker, by his wife.

✤ At **Thorpe Abbots** there is a cast iron village pump with a stone trough under a hexagonal shelter. A plaque on the central post of the shelter states that that the pump was given by Edward Kay in 1867. It was restored by Dr F.N. Kay Menzies in December 1924 and by the parish council in 1979.

✤ There's a thatched pump house at **Woodbastwick** on the village green; one of the beams is carved with the inscription 'In memoriam Marguerite Tournois December 19th 1888.'

✤ At **Worstead** there's a pump next to a well in the village.

Windmills

✤ More than 900 windmill sites in Norfolk have been identified. Even today, the remains of 120 corn mills can be found in the county, although only a quarter of these have either been restored or are almost complete. Of these mills, the majority (93) are tower mills; there are also five smock mills, 20 post mills and two composite mills. The last corn mill to stop working was the mill at **Billingford** in 1956. It was restored in 1962 and in 1998 was in full working order.

The corn mills used millstones, arranged in pairs, to convert wheat grain and other cereals into flour for baking. The earliest type of mills were post mills, which had a large oak post as the core and the body (or buck) of the mill would turn round it to catch the wind. The last original post mill is at **Garboldisham**; it's thought to date from the 1770s and was restored in the 1970s. At 6.7 metres, it's body is the longest in Norfolk. There is also a depiction of a post mill on the Walsoken Brass, dated 1349, in St Margaret's Church, **King's Lynn**. In 1994, at South Walsham, millwright Richard Seago began building the first post mill to be constructed in Norfolk for 150 years. Smock mills followed the post mills; the earliest remaining example in the county is at **Melton Constable**. Finally, the brick tower mill took over. Due to its design, it could hold the latest machinery and was also taller than the post mills and smock mills.

There were also watermills in the county; many of them were draining mills (there were 68 in Broadland alone). In 1906 there were still 72 watermills working in the county, but by 1969 that had dwindled down to just one.

Mills were used for other things besides grinding corn or draining land. In **Taverham** the mill was used to make paper between 1701 and 1899. In the early 19th century Fourndrinier machines were installed so the paper could be produced in a continuous roll instead of single sheets. Paper from Taverham was used to make banknotes and Bibles, and, in its heyday, the mill supplied half the paper for printing *The Times*. Other mills were used for fulling (a

Thurne Mill.

process involving the felting of wool), at **Hellesdon**; crushing bone for fertiliser, at **Narborough**; making mustard, at **Stoke Holy Cross** (before Colmans moved to Norwich); tanning, at **Whitwell**; and sawing, at **Gunton**.

Mills great and small

✳ At **Horning** you'll find the only open trestle mill with a scoop wheel in Britain. It was built pre-1930.

✳ The oldest watermill in the county is at **Burnham Overy**, dating from 1737.

✳ Sutton Mill, a nine-storey corn grinding mill near **Stalham**, is Norfolk's tallest surviving windmill, measuring 24.35 metres (or just under 79ft) in height. It was built in 1862 after a fire destroyed the previous mill on the site and was in use until 1940. It is no longer open to the public.

✳ One of the biggest windmills in the county was at **Bixley**: it was 137ft (41.76 metres) tall. As it ran at a loss it was dismantled and sold in 1865. Another monster was High Mill (also known as Southtown High Mill) in **Great Yarmouth**, which was 10-storeys tall and was possibly 41 metres tall. It was built in 1812 at a cost of £2,000 (the equivalent of just over £120,000 today). It stood on oak piles and a raft and supplied flour to the army during the Crimean War. It was demolished in 1904, after which the bricks were supposedly used to build High Mill Terrace (now Gatacre Road).

✳ The **Berney Arms** Windmill is another huge mill, built in 1870, and is Norfolk's tallest working marsh windmill. It was originally used to grind cement clinker, but later was used to pump water from the nearby marshes. It is acknowledged as one of the best in the county. The sails of the windmill span 25.9 metres, making them the longest in the UK.

✳ **Denver** Mill is the tallest working windmill in the county and measures 59ft (17.9 metres) to the top of the tower. It's open to the public.

✳ One of the largest mills ever constructed is **Old Buckenham**, which has five pairs of millstones all situated on one floor. It was built in 1818 for John Burlingham, and has the largest diameter of any tower mill in the country. It measures 8 metres at the base and 7 metres at the top of the tower, and has a boat-shaped cap on top that's 7.32 metres wide. The sails aren't much shorter than those at Berney Arms, with a diameter of 24.1 metres. It also has the biggest spur wheel found in a windmill, which is 3.96 metres in diameter and has 171 teeth.

✳ The mill at **Ringstead** was one of only six in the county that had six sails.

✳ The tower mill at **Great Bircham** was the first mill in the county to use wind power after it was restored. It was originally built in 1846, but was restored in the 1970s by the great-grandson of the miller who worked at the windmill in 1888.

✳ The only parish in Norfolk which has a windmill, a watermill and a combined wind-and-watermill is **Burnham Overy**. There are very few wind-and-water windmills in the UK; the only other one in Norfolk is at **Little**

Cressingham. It was built in 1821 and has two pairs of stones driven by water, with two on the floor above driven by wind.

✳ The windmill at **Cley**, which was built in 1819, was the first windmill to be converted into accommodation, in 1921.

✳ Two of the oldest mills in Broadland are at **Oby** (dating from 1753) and Brograve Level (at **Hickling**, dating from 1771). Both mills contain machinery dating from the mid-19th century.

✳ Clayrack Mill is a rare 17th-century hollow-post mill. It was found at Ranworth, but was moved to Ludham and rebuilt for the Norfolk Windmills Trust.

✳ According to Pevsner, **Tunstall** Dyke wind pump is the last 18th-century timber smock mill remaining in Norfolk.

✳ St Benet's Level Mill at **Thurne** is one of only two windmills in the country to have a fantail with 10 blades.

✳ St Benet's Abbey Mill at **Horning** was built in the ruins of the abbey gatehouse in 1740. It started out as a mill for crushing colza (rape) seed, turning it to oil and was then converted to a drainage mill. The sails were destroyed in a storm in 1863 and the mill stopped working; only the tower remains today.

✳ Modern windmills are a contentious subject; some love them and some loathe them. The first wind farm in the county was at Blood Hills in **East Somerton**. Ten turbines were commissioned in 1992; a large turbine, which took four days to build, was added in 2000. Two turbines have been built at **Swaffham**, one in 1999 and one in 2003. At **Scroby** Sands 30 turbines were built in 2004. They cost £75 million and each turbine generates two megawatts.

Bridges

✳ Bishop's Bridge in **Norwich**, dating from around 1340, is the only surviving mediaeval bridge in the city. The oldest river crossing in the city is Fye Bridge, and a timber causeway 100 yards long was discovered there in 1896. The earliest iron bridge in the city is Coslany Bridge, which was built in 1804.

✳ **Potter Heigham** has a mediaeval bridge which crosses the River Thurne and has three arches; the outer two date from the 14th century and the central arch dates from the 15th century.

Haveringland stocks.

❊ The Haven Bridge in **Great Yarmouth** was opened on 21 October 1930 by the Prince of Wales. The construction is double bascule (counterpoised) and it opens to let ships through.

❊ Nuns Bridges at **Thetford** is one of the oldest known crossing points in the county and follows the line of the Icknield Way.

Crime and punishment

❊ Most towns and villages in Norfolk had a set of stocks. Many have disappeared (including the ones in **Norwich** which used to stand next to the guildhall), but on Haveringland Road in **Haveringland** you can still see a complete set of village stocks, dated 1804. (Incidentally, only one leg was put in the stocks – so this would have accommodated five miscreants.)

❊ **Feltwell** once had an iron cage and any highwaymen who were caught were placed inside until they could be brought before the magistrate. Jackson Hill at Feltwell was named after a former highwayman who was hanged there. Apparently, his body was left there for two or three years as a deterrent. Records show that the body was still there in 1808.

✷ In Church Street, **Gimingham,** you can still see the triangular-shaped village pond, which was built in the early 19th century. Any stray animals found in the village would be kept there until the owner paid a fine.

✷ The Bridewell at **Aylsham** was built in 1543. The house was rebuilt in 1785, used as a prison until 1825 and is now offices. **Horsford** still has an 18th-century brick lock-up, 'The Clink', on Norwich Road. At **Little Walsingham** there is the Shirehall, which includes court fittings dating from 1805, a holding cell and the arms of George III; the last petty sessions were held there in 1971. There is also the Old Gaol on Bridewell Street, which was built in 1787 on the site of the leper hospital and has four treadmills; it was closed in 1861. **Norwich** has the Bridewell – now used as a museum (being refurbished at the time of writing). It has the largest known mediaeval undercroft in the city, and from 1583 it was used as 'a Brydewell to keep and stay ydle persons to somme honest woorke and labor.' Historian Michael Gibbs says that the prisoners had to work from 5am to 8pm, with a single 30-minute break for food and a 15-minute break for prayer. Apart from one flint wall and the crypt, the building was destroyed by fire in 1751 and rebuilt in 1786. The wall was described by travel writer Celia Fiennes in 1698 as the 'finest piece of flintwork in England.' **Thetford** has a lock-up behind the guildhall in Cage Lane. It was rebuilt in 1578, but placed in its current position after it was dismantled in 1968. The ground floor of the clock tower in **Watton** was once used as a lock-up.

Market Crosses

Most towns and villages which had the right to hold a market would have a cross in the market place. This could be a simple obelisk or marker, or it could be a more complex structure with a roof (such as those at **Wymondham** and **North Walsham**). The market cross was sometimes used as a place to preach and official measures might also be kept there. Very few have survived, but we know details of some of them.

✷ **Attleborough** once had a market cross; it was removed in 1787, and in 1897 the water pump (see page 165) was built on the site.

✷ The market cross at **Downham Market** is now in the base of the war memorial.

✷ The market cross at **Fakenham** was built in 1650; it was demolished in 1790 and the Cornhall was built on the site in 1855. The building was used as a Home Guard lookout in World War Two and it's thought that there is a 'tank trap' nearby.

✳ The cross at **Foulsham** was pulled down in 1760 and a war memorial is now on the site.

✳ The cross at **Great Yarmouth** had a very long history. It was rebuilt in 1385, 1509 and 1730, but was finally demolished in 1836.

✳ **King's Lynn** once had a domed, octagonal market cross in the Tuesday Market Place, which was built in 1707 on the site of an earlier cross. It was demolished in 1830 and no trace remains.

✳ The cross at **New Buckenham** is still there. It was originally the site of two 16th-century shops, which were bought by the town in 1715, and the market cross was moved there in the early 18th century. It has an open ground floor, and the columns date from 1754; the middle one was used as a whipping post. The upper floor was used as a meeting room. There's also a large hook, probably for a set of scales.

✳ The first market cross at **North Walsham** was built in 1550 by Thomas Thirlby, the Bishop of Norwich (who was also the lord of the manor and collected the market tolls). It was destroyed in the fire of 1600 and its replacement was built shortly afterwards – an octagonal structure with a three-tiered dome. It has been heavily restored, particularly in 1897 and 1983. The original clock came from Worstead Hall in 1787, with the chiming mechanism added in 1899.

✳ **Norwich's** market cross was first built in 1411 and was a stunning 60ft tall. It was later rebuilt opposite Davey Place in 1503. When the building deteriorated the city demolished it in 1732. The stone was sold for £125 (the equivalent of about £19,000 today) and the site was levelled. In 2005, archaeologists excavating the area during changes to the market discovered the foundations of the cross.

✳ The original market cross at **Swaffham** was in the Shambles, built in 1575. However, in 1783 it couldn't be seen properly and was demolished. The replacement cross was built between 1781 and 1783 by the Earl of Orford, and has the figure of Ceres on the top.

✳ The cross at **Walsingham** was removed in 1790 and there are no surviving traces.

✳ **Watton** appears to have had two market crosses. One stood in front of Wayland House and had wooden spandrels showing the town rebus of a hare (*wat*) and barrel (*tun*), which are now in the Clock House. The other, which wasn't as old, stood on the road outside the Clock House. It was demolished in 1820 and replaced with a milestone marker.

✴ The octagonal market cross at **Wymondham** was built in 1617, after the previous one (dating back to the 1300s) was burned in the fire of 1616. It has carvings of spoons, spindles, skewers and foliage in a depiction of the town's industries. In 1618 the lord of the manor, Sir Henry Hobart of **Blickling,** was invited to the grand reopening of the cross, where he dined on 'wine, sugar, beer and cakes.' In 1713 Robert Barret and William Broughton were hanged from a gallows there for robbery and for the murder of James Pointer on Silfield Common. The upper room was converted into a reading room in the 1840s. The cross was restored in the 1980s and is now Wymondham's tourist information centre.

Chapter 10

Rebels and rogues

Norfolk has a long tradition of protest, from Boudicca's rising against the Romans in AD 61, through to its part in the Peasant's Revolt of 1381, and on to Kett's Rebellion in 1549 and the agricultural disturbances of the 19th century. One of the most important rebellions was the school strike at **Burston** – and the placard that led the procession, loaned by the village shop, said it all: *Justice*.

And then there are the rogues, such as the notorious pirates, the smugglers and the hot-headed duellists...

The Burston School Strike

The longest strike in history was staged by children in **Burston** on 1 April 1914, in protest of their teachers Tom and Kitty Higdon being dismissed. The Higdons were committed Christians and Socialists, who believed that education should help the next generation to gain a better life. They began teaching at **Wood Dalling** in 1902, but ended up fighting with the owners of the school because the school buildings were in a bad state and because the local farm owners kept taking their children out of school as cheap labour. Tom was fined 11 shillings for assault after an argument with one landowner, so in 1911 the education authorities moved them to Burston.

Here the conditions were just as bad, with semi-derelict buildings and landowners valuing cheap labour above the children's education. Tom wrote in his diary, '...there was much radical wrong, which for very conscience sake, as well as for all practical and healthful reasons, must needs be faced.' They clashed badly with the vicar, Revd Charles Tucker Eland, who was also chair of the school. The school authorities said that Kitty must ask permission to light a fire to dry children's clothing when they'd walked miles to school in the rain, or heat water to bathe children who were ridden with lice. Tom stood for election to the parish council – and won with a huge majority, annoying Eland still further – but the landowners were still in control of the school. They dismissed Kitty on trumped-up charges of neglect and abuse, and the Higdons were told to leave the school by the end of March 1914.

On 1 April the new teachers came in to find a notice chalked on the blackboard: 'We are going on strike tomorrow.' They then discovered the children – led by Violet Potter and supported by the parents – marching outside, waving placards stating 'We want our teachers back' and 'Justice'. The parents, led by fishmonger George Durbidge, decided they wanted their children taught by the Higdons and set up a new school under a marquee on the village green. All bar six of the 72 children from the village school were taught by Kitty in the new 'Strike School'. In the winter they found an unused workshop to house the school.

Despite being fined for not sending their children to a recognised school, the parents continued to send their children to the Higdons. Tenants were sacked and threatened with eviction, but, with people going off to fight the war, the landowners couldn't afford to reject workers for long. When the lease on the workshop expired the following year people from across the country donated £1,250 via trade unions to help and a new school was built. The school was opened by Violet Potter, the leader of the strike, on 13 May 1917. Children were still sent to the 'Strike School' in the 1930s, and it only closed in 1939 after Tom's death, when 75-year-old Kitty felt she couldn't continue alone. The children returned to the village school (which had been improved to match the Higdons' school) and the strike finally ended after 25 years.

Kitty died in 1946 and was buried next to Tom in Burston. The 'Strike School' was given charitable status in 1949 and turned into a museum. From 1984 a rally has been held on the first Sunday in September to commemorate the protest.

The story was made into a BBC drama in 1985, starring Bernard Hill and Eileen Atkins.

Duellists

Sir John Heydon and Robert Mansfield, 1600

The severed hand of Sir John Heydon was an exhibit at the Canterbury Museum in the early 1800s. It was presented to the museum by Daniel Jarvis, a doctor from Margate. Gruesomely, the exhibit was described as a left hand 'carefully dried' and severed from the wrist an inch below the little finger. As the duel was fought with rapiers, the hand was probably amputated by a surgeon. Heydon was forever known after that as 'Heydon with one hand.'

Heydon was very much a hothead and clearly owed Mansfield some money, because Mansfield challenged him to a duel in January 1600, just outside Norwich. There were no witnesses and the only surviving account of the duel is by Mansfield, who was also suspected of foul play as there was an enquiry into the duel. According to Mansfield, when they measured their rapiers Heydon's was longer and their seconds argued, but eventually they agreed to fight with the rapiers. Mansfield led the way to the duelling ground (which was 'Rackeywards') on Heydon's directions and finally, at 'the top of a hill between two great high waies', they drew their rapiers.

They wounded each other and when Heydon fell, he begged to be allowed up rather than being killed 'baselie on the grounde'. However, when Mansfield let him up, Heydon drew his dagger and stabbed him. Finally, Mansfield took Heydon to 'the place where [he] left [his] purse and inkhorne' and told him to sign papers relating to their monetary rows. Heydon said he couldn't, as Mansfield had killed him and he was unable to write; Mansfield retorted that he'd kill Heydon if he didn't sign! Eventually, Heydon signed the papers, and Mansfield, after discovering that he couldn't use his right arm and that 'one of [his] wounds to rattell', left his ruff, spurs and scabbard behind and rode home to bed. Heydon was apparently lifted into a cart and carried home half an hour after Mansfield had left. Both men lived for some years after.

Thomas Berney and Thomas Bedingfield, 1684

This was more of a drunken brawl than a duel and ended badly for both. Bedingfield was the son of Sir Thomas Bedingfield of Darsham, and Berney was the second son of Sir Thomas Berney. During the assizes they were drinking with the High Sheriff in an inn in the parish of St Andrew's, **Norwich,** when Mr Bladwell, a fellow drinker, decided to start a game of 'six glasses of wine in a hand.' Bedingfield was rude about Bladwell's sister; Berney intervened and said that 'it was not kindly done to reflect on a gentlewoman.' In response, Bedingfield hit him!

Duel Stone at Cawston.

Shortly afterwards, another quarrel blew up between Berney and two other men, Mr Ellis and Mr d'Havers. While that was being settled Bedingfield and Berney staggered outside and drew their swords. Berney ran his sword through Bedingfield, who died at once. As it was the middle of the assizes and the authorities wanted to make an example of Berney, it was alleged that Berney was quarrelsome and that Bedingfield was stabbed from behind. Berney was found guilty and sentenced to be hanged. At his execution on the 8 August 1684 he said he believed he drew first: 'I heard ye blood pour upon ye stones, and this is all yt I know of the barbarous murder done by me as ye jury or law found it.' He added that people should repent and avoid strong drink, and said: 'I do admonish them also to have a care of all manner of passions in all acts and attempts of revenge upon any provocation whatsoever, never to draw sword but for personall defence upon assaults, but suffer repeated injuries rather than to attempt revenge upon any sense of honour w'soever.'

A pamphlet in London Guildhall library, written by George Croom, is entitled: *A full relation of a Barbaraous Murther, committed on the body of Esq. Beddingfield on Sunday, the 20th day of July, 1684, by Mr Barney*. Croom said that Berney was quarrelsome and had stabbed Bedingfield eight times (half of those in the back). Berney had tried to escape, but the city gates were shut, so he was easily pursued and taken. According to Croom, Berney had said that if he wanted money and someone refused, he'd threaten them with a sword, and had wounded several people in the past. At the trial Berney said he was drunk and was greatly repentant. He was executed at the market cross.

However, Berney's funeral service stated that he was executed at the common place of execution, not the market cross; that he stabbed Bedingfield in the back in the course of a struggle, rather than on purpose; and that he had spent the time between his sentence and execution reading religious books. A note on the pamphlet in contemporary handwriting said that Croom was unreliable, printed things without checking that they were true and 'often obtrudes falsities on the public.'

Amelia Opie used the story as the basis for 'Henry Woodville' in *New Tales* (1818). However, her footnote states that a French dancing-master called de Havers had had an argument with 'Bennefield', took Berney's sword while he was in a drunken stupor and stabbed 'Bennefield' to the heart, and then returned the sword to the scabbard. On this circumstantial evidence Berney was executed in Town Close. According to Opie, de Havers fled to France and only finally confessed to the murder on his deathbed.

Sir Henry Hobart and Oliver le Neve, 1698

The Duel Stone in **Cawston** marks the duel between Sir Henry Hobart of **Blickling** Hall and Oliver le Neve of **Great Witchingham** Hall. Hobart believed that le Neve had spread rumours about him being a coward, which had lost him his parliamentary seat, and called him out. Hobart was known as a brilliant sportsman, while le Neve spent his time drinking and fishing. The duel took place on 20 August 1698, illegally as there were no seconds present. Hobart wounded le Neve, but then his sword tangled in le Neve's coat so le Neve was able to stab him in the stomach. Hobart died the next day – it's said that his dying groans can still be heard at Blicking Hall – and le Neve fled to Holland. He lived there under an assumed name (including, at the end, as a Mr Browne, a sword cutler). However, he finally returned home and stood trial at **Thetford** assizes in 1700, where he was acquitted of the murder.

Smugglers

- When taxes rose dramatically in the 18th and 19th century, so did levels of smuggling – particularly cargoes of tobacco, spirits and tea. Some estimates say that 80 per cent of tea in Britain hadn't had duty paid on it. Taxes were also payable on playing cards and dice.

- Parson Woodforde of **Weston Longville** mentions smugglers in his diary. It's not clear whether he helped them, but he certainly bought gin, tea and brandy from them. The smugglers would give him a scare by whistling unexpectedly under his window and waiting for money (as Richard Andrews did in March 1777), while others would knock on the door and vanish, leaving kegs on the doorstep to be bottled.

- Windmills on the Broads were used as a signalling system, as the wherries used to carry smuggled goods in addition to their normal cargo. If the watch was suspected, a warning was sent to the nearest marshman, who would stop his mill so the sails were set at a St Andrew's (diagonal) cross. He would wait until the next mill along had seen the signal and copied it and would then let the mill's sails continue as normal. When the all-clear was given the marshman would stop his mill's sails at a St George's (square) cross. The wherryman would then sink the contraband tubs in the Broad and mark the hiding place with reeds; the marshman would pick it up later. On other occasions the wherryman would put his tubs in the drainage ditch so it would go straight to the marshman.

- Smugglers on the coast would use the legend of Black Shuck to keep their paths clear, especially around **Happisburgh** and **Weybourne**. At night they'd put a black sheet over a small pony and hang a lantern round its neck, so it would make people think of the giant dog with one blazing eye – and they'd steer well clear of the cliffs.

- The smugglers at **Stiffkey** were led by John Dunn. In 1817, when horse racing at **Wells** took place on a rack on the beach, he organised a landing of spirits during a race meeting. Obviously people in the crowd were looking forward to some smuggled gin and brandy later that day, so the customs men were heavily outnumbered. Even when they were helped by a yeomanry major, who managed to form an impromptu cavalry, they didn't manage to stop the smugglers getting away.

✳ At **Blakeney**, there's a story that a farmer who was caught smuggling and had his horses confiscated. On the day they were to be auctioned, he went along and pulled out a handful of hair from one of his horses (knowing that it was the season for moulting) and told the revenue men that it was a sign of mange and would spread to all the horses, including the revenue men's own horses. The revenue men were seafarers and were not used to horses; suspiciously, they checked the other horses and were horrified to discover that they could pull out handfuls of hair. Wanting to get rid of the problem, they sold all the horses to the farmer for £5 – and the farmer made a handsome profit.

✳ There's a secret room in a cottage in Northgate Street, **Great Yarmouth**, which is only accessible from the roof space. It may have been used to store smuggled tea, as one of the occupants of the cottage was arrested for smuggling the beverage in 1760.

Sadly, the struggle between the smugglers and the revenue men didn't always stop at good-natured trickery. With the large sums of money involved, the smugglers were prepared to resort to violence.

✳ The Old Mill House at **Overstrand** had a smugglers' squint. The smugglers used to bury their cargo in a field near Mill Hill, and, according to William Dutt, the field was once called 'Hickerman's Folly' after a customs officer in **Cromer** who tried to impound the cargo. The smugglers pulled him off his horse, gagged and blindfolded him, and then tied him to the gate. By the time he was freed again, the smuggled goods had long since gone.

✳ In 1822 smugglers landed at **Snettisham** with 80 tubs of gin and brandy. The tubs and the boat were seized by the Preventive Men, but were rescued by the smugglers, assisted by more than 100 people carrying bludgeons and fowling pieces. The smugglers escaped along Peddars Way and afterwards called at houses in the village to see if a 'basket of fish' was wanted.

✳ An even more violent struggle ended at **Great Yarmouth** on 19 March 1817. The fight originated further up the east coast at Robin Hood's Bay, when the revenue cutter *Ranger* fired over the bows of a lugger, signalling that it needed to stop for customs inspection. The lugger was heavily armed (not to mention stuffed with illegal cargo) and fired back. After an hour and a half of fighting, the smugglers abandoned ship, along with £10,000 worth of cargo: 507 ankers (each equivalent to 8.5 gallons) and 945 half-ankers of Geneva (gin); 206 bags of tea; 9 boxes of playing cards; 27 bales of tobacco; and 47 bales of silk bandana handkerchiefs. Two smugglers were killed, along with three revenue men; seven were injured, three of them so badly that they had to be pensioned off. The officers were buried at St Nicholas's Church, Great Yarmouth.

❋ In the churchyard of St Mary's in **Old Hunstanton** there are epitaphs to two revenue men who were killed by smugglers:

In memory of William Webb, late of the 15th D'ns, who was shot from his Horse by a party of Smugglers on the 26 of Sepr. 1784
I am not dead but sleepeth here,
And when the Trumpet Sound I will appear
Four balls thro' me Pearced there way:
Hard it was. I'd no time to pray
This stone that here you Do see
My Comrades Erected for the sake of me.

Here lie the mangled remains of poor William Green, an Honest Officer of the Government, who in the faithful discharge of his duty was inhumanely murdered by a gang of Smugglers in this Parish, September 27th, 1784.

The gang were based at the Cutter pub. On this particular day, William Kemball of Thornham was unloading his contraband from the *Lively* near the cliffs at Hunstanton, intending to stash the goods in the cellars at the Cutter. The revenue men had heard rumours of the run of gin, brandy, tea and silk and disturbed the smugglers, who abandoned their cargo and rowed back to the *Lively*. Kemball, desperate to avoid a huge financial loss, armed his crew with muskets and cutlasses and went to recover the goods. The smugglers were ambushed outside Hunstanton and fired a volley of shots, killing William Webb and William Green. Kemball was caught and brought to trial and, according to contemporary accounts, although the jury knew the gang were guilty, they found him innocent. The prosecutors protested and asked for a new trial and jury but the second jury reached exactly the same verdict.

❋ However, the smugglers didn't have it all their own way. In the 1780s the *Norfolk Chronicle* reported many instances when the revenue men had won. Examples of this include 200 casks of liquor seized at **Bacton** in November 1781; '27 ankers of brandy, a like quantity of rum, 162 half-ankers of geneva, and 850 pounds of tea' seized at **Hunstanton** in March

1782; and 110 gallons of Holland's gin at **Weeting** in January 1783. Finally, Lieutenant Williams of the *Advice* cutter chased two smuggling cutters from **Cromer** to **Yarmouth** for seven hours in January 1783. Despite the fact that the smugglers were more heavily armed than the revenue men, Williams managed to seize 582 half-ankers of geneva and brandy and took the cutters into **King's Lynn**.

Pirates

✳ Pirates were even more of a problem than the smugglers. James I gave **Great Yarmouth** a charter in 1608 that included the right to try pirates at Yarmouth Admiralty Court, and the first piracy trial was held on 25 March 1613. Five men were accused of capturing the *Seahorse* and her cargo (22,000 lamphreys, 30 barrels of beer and six barrels of red herrings) at sea, and three of the pirates (Thomas Jinkins, Michael Muggs and Edward Charter) were hanged. The last case was heard in 1823 and the court was abolished in 1835.

✳ William Payne was one of the most infamous of pirates. He terrorised shipping along the east coast, and was tried and executed in London in 1781. The *Norfolk Chronicle* of 12 December 1781 explains what happened to his body: 'William Payne, lately executed for piracy on this coast was yesterday hung in chains upon a gibbet, above fifty feet high, erected on the Denes for that Purpose.' Allegedly, his body was brought to Yarmouth in a wooden box labelled 'Glass With Care', and his body hung on the gibbet until 1804, giving the area the name Payne's Hill.

✳ In January 1783 the pirate Captain Roberts tried to escape from the prison at Yarmouth. He managed to free himself from his irons, pushed the keeper's daughter to the floor and took the key from her. However, she hung onto his clothes screaming, 'Murder!' People came to her aid and locked him up again. His accomplice (from Ostend, according to the *Norfolk Chronicle*) managed to escape on horseback and Roberts was taken to London.

✳ Later that month, the brig *Alexander & Margaret* was attacked by pirates. The gravestone of David Bartleman, the Master of the brig, is in the churchyard of St Nicholas at Great Yarmouth and explains the story:

To
the memory of
David Bartleman

Master of the brig *Alexander & Margaret*
of North Shields
Who on the 31st January 1781 on the Norfolk Coast
with only three 3 pounders and 10 Men and Boys
nobly defended himself
against a cutter carrying eighteen 4 pounders
and upwards of a hundred Men
commanded by that notorious English Pirate
Fall
and fairly beat him off.
Two hours after the Enemey came down upon him again
When totally disabled his Mate Daniel MacAuley
expiring with the loss of blood
and himself dangerously wounded
he was obliged to strike and ransome.
He brought his shattered vessel into Yarmouth
with more
than Honours a Conqueror
and died here in consequence of his wounds
on the 14th February following
in the 25th year of his age.
To commemorate the Gallantry of his Son
the Bravery of his faithfull Mate
and at the same time Mark the Infamy of a
Savage Pirate
His afflicted father Alexander Bartleman
has ordered this Stone to be erected over his Honourable Grave.
'Twas Great
his foe tho' strong was infamous
(the foe of the human kind)
A manly indignation fired his breast
Thank GOD my son has done his Duty.

Bodysnatchers

❋ Before the Anatomy Act of 1832 was passed, it was very difficult for English surgeons to teach students as so few bodies were available for dissection. The only legal source of corpses were the bodies of hanged criminals – and so a new industry grew up. Bodysnatchers, also known as the 'resurrection men', would dig up recently buried corpses to sell to anatomy students, and the **Brooke**-born surgeon Astley Cooper (see page 124) ran a cartel of bodysnatchers to try to keep the price down. Even the

Norwich doctor John Greene Cross admitted later that he'd been involved with the resurrection men. As it was regarded a misdemeanour rather than a felony, a conviction for bodysnatching carried a sentence of a fine or a few months in prison, rather than execution or transportation.

✳ There was a notorious case in **Norwich** in 1823. Many parcels of the same size were sent to London from the Rampant Horse Inn. The coach office became suspicious and told the inn that the next time a porter brought one of the parcels in, they should detain the porter and examine the parcel. On 15 February 1823 they stopped Ephraim Ulph and discovered a body. The vicar of **Lakenham** identified it as Mr Brundall, who had been buried a few days before. Ulph was made to talk and he admitted that he'd been paid by Joseph Collins. Collins and his accomplice Thomas Crowe were arrested and it was discovered that they owned skeleton keys that fitted various churches. At their trial they were found guilty of bodysnatching and sentenced to three months' imprisonment, as well as a fine of £50 (the equivalent of about £3,600 today).

✳ More cases of bodysnatching were reported in the *Norfolk Chronicle*, including that of Mr Wiseman from Hardingham in April 1824, an old man from Hethersett and another in Thorpe in February 1825.

✳ Public hysteria grew and in December 1826 George Carter, the vicar of Lakenham, had to put an advert in the *Norfolk Chronicle* saying that, contrary to reports, the body of William Tounshend, buried the previous month, had not been disinterred by resurrection men. He opened the grave in the presence of distressed relatives and 'it was discovered that the body reposed in its peaceful abode undisturbed.'

✳ The most famous case in **Great Yarmouth** was that of Thomas Vaughan (alias Smith). In 1827 he rented a room in Row Six (later called 'Snatchbody Row'), dug up bodies and sent them over to London. In December 1827 baker George Beck was horrified to find his wife's grave disturbed in the churchyard at St Nicholas. He went to the authorities and consequently 20 more graves were found with their bodies removed. Robert Barber, one of Vaughan's accomplices, turned King's evidence at the trial in Norwich in August 1828 and told how the graves were robbed, the bodies put in boxes and shipped to London 'by the wain'… to none other than Astley Cooper. Vaughan claimed that he was driven to his deeds by poverty, and was sentenced to six months in the House of Correction in **Norwich**. Cooper's account book for May 1828 shows that he paid Vaughan £13 (10 shillings a week) during his prison sentence and also paid money to Vaughan's wife. Later, when Vaughan was caught in the possession of clothes taken from a dead body in Plymouth, he was transported to Australia.

✳ More cases came to light: in January 1828, a resurrection man was shot in **Bacton** churchyard as he was disinterring the body of James Howlett, who had been killed in an accident. He was badly wounded but managed to escape in the darkness. In February 1829 there was much panicking in **King's Lynn**; one family put 13 iron hoops round the coffin and 50 screws in the lid to make sure the body stayed put. In September 1829, Ann Coe, who had been buried in **Fincham** churchyard, was disinterred and her body stolen.

✳ Thankfully, in Norfolk there were no reported cases like the Burke and Hare scandal of 1827 and 1828 in Edinburgh, where 16 people were murdered in order to supply corpses to hospitals. Their methods were copied by the London 'burkers' until they were caught. The Anatomy Act was passed in 1832, which allowed unclaimed or donated bodies to be used for dissection and licensed anatomy teachers so there was no longer a need for a trade in bodysnatching.

✳ There was, however, a very odd case in **Norwich** in 1833, when blacksmith James Maxey died. His boss, veterinary surgeon George Perowne, said that he would pay for the funeral and sent a coffin to the house. He removed the coffin – with the body in it – while Mrs Maxey was out. She demanded it back, but he promised that the funeral would take place from his premises. When she turned up the following day she noticed that the coffin had been nailed down. She insisted on seeing the body, upon which Perowne threatened to shoot her! She left the premises, and on her return the coffin lid was open and the body was there… except it looked as if it had been used for dissection. She called the magistrates, who put Perowne (who was drunk) in the cells for the night. When he'd sobered up he claimed that he'd done a deal with Maxey 16 years before and bought the body. The magistrates said that nobody owned dead bodies, and he wasn't licensed for anatomical studies – he was a vet, not a doctor. Perowne was brought to trial, but discharged on the same day.

Wife-sellers

✳ February 1805 saw a strange case in **Norwich**: a woman who had eloped with a horse dealer was found by her husband in a house in St Peter Mancroft. She refused to return to her husband and the horse dealer offered to buy her for £5 (worth around £300 today – very insulting!). In an act very similar to that of Hardy's Mayor of Casterbridge, the husband put a halter round his wife's neck and sold her to the horse dealer.

✳ A similar tale is told of John Green, who was a shoe-blacker in **King's Lynn**. He had spent all his money betting on horses and cockfights and so to get out of monetary difficulties, he decided to sell his wife. When nobody would bid cash, he sold her for a gallon of beer. Contemporary newspaper reports say that Mrs Green stayed with her 'purchaser' until she died.

✳ Finally, in May 1842 Samuel Wilkinson asked the magistrates in **Norwich** for permission to sell his wife. They refused but he went ahead anyway, selling her for a guinea to Samuel Springle near the Prussia Gardens in **Lakenham**.

And a nasty taste…

✳ According to the *Norfolk Chronicle*, in January 1868 Orlando Barnes of **Beeston** sent 100 coombs of wheat to New Mills to be dressed for the preparation of human food. So far, so ordinary. However, the miller discovered that it was 'a mass of filth, 1/10 wheat and 9/10 rats' dung and maggots.' The magistrates ordered the wheat to be destroyed and it was publicly burned on the 22 to the 23 January in the cattle market. On 7 February Barnes was summoned to Norwich Police Court and fined 40 shillings and costs. The paper reported that several thousand people had visited the farm to protest at Barnes's behaviour, so the police were forced to send 30 police officers and eight mounted inspectors to prevent trespass on the farm – and presumably to protect the rogue!

Chapter 11

Particular to Norfolk

Norfolk is renowned for many things, including its people, its peace and its beautiful skies. Here are just a few of them:

Food and drink

✳ **Norfolk Dumplings**

These have to be one of our most famous exports. Simply mix eight ounces (200g) of plain flour with a pinch of salt and a teaspoon of baking powder, then add enough water to make into a firm dough. Divide the dough into four pieces, roll each into a ball and either steam or place them on top of a stew for 20 minutes.

A Norfolk Dumpling is also a description of what you might call 'a plump li'l mawther.' There are also a couple of intriguing references in John Day's play *The Blind Beggar of Bethnal Green*, performed in 1600 but not published until 1659: 'As naked as your Norfolk dumpling' and 'Make me your cheat, your gull, your strowd, your Norfolk dumpling.' Clearly, in Tudor times it was the equivalent of calling someone a country bumpkin.

✳ **Norfolk Shortcake**

Norfolk Shortcake is a sweet, unleavened cake made with raisins. How it's actually made is a matter of opinion. One school of thought is that you put raisins and sugar between layers of shortcrust pastry and bake it; others treat it more like a biscuit, adding the raisins and sugar before rolling it out.

✳ **Norfolk Biffins**

A biffin (or Beefing) is a variety of apple which has a green skin streaked with maroon. The name 'beefing' apparently came about because of the way they were cooked, which made them look like a slab of beef. They were slow-baked between layers of straw on wire racks for about five hours, then taken out and carefully pressed flatter (without breaking the skin), baked for another hour and sprinkled with sugar when they were cold. The estate records at Mannington Hall from 1698 referred to biffins, which they sent up to London for Robert Walpole. Norwich bakers used to send biffins up to London for Christmas, and Charles

Dickens described them in *A Christmas Carol*: 'Biffins, squab and swarthy, setting off the yellow of oranges and lemons, and in the great compactness of their juicy persons, urgently entreating and beseeching to be carried home in paper bags and eaten after dinner.' The Victorian food writer Eliza Acton said in 1845 that they were the best variety to use when baking with wine and lemon. They've also been used in cider-making and for apple crisps. Biffins are no longer grown commercially in Norfolk, although trees are available from specialist nurseries.

✳ Fair Buttons

Fair Buttons were biscuits, traditionally sold at the Easter fair in **Norwich** and **Great Yarmouth**. Sift eight ounces (200g) of plain flour with a pinch of bicarbonate of soda, four ounces (100g) of soft brown sugar and ½ an ounce (15g) of ground ginger. Rub in four ounces (100g) of butter until the mixture looks like fine breadcrumbs, then mix in four ounces (100g) of golden syrup. Roll out thinly and cut into rounds. Place on a greased baking sheet and bake for 10-12 minutes at 180°C (gas mark 4).

✳ Yarmouth Bloaters

Bloaters are believed to have been invented in **Great Yarmouth** in about 1835, when a herring-curer named Bishop discovered that a batch of fresh herrings hadn't been processed. To avoid wasting them, he covered them in salt, spitted them and hung them up in the smokehouse. (Unlike kippers – also a form of smoked herring – bloaters are smoked with the fish's innards intact. Herring-curer John Woodger claimed to be the first to kipper herrings, in 1846). When Bishop returned the next morning he was delighted with the result and went on to experiment until he found the perfect cure.

At the height of the herring trade, on 23 October 1907, 60,000 lasts of herring were delivered to the Fishwharfs. Each last contained 13,200 fish, so that was more than 80 million fish in just one day! During that era more than 9,000 fishermen were employed on the boats each season, with around 8,000 women preparing the fish (the Scots fisher girls could gut and pack the herring at the rate of one a second) and 2,000 more working in the smokehouses.

Yarmouth also produced red herrings, known as 'militiamen' because their deep red colour was the same as a military jacket. These had a strong cure and were brined, dried and smoked for up to six weeks. However, it fell out of favour as the milder bloater took over the public taste.

✳ Samphire

Samphire (*Salicornia europea*) is known as 'poor man's asparagus'. It's usually boiled (for about 10 minutes) or steamed, and you simply add a little melted butter and suck the leaves from the stalks; it can also be blanched for use in a salad. Although it grows in other places on the British coastline, the best samphire comes from North Norfolk. It used to be pickled and taken on long sea voyages to prevent scurvy, and, interestingly, it was also used to cure flatulence!

✳ Cromer Crabs

The crabs from **Cromer** are known for their high proportion of white meat to dark, and their flesh is slightly sweeter than crabs caught in other areas – possibly due to the chalk shelf off Cromer, which may affect their diet and stop them being tainted with mud. There were once around 50 crab-fishing boats, but nowadays there are only about a dozen looking after 200 crab pots, so Cromer crabs are a real speciality.

✳ Norfolk 'venison'

According to the *Spectator* of August 1898, swan was known as Norfolk venison because it was so abundant. There's a swan pit behind the Great Hospital in **Norwich**, where swans were once fattened. An article in the *New York Times* of 1904 refers to 'swan upping' taking place and states that it was one of the few places in England where swans were still fattened for eating. The same article goes on to say that there used to be a city swanner, who would search the river during the nesting period, mark the cygnets and deliver them to the master of the Great Hospital, who would pay him two guineas.

There's a Swan Roll in the Norfolk Record Office, which contains a pictorial and written register of the ownership marks of swans of the Broadland area of Norfolk at the turn of the 15th century. The Swan Roll shows 99 illustrations in red and black ink, displaying the marks on the swans' beaks. Although swans are royal birds, the Crown granted private individuals the right to own swans under the Swan Act of 1482. The roll records owners included the Duke of Norfolk, the Mayor of **Norwich**, the Abbot of St Benet's near **Horning** and – surprisingly – the churches of **Acle**, **Billockby** and **Hickling**.

Clothing and shoes

✳ Worsted

Worsted is a cloth made from the long wool of sheep. The fibres are combed to lie parallel and the cloth is lightweight with a coarse texture. In the 14th century Yarmouth handled three quarters of all worsted exports. In 1465 John Paston wrote, 'I would make my doublet all worsted, for worship of Norfolk.' The name is taken from the village of **Worstead**, where much of the cloth was woven.

✳ 'Aylsham Web'

Until the 15th century, the linen and worsted industry was the main industry in **Aylsham**. 'Aylsham Web' or 'cloth of Aylsham' was supplied to the royal palaces of Edward II and III, and there's an entry in the Bishop of Hereford's house book from 1291 for four yards of Aylsham linen (costing 18 shillings – equivalent to £342 today). Aylsham linen was usually used for leggings. The industry declined after the 18th century.

✳ Norwich Burying Crape

In 1575 Dutch weavers in Norwich developed a material known as bombazine: it was made from a silk warp and a worsted weft. It was durable enough to wash well, but at the same time the silk gave it enough gloss for it to be suitable as mourning clothing when dyed black. It was also known as the 'Norwich Burying Crape' and was used by funeral directors.

✳ Norwich red

Norwich red was a brilliant red dye invented by Michael Stark, a dyer in Norwich (whose son James was one of the Norwich School of painters). His dye would turn both silk and worsted yarns exactly the same shade of red – the first time mixed yarns had been uniformly dyed – and manufacturers from Scotland and other parts of England would send their yarn or cloth to be dyed by him. An analysis of the dye showed that the colour came from madder with a tin mordant (which set the dye by forming an insoluble compound with it). Even 200 years later, materials dyed with Norwich red are still brilliantly coloured.

✳ The Norwich Shawl

In about 1780, alderman and manufacturer John Harvey introduced shawl-making to **Norwich**. Kashmir shawls had become fashionable and textile centres in Britain attempted to produce shawls which were as soft, colourful and good quality as the Kashmir ones. Norwich produced some of the finest. In the early stages the design was embroidered upon because it was cheaper and much quicker than weaving. However, Norwich gradually introduced woven borders, known as 'fillover', woven with the shawl face-down. The 'pine' motif was particularly popular (and is why Norwich shawls are sometimes described as 'paisley'), and by 1800 there were a dozen shawl manufacturers in the city. Gradually, the 'turnover' shawl was developed, where one triangle of the border was sewn in reverse so that when it was folded over it fitted into the triangle of the other border and matched exactly.

Norwich shawls did well in the Great Exhibition of 1851, and Queen Victoria is known to have bought shawls from the Norwich manufacturer

Clabburn Sons and Crisp. However, the shawl fell out of fashion when the bustle became fashionable in the 1870s – shawls didn't drape properly over a bustle – and the industry declined.

✳ Norwich Shoes

Shoemaking was also important in **Norwich** and in 1860 it became the city's major industry. A particular speciality was the turn shoe, which was a light shoe constructed inside out and then turned, leaving the seams on the inside and the finished (possibly decorated) surface of the leather on the outside.

James Smith was the first person to make and sell ready-made shoes, and opened a shop in the Upper Market Place in 1792 to sell them. His company also became the first shoemakers to use Singer sewing machines to make shoes, in 1840 (producing an incredible 3,000 stitches per minute).

Sadly, the industry declined after World War Two, partly due to the loss of factories and markets and partly due to competition from cheap imports.

✳ Sheringham Ganseys

There is a tradition in many maritime areas of special sweaters for fishermen, and in Norfolk we have the **Sheringham** gansey. The sweater was tight-fitting to protect against the cold and damp and was knitted 'on the round', like a sock, on five size 16 or 17 needles, using three-ply oiled worstead wool. Fishermen tended to have one for work and one for 'Sunday best', and several dozen patterns are known from Sheringham, including the zig-zag, ladder, 'flag and rig', herringbone and 'coil o' rope'. Patterns weren't written down; it was all done by eye and experience.

There are also traditions of ganseys at **Caister** and **Winterton** – rivalling Sheringham!

Animals and birds

Various breeds of animals and birds are associated with Norfolk, including:

✳ Red Poll Cattle

In the 19th century farmers wanted a cow that would make good dairy produce and also fatten well, without being oversized. The Suffolk Polled cow was noted for the quality of its butter, while the blood-red Norfolk cow was described in 1787 as 'fattening as freely and finishing as highly at three years old as cattle in general do at four or five'; therefore the obvious solution was to cross a Norfolk cow and a Suffolk bull. The result was exactly as farmers had hoped. By 1863 the cattle became known as Norfolk and Suffolk Red Polled, and in 1888 the Red Poll Cattle Society was formed.

❋ Norfolk Horn Sheep

The Norfolk Horn is a success story. It's been recognised for almost 400 years (it was mentioned in Robert Reyce's *The Beauties of England* in 1610) but almost died out in the early 20th century. It's a black-faced healthland breed which evolved in Breckland. However, in the middle of the 19th century, when farmers were looking for 'improved' breeds, it was replaced. By 1919 there was only one remaining flock, conserved by Mr J. Sayer, and in 1950 there were only 10 registered ewes and two rams. They were transferred to the National Agricultural Centre at Stoneleigh in Warwickshire and a breeding programme resulted in the breed's revival.

❋ Norfolk Trotter

The Norfolk Trotter (also known as the Norfolk Roadster or the Norfolk Cob) was a large horse used in a carriage harness. The breed originated in the mid-18th century, and, although the horse was purely a road horse, its speed meant that it was used for road racing. The races usually involved trotting over a certain distance in a specified time. The breed is now extinct, although Hackney horses are descended from Trotters, from the time when they were crossed with thoroughbreds in the mid-19th century. A Norfolk Trotter was imported to America in 1822 and was a major influence in the founding of the Standardbred breed.

❋ Norwich Canary

The **Norwich** Canary was introduced to the country by Flemish refugees and took the name of the city where the refugees settled. It was one of the earliest types developed in the country and became the leading exhibition variety before 1850. The Norwich Canary is also known as the 'John Bull' because it's a thickset bird, about 6.5 inches long, with a thick neck and a large head. Despite the fact that the bird on Norwich City Football Club's badge is yellow, if the Norwich canary is 'colour fed' its feathers will become deep orange. Back in the 1880s breeders added small quantities of cayenne pepper to the bird's food to produce the colour, but nowadays a commercial colouring is used.

❋ Norfolk Turkeys

Turkeys have had an extremely long association with Norfolk; the birds were first introduced into the county in 1542. There was a turkey market at **Attleborough** in the 1930s, where thousands were sold every Thursday, and which is commemorated on the town sign. Before turkeys were taken to London by car and train, drovers used to tar the turkeys' feet and wrap them in hessian to protect them while they were being herded to London.

Nowadays, Norfolk Black Turkeys are a rare breed. They almost died out after being cross-bred to improve them (as they have smaller breasts and are slower to grow than bronze turkeys), but when Ernest Peele moved from Lincolnshire to **Wymondham** in the 1880s he began raising black turkeys. His son Frank set up a breeding programme at **Thuxton** in the 1930s to make the flock sustainable.

Whifflers and Old Snap

✳ A whiffler was one of six city officials who would clear the way during the mayor's procession in Norwich. Originally they were pipers, but over the years they stopped using pipes and instead carried blunt swords with short blades and long handles. Their costume in the ceremony included a white cotton doublet with blue ribbons and gilt buttons, crimson or blue satin breeches, white stockings gartered with crimson ribbons, shoes with white rosettes and a crimson hat edged with white ribbons, a large blue bow and white feathers. There were also two Dick Fools, who wore painted canvas coats, with fox or cats' tails and small bells sewn on their red and yellow cloth caps. They were usually accompanied by Snap the Dragon – that is, a person wearing a 'hobby horse' costume in the shape of a dragon. The Norwich Snap is probably the most famous British pageant dragon.

The earliest reference to Snap in Norwich is in the guild assembly minutes in 1408, when the members agreed 'and the George shall go in procession and make conflict with the Dragon.' The guild procession took a particular

Snap the Dragon.

route in the city which included stopping at the cathedral and leaving the dragon on the 'dragon's stone' outside while they heard the service. In 1429 the dragon was able to breathe fire and smoke to amaze the crowds, thanks to a judicious use of gunpowder. After the Reformation, St George vanished from the procession but the dragon still made an appearance. From 1584 the St George's Day Festival was on the same day as mayor's day, and so the dragon remained part of the procession. Even after the Company of St George was abolished in 1731, the dragon remained until 1835, when the last Guild Day was abolished by the Municipal Corporations' Act. Snap made a few appearances until his retirement in 1850, minus the whifflers or Dick Fools. However, the Norwich Whiffler group revived the tradition of the whifflers for the Lord Mayor's Procession in 2008.

Eighteenth-century historian Benjamin Mackerell described the parade in his lifetime: on Guild Day, the outgoing city officials would meet at the new mayor's house for 'sugar rolls and wine' and then paraded back to the old mayor's house for a breakfast of 'pasties, roast beef, boiled legs of mutton and wine.' Then, accompanied by the whifflers, Dick Fools and the dragon, they went to the cathedral. Mackerell added, 'The Dragon, carried by a Man in the body of it, gave great diversion to the common People: they always seemed very much to fear it when it was near them, but always looked upon it with pleasure when it was a little distance from them.'

There were other dragons around the county; records show they were used in guilds at Wymondham and at Walsingham. The first Norwich Dragon Festival took place in January 2009.

Wherries

✳ Wherries were flat-bottomed boats with a square sail, specially designed to carry cargo and passengers on the Broads. In order that they could navigate swiftly under the bridges, the mast on a wherry was hinged at the bottom and counterbalanced with a 1½ ton lead weight. When the wind was coming from the wrong direction, though, the boat had to be 'quanted' – this meant digging a sturdy 24ft-long 'quant' or pole into the river bed at the bow, then walking the full length of the vessel pushing against the pole to punt it along the broad.

The trading wherries had black hulls, with a white nose to help visibility after dark, and black sails, protected with fish oil and tar. They could carry up to 25 tons of goods. Most of the trading wherries were clinker-built (with overlapping planks), but the *Albion* was carvel-built (with the planks abutting each other, giving a smooth hull). The last trading wherry, *Ella*, was built in 1912. Special wheelbarrows were made for unloading cargo. These were made from wood, strengthened with iron bands, and instead of having legs they rested on planks on the side of the wherry.

As tourism developed in the Broads, pleasure wherries were built. The cargo hold was replaced with living quarters and had a white sail. *Hathor*, built for the Colman family, had an Egyptian theme in its decoration (and the name, too, was Egyptian – pronounced Hart-or). It has been restored by the Wherry Yacht Charter Charitable Trust and sails the Broads today.

Wherry yachts were the next to be developed and were smaller than the other two types. They had white hulls, were carvel-built and were fitted with engines, as well as a white sail.

During World War Two wherries were sunk in the Broads in case enemy seaplanes tried to land there, and in the 1960s several more were sunk to protect the river bank. However, since then, seven wherries have been restored and can still be seen on the Broads.

Cosseyware

* Cosseyware was a type of moulded and decorative brickwork. It was made by George Gunton in his brickworks at **Costessey** in the mid-1800s. Originally it was developed to decorate Costessey Hall, but it was also used on buildings in **Norwich**, including on the first and second floor of Edward Boardman's former offices at No. 7 London Street (now part of Jarrolds) and a gothic fountain in the Plantation Garden on Earlham Road. The brickworks at Costessey closed after World War One, but William Gunton still produced some cosseyware in his works at **Barney, Little Plumstead** and **East Runton**. Cosseyware was last produced in 1939.

Jack Valentine

* Jack Valentine is a tradition that's definitely particular to Norfolk. In Victorian times Valentine's Day saw as many gifts as Christmas. Parents used to knock on the front door and run away, leaving small gifts on the step for the children of the house to find. The custom is mentioned in the diary of the Reverend Benjamin Armstrong, vicar of Dereham, in 1858. There were also special Valentine buns and lemon-flavoured Valentine biscuits.

Harry Carriers and Swills

* Great Yarmouth has two particular things found nowhere else. The first is the 'trolly cart', which was also known as the 'Harry Carrier' because it was invented in the time of Henry VIII. The cart was 12ft long and 3ft 6in wide, with wheels 2ft 9in high. It was drawn by a single horse and the driver stood on the cross-staves. The cars were specially designed to fit through the narrow Yarmouth Rows – the grid-shaped housing system on

which old Yarmouth was based. In the 18th century the Harry Carriers were used as pleasure vehicles in the bathing season for people who wanted to go to the Denes.

The second unique thing is connected to the first because it was used in the Harry Carrier: a swill. This was an oval-shaped basket, used only in Yarmouth in the herring trade. It measured 1/3 of a cran (a cran was a measure of 37½ gallons, or approximately 1,300 fish) and it was made to fit Harry Carriers, which were used to haul the fish from the beach through the Yarmouth Rows.

Norfolk brands

There are certain brand names that instantly say 'Norfolk'...

✳ Colman's Mustard
Jeremiah Colman said that he made most of his money from what people left on their plates. He was a truly philanthropic employer, and the company was involved in several pioneering events (see chapter 13). The company was awarded royal warrants from Queen Victoria and various European monarchs, and its products (including starch and laundry blue) won awards, including one of only two gold medals awarded at the 1872 Moscow Exhibition, and the French Cross of the Legion of Honour.

After Colman moved his family's mustard business from **Stoke Holy Cross** to Carrow, **Norwich**, in 1856, he brought in completely different operational procedures. Before then, mustard powder was delivered to grocers in wooden casks, which contained between nine pounds and a hundredweight of mustard. Colman introduced the idea of using small decorated containers and bright yellow labels so his product would be recognised on the shelves. The bull's head trademark was introduced in 1855 and was one of the first registered under the Trade Marks Act of 1875.

Although Colman's is now part of Unilever Bestfoods UK, the works at Carrow still produce Colman's mustard.

✳ Caley's Chocolate
Caley originally started making eating chocolates in 1886, and, despite having worldwide sales in the early 20th century, the firm stuck to their recipe using milk from local Red Poll cattle at **Whitlingham**. Caley's Marching Chocolate (known as 'Marcho') was given to the troops in World War One as part of their rations to help them 'fight fatigue' and give them strength. It gained the Royal Warrant in 1932 and was still part of army rations into the late 1930s. At the coronation of George VI one of the soldiers lining the procession gave a small boy the chocolate from his rations. The small boy never ate it – and when he read about the proposed

revival of the Caley's name in 1996 he sent the original bar to the company, explaining that he'd kept it all those years. Nestlé had bought the firm in 1988 and closed the factory in the city in 1996. However, three former executives had acquired the Caley's brand and reintroduced the chocolate, including Marching Chocolate, in 1998. Chocolates are still handmade in **Norwich,** by Angela Ruthven from Saffire Chocolates. She's an artisan chocolatier who was the valedictorian graduate of the Ecole Chocolat – she came top of the class in her course, with an incredible 97 per cent. Initially, she made chocolates for her family and friends in a converted log cabin in her garden. Now, her chocolate has gone as far afield as Brazil, India, Australia, Peru and Spain. They still contain a bit of Norfolk: one of her specialities is white chocolate with a Norfolk Lavender centre.

✳ Norfolk Lavender

The company was started in 1932 by Linn Chilvers, a botanist from **Heacham** who owned a nursery. He went into partnership with Francis Dusgate and they planted 13,000 lavender plants in six acres. Mr Avery, a chemist from Leicester, had the recipe for a perfume used by George IV, which the company then started to produce. Norfolk Lavender bought Caley Mill in 1936. It has the national collection of lavenders – more than 150 different varieties. The lavender used to be harvested by hand, but nowadays it's all done by machine. The lavender is dried and distilled at Heacham, and more than 60 different Norfolk Lavender products are sold in more than 25 countries.

✳ Lotus Cars

Lotus Engineering was set up by Colin Chapman in Hornsey in 1952 and moved to **Hethel** in 1966, which had a test track that incorporated part of the old runway from the RAF base. The company designed and made sports and racing cars. Stirling Moss won the 1960 Grand Prix at Monaco in a Lotus 18. Successful road cars include the Elite, the Elan, the Esprit (which was used as the Bond car in *The Spy Who Loved Me*; the Esprit Turbo followed suit in *For Your Eyes Only*) and the Elise. The Evora, lauched in 2008, is also doing well, boasting a clutch of awards.

✳ Bernard Matthews

It's the largest food company in East Anglia and was founded in 1950 with 20 turkey eggs and a second-hand incubator. Within three years Matthews was hatching more than 3,000 eggs and rearing turkeys in his back garden. The company moved to Great Witchingham in 1955, and by 1968 Matthews was in the Guinness Book of Records as Europe's largest turkey farmer. The company produces around seven million turkeys a year in the UK, and it's thought that one in four turkeys eaten in the UK on

Christmas Day are Matthews turkeys. The company introduced the catchphrase 'Bootiful' in 1980, and although the phrase hasn't been used for years, it's stayed in the public consciousness.

A bit of a mardle

Norfolk dialect could take up a whole book on its own, so the section below barely scratches the surface. (Mardle, incidentally, comes from the Old English *mapelian*, meaning 'to talk' – exactly what the dialect word means). Here are some of the more colourful words from our history:

✳ A bishy-barney-bee is a ladybird. The name may come from Bishop Bonner, who lived in **Dereham** and burned heretics in the name of Mary, Queen of Scots. The red colour of the ladybird is meant to be similar to the sparks from those fires. There's an old children's rhyme about ladybirds which uses the Norfolk dialect phrase:

> Bishy, Bishy Barnabee,
> Tell me when my wedding be;
> If it be to-morrow day,
> Open your wings and fly away.
> Fly to the East, fly to the west,
> And fly to him that I love the best.

✳ A dodman is a snail. Dickens used the term in *David Copperfield* when he had Mr Peggotty saying, 'I'm a reg'lar Dodman, I am,' and even explained it for his readers. Where did the word come from? One explanation is that the name may have come from a cloth seller called Dodman, who apparently carried a large roll of cloth on his back. Alfred Watkins, the discoverer of leylines, thought that it came from an old term for a surveyor, as a snail's horns reminded him of surveying rods. There's also an old rhyme about snails, quoted in the *Dictionary of Phrase and Fable*:

> Doddiman, doddiman, put out your horn,
> Here comes a thief to steal your corn.

✳ A dorhawk is a nightjar (*Caprimulgas europaeus*); the Norfolk version of the name came about because it fed on cockchafers (known in Norfolk as a dor beetle).

✳ If someone tells you 'dew you keep a troshin', it would've originally been an instruction to carry on with the threshing, but it also tells you to take care of yourself.

✳ Some critics have puzzled over Shakespeare's use of 'I am but mad north-northeast; when the wind is southerly I know a hawk from a handsaw' in *Hamlet*. Had they spoken to someone from Norfolk they would've learned that 'handsaw' is actually a 'harnser', meaning a heron. Therefore being able to tell the difference between a bird of prey and a wading bird means that Hamlet isn't mad.

✳ A dickey is a donkey, and it's said that you can tell a Norfolk person from the answer to the question: 'Ha' yer fa' got a dickey, bor?' (The correct answer being, 'Yis, an' he want a fule to roid it, will yew cum?') The Light Horseman pub in Westlegate, **Norwich** (currently Carsaccio's) was once known as the Barking Dickey because of the pub sign. It had been painted so badly that the horse looked like a cross between a dog and a donkey – hence the nickname.

Chapter 12
Norfolk and the Arts

Norfolk on film and TV

Norfolk has been used as the location for various films, including:

✳ *A Cock and Bull Story* (2005), an adaptation of Laurence Sterne's novel *Tristram Shandy*, starring Steve Coogan, Gillian Anderson and Rob Brydon, was filmed at **Felbrigg** Hall, **Blickling** and **Heydon**. During filming, for the first time in more than 100 years, Felbrigg's dining room was candlelit.

✳ *Atonement* (2007) has scenes filmed at **Denver** and **Walpole St Andrew**.

✳ The Ealing comedy *Barnacle Bill* (1957), starring Alec Guinness (in his last role for them), was filmed partly at **Hunstanton**.

✳ *The Dambusters* (1955), one of Britain's biggest box office successes, used the airfield at **Langham** as a location, as well as using **King's Lynn** and the Wash as the Dutch coast.

✳ *Die Another Day* (2002) – the scene in the paddy field was shot around **Burnham Deepdale**.

✳ *The Duchess* (2008), starring Keira Knightley as Georgiana, the Duchess of Devonshire, was filmed at **Holkham Hall**. A casting session for extras was held in **Fakenham** Methodist Church and proved so popular that the doors had to be closed after two hours.

✳ Stanley Kubrick's movie *Full Metal Jacket* (1987) was partly filmed around the Norfolk Broads.

✳ *The Go-Between* (1970), starring Julie Christie and Alan Bates, was filmed largely at **Melton Constable** Hall, but scenes were also filmed at **Heydon**, **Norwich** (particularly Tombland), **Thornage** and **Hickling Broad**. In the novel L.P. Hartley's 'Brandham Hall' is based on **West Bradenham** Hall, where he stayed with the Rider Haggard family as a boy.

✻ *The Grotesque* (1977), starring Sting and Alan Bates, was filmed at **Heydon** Hall.

✻ *Julia* (1977), based on Lillian Hellman's autobiography *Pentimento* and starring Jane Fonda and Vanessa Redgrave, used locations in **Winterton-on-Sea.**

✻ *The Mill on the Floss* (1997), starring Emily Watson and Bernard Hill, was shot partly at **Bintree** Mill.

✻ *Revolution* (1985), starring Al Pacino, turned **King's Lynn** into 18th-century New York; the Saturday Market Place became Wall Street and the quayside became William Street.

✻ In *Out of Africa* (1985) the opening shots which showed Denmark were actually filmed in **Castle Rising.**

✻ *Shakespeare in Love* (1998) used **Holkham** Beach for the film's closing shots.

✻ During filming for *Stardust* (2007) the Briton's Arms in Elm Hill, **Norwich,** became 'The Slaughtered Prince'.

✻ Scenes for *Tarka the Otter* (1979) were shot on location at **Bintree** Mill. Henry Williamson, the author, lived at Stiffkey for a while during the World War Two.

✻ *The Wicked Lady* (1945), starring Margaret Lockwood and James Mason, was filmed at **Blickling** Hall.

Many TV dramas have also been filmed in Norfolk, including:

✻ *'Allo 'Allo* – scenes were filmed at **Lynford** Hall and also at the railway bridge at **Briston.**

✻ *All the King's Men* (1999), a drama about the Sandringham Company which went missing at Gallipoli in 1915 and starring David Jason and Maggie Smith, was filmed at **Sheringham, Cromer, Blickling, Burnham Deepdale** and **Holkham** Hall.

✻ *Backs to the Land* (1977–78), a drama about land girls in World War Two, was filmed at **Heydon.**

✻ *Dad's Army* (1968–77) was filmed at **Thetford;** the guildhall was once Walmington-on-Sea's town hall. **Weyborne** railway station was also one of the locations for the series.

✳ *David Copperfield* (2000), starring Bob Hoskins and Nicholas Lyndhurst (and a very young Daniel Radcliffe), was filmed at **King's Lynn**.

✳ *Great Expectations* (1999) uses the 'coalhouse' barn at **Thornham** as Pip's childhood home.

✳ When the soap opera *Eastenders* showed characters on holiday on the Broads, filming took place at **Horning**.

✳ *The Evacuees*, a BBC children's show from 1975, was filmed partly at the steam railway station at **Sheringham**.

✳ Stephen Fry's drama *Kingdom* has a number of locations in the county, including **Swaffham**, the lighthouse at **Happisburgh** and **Wells** quayside.

✳ BBC drama *The Lost Prince* (2003), the story of George V's son Prince Johnnie, was filmed at **Holkham** Hall (standing in for Buckingham Palace) and **Weybourne** railway station.

✳ *Love on a Branch Line* (1994, based on the 1959 novel by John Hadfield) was filmed at **Oxburgh** Hall and the North Norfolk Railway at **Weybourne**.

✳ The London street scenes in *Martin Chuzzlewit* (1994) were filmed at **King's Lynn**.

✳ The TV adaptation of Nina Bawden's *The Peppermint Pig* (1977) was filmed at **Heydon**. Heydon was also the setting for *The Moonstone*, *Vanity Fair*, Jilly Cooper's *Riders* (1993), the 1997 production of *The Woman in White* and the drama series *Up Rising* (2000).

✳ Episodes of *Tales of the Unexpected* (1979–88) were shot in various locations in Norfolk, including **Corpusty**, **Hunworth** and Lime Tree Farm in **Thurning**.

✳ *Weavers' Green* was Anglia TV's first 'soap', a serial produced in 1966 about life in a veterinary practice. The cast included Susan George, Kate O'Mara, Wendy Richards and Dennis Waterman. It was one of the first TV programmes to be shot on location using videotape and outside broadcasting equipment, rather than film. It was filmed at **Heydon**, with some scenes shot at **County School** railway station, near **North Elmham**.

✳ Many of P.D. James's serials have been filmed at locations in Norfolk, including **Reepham**, **Thurning** Hall, **Cley** Mill and **Stiffkey**.

Actors and comedians with a Norfolk link

✳ Writer and comedian Charlie Higson studied at the University of East Anglia, as did Paul Whitehouse, Eddie Izzard and Arthur Smith. Actors Jack Davenport, James Frain and Tim Bentinck also studied there, and the new Dr Who (the 11th Doctor), Matt Smith, studied drama and creative writing at the UEA.

✳ Actor Hugh Jackman's mother lives in Norfolk and because of this he's one of **Norwich** City Football Club's most famous fans (along with writer, actor and comedian Stephen Fry).

✳ Welsh actress Ruth Madoc was actually born in **Norwich**, while actor Rupert Everett was also born in the city. Sir John Mills was born in Norfolk and went to Norwich School for Boys; it's said that his initials can still be seen carved into the brickwork.

✳ Actress Sienna Guillory, star of *Inkheart*, moved to Norfolk when she was 11 and won her first major role (in *Riders*) while she was studying for her A levels at Gresham's school in **Holt**.

✳ Terry Molloy, who lives in **Bawburgh**, terrified children as the evil scientist Davros, creator of the Daleks, in *Dr Who*. He has also played Mike Tucker from the BBC Radio Four serial *The Archers* for more than 30 years.

✳ Actor Chris Rankin, who plays Percy Weasley in the *Harry Potter* films, grew up in **Dereham**, and actor Matthew Macfadyen, star of *Spooks* and *Pride and Prejudice*, was born in **Great Yarmouth**.

Norfolk music

✳ Many bands have played at the **West Runton** Pavilion over the years, including T.Rex (it was Marc Bolan's penultimate live performance before his death), the Sex Pistols (who played there twice), Duran Duran, Chuck Berry, Dire Straits, the Jam, Def Leppard, Black Sabbath and AC/DC.

✳ The Beatles played at the Grosvenor Rooms on Prince of Wales Road, **Norwich**, in 1963. After the gig they went round the corner to Valori's for fish and chips.

✳ The Orford Cellar in **Norwich** has seen many famous faces over the years, including Jimi Hendrix, Rod Stewart, Eric Clapton and David Bowie.

✳ The Wilde Club introduced several bands to the **Norwich** Arts Centre, including Nirvana and Coldplay (both as support bands!), Oasis, Snow Patrol and Muse.

✳ Songwriter Cathy Dennis (whose 'Can't Get You out of my Head' kept Kylie Minogue at the top of the charts for four weeks in 2001 and has sold over 10 million copies worldwide) was born in **Norwich**.

✳ Neil Innes (famous for his comedy songs in the Rutles and the Bonzo Dog Doo-Dah Band) attended **Thorpe** Grammar School and **Norwich** School of Art.

✳ Classical pianist and former member of Hear'Say Myleene Klass was born in **Gorleston**, as was Hannah Spearritt, former S Club 7 singer.

✳ Singer-songwriter Beth Orton was born in **Dereham** and grew up in **Norwich**.

✳ Roger Taylor, drummer and vocalist with Queen, was born in **Dersingham** and grew up in **King's Lynn**.

✳ One of Norfolk's most famous musical exports is the Singing Postman, Allan Smethurst (1927–2000). Although he was born in Lancashire, his mother came from **Stiffkey** and he grew up in **Sheringham**. He experimented with singing in the Norfolk dialect and was the only 20th-century performer of dialect songs to gain a national audience after his demo tape was taken up by BBC presenter Ralph Tuck. His single *Hev Yew Gotta Loight, Boy?* won the Ivor Novello Award for best comedy song in 1966 and, within East Anglia, outsold the Beatles and the Rolling Stones. Sadly, a combination of stage fright and alcohol dependency ended his career only a couple of years after it had started.

Norfolk and the fine arts

✳ Norfolk has a strong tradition in the fine arts. The first British art movement based outside London was the **Norwich** School of Artists in the early 19th century, which included John Crome, John Sell Cotman and Joseph Stannard.

✳ The Pre-Raphaelite painter Frederick Sandys was born in **Norwich**, as was Post-Impressionist artist Edward Seago (who also created the solid silver mascot of St George slaying the dragon, which is used on any limousine in which the Queen is travelling, in place of the manufacturer's mascot) and pop artist Colin Self.

❉ Many well-known artists have studied at the **Norwich** University College of the Arts (formerly the Norwich School of Art and Design), including artist (and President of the Royal Academy) Alfred Munnings, landscape artist Horace Tuck, sculptor Bernard Meadows, animator Keith Chapman (creator of Bob the Builder and Fifi and the Flowertots) and games designer Jamie Durrant.

❉ Silver was assayed at **Norwich** during three periods between 1565 and 1702 on a site now occupied by Jarrolds. Norwich was only the second provincial town after York where goldsmiths were allowed to use a town mark. The most important collection of Norwich silver is at the Castle Museum in the city, and contains 100 pieces of Norwich silver.

Chapter 13

Pioneers and record-breakers

Writing in 1607, William Camden said of Norfolk: 'the inhabitants are of a passing good complexion, to say nothing of their exceeding wily wits, and the same right quicke in the insight of our common lawes, in so much as it is counted, was well now as in times past, the onely country for best breed of Lawyers.'

Those 'wily wits' have led to an awful lot of pioneering over the years. Norfolk can justifiably lay claim to many firsts, including:

The King's Lynn Mart

✶ Henry VIII granted **King's Lynn** the right to hold the Mart in 1537. The fair begins on Valentine's Day in the Tuesday Market Place and goes on for two weeks. Traditionally, it's the first funfair in the Showmen's Calendar and new rides are tried out. Frederick Savage, who lived in King's Lynn, worked in partnership with the Showmen's Guild to develop new rides. He pioneered fairground barrel organs driven by steam and developed steam-powered roundabouts, swings and joy wheels (some of which can still be seen in the fairground at **Thursford**). In 1897, Randall Williams was the first showman to show moving pictures to the public at the fair.

Boulton and Paul's aircraft

✶ Boulton and Paul of **Norwich** made the first metal-framed aircraft in 1915. The prototype, the FE2B, flew from the airfield at Cavalry Drill Ground on Mousehold Heath and reached a top speed of 60mph. At the peak of production in World War One they made 28 Sopwith Camel fighter aircrafts per week. They made an all-steel P10 biplane which was exhibited at the 1919 Paris Air Show, and also developed the first plane in the world to use plastic components. The most famous plane they produced was the Boulton Paul Defiant, which was a night fighter. They also produced a R101 airship. In 1930 one of their ships embarked on a long-distance flight to India. Sadly, it crashed into a French hillside, killing the air minister and vice marshall, along with two passengers. Although Boulton and Paul were cleared of any blame in an inquiry, the British airship programme was halted after that.

The Pulham Pigs

✳ Pulham St Mary was involved in the first double air crossing from England to America and back again in 1919. The first coastal airships started patrolling from Pulham in August 1916. These airships were called 'Pulham Pigs' because of the colour of their yellowish-buff envelope (and, allegedly, one farmer said that the airships looked like pigs in the sky). The name stuck, even after the envelopes were painted silver. Pulham became a staging post on the route for airships between Kent and the north of England, and the R34 rigid airship was based there from 1918.

When a ship was expected lorries would drive round the Pulhams, sounding their horns. Up to 400 people were needed to catch the holding ropes and then walk the ship to the hangar. They were paid five shillings each for the job, but it was dangerous as the ship could rise up while people were still hanging on to it.

On 2 July 1919, the R34 set off from East Fortune in Scotland at 1.42a.m. on its historic voyage to America. William Ballantyne was so disappointed at not making the crew list for the voyage that he stowed away; he hid on a girder between the gas bags and was discovered well into the voyage. Although he was reprimanded, he later became an airship pilot. On 5 July the ship crossed the Newfoundland Coast. There were electrical storms on the approach to New York, but they finally landed at 9.45 after a journey of 108 hours and nine minutes. On the homeward voyage the ship was crossing Ireland when it was ordered to go to Pulham; high winds in Scotland meant that it would be too dangerous to go back to East Fortune and the crew could moor the ship safely on the mast at Pulham. It finally landed at Pulham on 13 July 1919, and the entire trip (excluding a stopover) from Britain to America and back again took seven days, 15 hours and 15 minutes. In 1979, on the 60th anniversary of the flight, Concorde made the same return trip in only six hours and 59 minutes.

Postal codes

✳ After World War Two the volume of mail greatly increased and so the Royal Mail decided to introduce a postal code system. The first test of the system was at **Norwich** in 1959. The code had six characters, with the first three characters (NOR) designating the city and the last three characters identifying the street. The city had eight new sorting machines and operators keyed in the postcode to sort the letters for delivery. As the trial progressed, the Post Office realised that they needed more codes to help specify the addresses within the street, so the postcode system was modified and the first half of the Norwich district was reconfigured as NR (plus 1–2 digits) as part of the national system in 1974.

Medical pioneers

❋ The Norfolk and **Norwich** Hospital developed gallstone surgery, and was one of the first hospitals to use antiseptic and anaesthetic.

Surgeon Ken McKee pioneered total hip replacement surgery in 1951 (known as McKee-Farrar hip replacements and used throughout the 1950s and 1960s). He began working on the models in 1938 and got local firms and dentists to help him make brass mock-ups. Working with John Watson Farrar, he developed a joint made from chromium cobalt and molybdenum, which cemented into the existing bone structure with plastic and was much more durable than its stainless steel predecessor. Until his retirement in 1971, he replaced more than a thousand hips, and he also pioneered knee replacements in 1963. However, he was incredibly modest about his achievements, saying, 'It doesn't matter so much who started the concept of total hip replacement or whose name is attached to it. Remember, one of the objects of our journey is to help others to be less crippled and to suffer less.' He was made a CBE in 1972, and one of the halls of residence for junior doctors at the Norfolk and Norwich Hospital is named after him.

The first pneumothorax operation was carried out at the tuberculosis hospital in **Mundesley** in 1910.

Pioneers in science and industry

❋ William Bateson, the first director of the John Innes Institute in **Norwich**, was a leading light in the early days of genetics and was the first person to use the term in 1905.

❋ The John Innes Centre in **Norwich** was the first to clone the gene Rht, which increases the yield of wheat, and to identify how it works so wheat breeders across the world could use it.

❋ Terry Galliard at the Institute of Food Research in **Norwich** discovered colnucleic acid (produced by potatoes when attacked by fungal diseases) in 1972. The name comes from **Colney** Lane, where the institute is based.

❋ The first sugar beet factory in Britain was built at **Cantley** in 1912 by the Dutch. It closed in 1916 and reopened under British Sugar in 1921. It could process 800 tons of beet a day; nowadays the average daily throughput is 9,000 tons. The factory provides its own electricity.

❋ The first refinery to produce bioethanol ('green' fuel) from sugar beet was opened at **Wissington** in 2007. The £10 million plant was built next to the world's largest beet sugar factory and produces about 70 million litres of bioethanol a year. The sugar factory's plant provides energy for the bioethanol plant; and 70 million tomatoes are grown each year in the UK's largest glasshouse (a staggering 11 hectares) using waste heat from the power plant.

✳ Burrell's of **Thetford** were the first to introduce a practical heavy-duty traction engine for use on roads. They started with a steam engine in 1846, which was towed to its worksite by a horse, and by 1856 they had produced the Burrell-Boydell heavy traction engine, fitted with an 'endless railway' system of boards. The system meant that the wheels had a smooth surface to run on, and it also spread the load, which helped to stop the engine getting stuck in soft ground.

✳ Charles Barnard (from the **Norwich** firm Barnard, Bishop and Barnard) built the first wire-netting machine in 1844, based on a weaving loom. It operated manually, with a man doing the weaving and a boy turning it. He also exhibited galvanised wire netting at the Great Exhibition in Crystal Palace in 1851 and patented a self-rolling mangle. The firm produced an iron lighthouse in 1860 for the Brazilian government. The 46ft-high building was made in sections and had 144 iron plates. The company's wrought and cast iron pagoda won a medal at the Philadelphia Exhibition in 1872, and they also made the station platform canopy for Thorpe station in Norwich.

Literary firsts

✳ The first provincial newspaper (the *Norwich Post*) was published by Francis Burges near the top of Redwell Street in **Norwich** in 1701 – a year before the first London newspapers were produced.

✳ The first recorded monastic library was at **Norwich** Cathedral. The first provincial public library under municipal control was set up in 1608 over the south porch of St Andrew's Hall, Norwich. Norwich was also the first city to adopt the Public Libraries Act in 1850, which allowed any municipal borough of 100,000 people to introduce a halfpenny rate to establish public libraries. The foundation stone was laid in 1854 and the library was opened in 1857.

✳ The first book written in English by a woman was in Norfolk: Mother Julian's *Revelations of Divine Love*, written in 1395. The first biography of a woman written in English is also by a Norfolk woman, Margery Kempe (see page 129).

✳ One of the earliest dictionaries for schools – called the *Promptorium Parvulorum* – was compiled in 1440 by Geoffrey, a monk who lived at the Dominican friary in **King's Lynn**. According to mediaeval historian Nicholas

Orme, this was the first significant dictionary of English to Latin words, the first English dictionary that had a large number of English words in alphabetical order and the first dictionary that took an interest in children.

✳ The first recorded Valentine letter in English was written by Margery Brews, from Topcroft, near Bungay, to John Paston III of **Norwich** in 1477, calling him her 'right worshipful and well beloved Valentine.'

Norwich firsts

✳ The first industrial nurse in the country, Philippa Flowerday, was employed by Colman's in 1878. Thirty-two-year-old Philippa's duties involved helping the doctor each morning in the dispensary and then making 45 home visits per week in the afternoons to sick employees, taking them meals from the works' kitchen.

✳ The first long-distance telephone call was made in Norwich on 1 November 1878, from Colman's accounting house in Carrow to Cannon Street in London.

✳ Colman was also one of the first to introduce the idea of paid holidays for staff. He instituted an annual tea party on Whit Tuesday, but in 1877 there were too many employees to sit down, so he gave them a day's paid holiday instead. The office staff had a day off in September after the annual mustard delivery.

✳ The Rosary, which was the first non-denominational cemetery in the country, was founded in Norwich in 1821 by Thomas Drummond.

✳ The first full-time amateur dramatics company in the country was the Guild of Norwich Players, formed by Walter Nugent Monck in 1911. They performed in Monck's house and later at the Music House in King Street. Monck then bought a grocery warehouse that had been converted from a Roman Catholic chapel and remodelled it as the Maddermarket. The theatre opened in 1921 and was the first permanent recreation of an Elizabethan theatre. It was also the only theatre in the UK to have staged all of Shakespeare's plays as he had intended them to be performed, according to Mike Loveday, the CEO of Norwich HEART.

✳ The earliest known reference to a barber in England is to John Belton, a Norwich barber, who was recorded as resident in the city in 1163.

✳ The first council estate built outside London was the Mile Cross Estate in Norwich, which started out in 1918 with 200 houses.

✻ The annual Norfolk & Norwich Festival is the oldest city-based arts festival in Britain.

✻ According to historian Susanna Wade Martins, Norwich was the first city to adopt a system of poor relief that included financial help for poor families and education for poor children, all in place by 1570.

✻ Eighteenth-century historian Francis Blomefield has said that Anne of Bohemia introduced side saddle to East Anglia during her royal visit to Norwich in 1383: 'The English ladies, after the example of Queen Anne, daughter to the King of Bohemia, and wife to King Richard, began to ride on side saddle; this Queen first brought this fashion into the land, for before, women used to ride like men.'

The first anti-aircraft rocket

✻ The first public demonstration of an anti-aircraft rocket had the code name 'UP', standing for 'Unrotated Projectile', and it took place in 1940 at **Weybourne** in the presence of Winston Churchill. Unfortunately, it didn't go quite to plan as none of the experimental shells hit the the radio-controlled aircraft (a converted Tiger Moth biplane known as the Queen Bee). The team had to fire the anti-aircraft artillery, which finally destroyed the aircraft (though its engine landed on the beach and exploded a mine).

The first lottery

✻ **Great Yarmouth** Town Council entered the first lottery in England in 1567, to raise money to strengthen the harbour. It was described as 'a very rich lottery, generally without blankes, containing a great number of good prizes as well as ready money as of plate and certain sortes of merchandizes. The number of lottes to be 400,000 and no more; and every lot to be the sum of 10 shillings sterling and no more.' However, as no mention of prizes was made, it's likely that the councillors were unsuccessful in their bid to win.

Boats

✻ In 1850, the Duke of Northumberland offered a prize of 100 guineas (equivalent to £8,650 today) for the best lifeboat design. There were 280 entrants and a committee assessed each one – including testing models in the Thames. James Beeching from **Great Yarmouth** won the competition; his lifeboat was designed to be self-righting if it turned over. After the lifeboat was built, it was modified to include the best features from other entries and the design for the new boat was used by the RNLI for the next 50 years.

✳ The *Ra*, Britain's first passenger-carrying solar-powered boat, had its first voyage on Barton Broad in September 2000. It has 12 seats (including room for a wheelchair) and is powered by three rows of seven solar panels. There are other electric boats on the Broads, including an Edwardian-style boat at **How Hill** and an electric ferry (*Helen of Ranworth*) on **Malthouse** Broad.

The first bowler hat

✳ William Coke of **Holkham** Hall was the first man in England to wear a bowler hat. He asked James Lock & Co of London to design a hat that would be tough enough to protect a horserider's head from branches, and gamekeepers from poachers. Lock's usually named their hat designs after the customer who commissioned them; however, because the hat was manufactured by Bowler Bros, it became known as the Bowler.

Food for thought

✳ Although the Dunmow flitch originates from the village of Great Dunmow in Essex, the first person to win it was a Norfolk couple – yeoman Richard Wright and his wife from **Bawburgh**. The trials for the flitch (a side of bacon) take place every four years and the flitch is awarded to a married couple from anywhere in the world, provided they satisfy the judge and jury (made up of 'six maidens and six bachelors') that in 'twelvemonth and a day' they have 'not wisht themselves unmarried again.' The trials are mentioned in Langland's *Piers Plowman* in 1362 and Chaucer's *Wife of Bath's Tale*. In the cartulary of Dunmow Priory an entry in 1445 records that: 'One Richard Wright of Bawburgh next Norwich, in the County of Norfolk, came here and pleaded for the bacon of Dunmow on the 17th day of April... and was sworn according to the form of the gift aforesaid, &c before John Canon, then Prior of this place aforesaid.'

✳ The world's first fish finger was invented and produced by a frozen food company in **Great Yarmouth** in 1955 by inventor Clarence Birdseye. He patented frozen fish fingers in the UK in 1927, after having worked as a biologist in Canada and noticing that fish froze solid almost immediately if exposed to sub-zero temperatures. However, it took him years to find a freezing method that would work commercially. He asked the female workers in the factory to vote in a poll for the name – they rejected 'Battered Cod Bites' and voted for 'Fish Fingers'. When they were launched, few people had freezers, so the fish fingers had to be cooked immediately.

✳ 'Farmer's Glory' wheat flakes, one of the earliest breakfast cereals, was produced in Norfolk in 1933 by the Allen Brothers in Bluestone Farm,

Creake. (Bluestone Farm was also the first mechanised farm in the country). Weetabix was founded a year earlier, in 1932; Huntley & Palmer introduced Tribrek in 1934, and in the same year Brown and Polson developed Zesto cornflakes. The Allens sold the brand to Colman's in 1938, and sales figures from 1935 suggest that three million packs of Farmer's Glory were produced in that year.

Windmills

✱ William Cubitt, the son of a Norfolk miller, invented a new sail for windmills, called Cubitt's patent sails. It had adjustable shutters, so you could close them to catch the wind or open them to let the wind go through the sail. You could adjust all four sails at the same time without having to stop the mill. One of the first windmills to use the new sail was Cooke's windmill at **Stalham**, which burned down in 1903.

The first recorded steeplechase

✱ On 12 April 1884, a horse called Useful won the first recorded steeplechase over an improvised course at **East Winch**. Racing continued on the East Winch course until Easter Monday 1905, when it moved to **Fakenham**. Since 1905 racing at Fakenham has been uninterrupted (except for during the two world wars). The queen was the patron of the course for nearly 50 years, until Prince Charles took over on 1 January 2000.

The first turnpike in England

✱ When the Act of Parliament was passed to allow turnpike (toll) roads to be built in England, one of the first three roads authorised was between **Wymondham** and **Attleborough**. It was the first turnpike road to be built after the Great Northern Road and was constructed in 1695. Sir Edwin Rich donated £200 to repair and make the road in 1675, and a pillar commemorating his donation was set up at **Besthorpe**. It was known as the Dial Stone, as it used to have a sundial on the top. The wording on the pillar says:

This pillar was erected by order of the sessions of the
peace of Norfolk as a grateful remembrance of the charity
of
Sir Edwin Rich K
who freely gave ye sum of two hundred pounds towards
the repair of ye highway between Wymondham and
Attleborough
AD 1675

The traveller Celia Fiennes, who visited every English county between 1697 and 1698, recorded her journeys in *Through England on a Side Saddle in the Time of William and Mary*. She noted having to pay 'a penny a horse' at the 'barr' (the turnpike) to go towards 'mending the way'.

The pillar was restored in 1985 and reset after the Attleborough bypass was built. It's now in a little layby just off the roundabout at Besthorpe which leads to the A11.

Record-breakers

✳ In 2007, Suzannah Sorrell from **Welbourne** and a team of eight British Siberian Huskies set a world record, crossing a 100-metre course on Holkham beach in 10.65 seconds.

✳ 2008 saw a new British angling record on the River Wensum, when Chris Mack from **Elsing** landed a 21lb 2oz barbel.

✳ The same year also saw a new world record for the biggest marrow. Grown by Ken Dade from **Terrington St Clement** and weighing in at 65 kilos, the marrow needed two people to carry it to the stand at the National Amateur Gardening Show in Somerset.

✳ In 2007, Lotus enthusiasts set a new Guinness World Record at Brands Hatch for the highest number of cars in a parade. The cars included the Gold Leaf F1 Type 49B; the Lotus Sunbeam works rally car; the extreme Lotus 2-Eleven; and concept GT3. It wasn't Lotus's first record – the Lotus Type 119c Gravity Racer set the record for the quickest run down the hill at the Goodwood Festival of Speed in 2003, more than 1.3 seconds faster than its nearest rival. It also set a new record at the Brooklands Soapbox Derby in Surrey in 2006; the engineless vehicle's time of 67.7 seconds was more than four seconds faster than the previous record.

✳ One of Norfolk's youngest record-breakers is little Leah Robbins from **Gorleston**, who won her Amateur Swimming Association for swimming five metres when she was just 13 months old, adding her 10, 25 and 50 metres by the age of two, and following it up with her 400-metres certificate at the age of three in March 2008.

✳ In March 1785 the first mailcoach ran from London to **Norwich**. The last mailcoach trip before the trains took over completely was on 6 January 1846. One of the few surviving mailcoaches, number N205, was originally assigned to that route. It was re-registered in 1967 so it could carry mail again. Nowadays, it's driven by John Parker from Swingletree, near **Diss**,

The Dial Stone at Besthorpe.

and his team of Hungarian Greys. It weighs 1.25 tons without passengers. A former owner, James Selby, set two records in the 19th century just before his death in 1888: for the longest distance ever driven by a coachman, and for the fastest time changing one set of horses for another (47.2 seconds). However, John Parker broke both those records. His team changed the horses in less than half the time (21.2 seconds); and in 1996, on the 150th anniversary of the last mailcoach run from London to Norwich, he drove his horses non-stop on the 139-mile route from London Guildhall to Norwich Cathedral – in an amazing 21 hours 30 minutes.

✳ Wing Commander Ken Wallis, who lives at **Reymerston**, invented and built the autogyro. His most famous one is probably 'Little Nellie', which starred in the Bond film *You Only Live Twice*. He built his first plane in the 1930s, a 'Flying Flea'. Knowing that his poor sight in one eye would scupper his dreams of flying in the RAF, he found a way round it and wore corrective goggles while flying. After his retirement from the RAF he moved to Norfolk. He's the holder of 34 world records for autogyros, including:

The longest non-stop distance in a straight line (543 miles, in 1975);
The longest flight (6 hours 25 minutes, in 1975);
The fastest speed over 15km (189.6km per hour, in 1984);
The fastest speed over 100km closed circuit (190.4km per hour, in 1985);
Time to climb to 3,000 metres (7 minutes 20 seconds, in 1998 – which also made him the oldest pilot to set a world record, at 81 years and 336 days).

✳ Kieron Bradley of **Taverham** and Peter Ash, also of Norfolk, set the world record for the longest distance travelled in a kite buggy between 5 and 21 September 2004 – an incredible 1,015km across the Gobi Desert. Kieron, an ex-Formula One engineer, designed the three-wheel aluminium-framed buggies, which had wide tyres and roll-bars to protect the pilots. The terrain was far from smooth, and included thorn bushes growing out of sandy mounds and temperatures of up to 40 degrees C. However, on good days they were able to travel at 41mph before the wind. Before they set off, they were given three red strings from the Dalai Lama, via the Mongolian Ambassador, Dalrain Davaasambuu. Known as the 'Dalai Lama ties', the strings were a blessing for the journey. Next up for Kieron is the Moon Regan TransAntarctic Expedition. He helped to design the new Lotus Concept Ice Vehicle for the expedition, which is a cross between a skidoo and a microlight. The biofuel-powered, propeller-driven trike on skids has an ice-penetrating radar.

Chapter 14

This and that

A miscellany of facts and figures about Norfolk, its people and its places:

✳ The **Wells** and **Walsingham** Light Railway is the longest 10¼-inch narrow-gauge steam railway in the world.

✳ The Twining Teapot Gallery in the Castle Museum at **Norwich** contains the greatest specialist collection of British ceramic teapots in the world. There are more than 3,000, dating from the 1730s right through to the 1980s. The collection includes a teapot with two spouts; a teapot in the shape of a World War One tank; one in the shape of a monkey; and another in the shape of a castle. Early teapots were often small as tea was expensive; in the early 18th century, a pound of tea could cost three months' wages. Tea was often smuggled in the late 18th century because of the high taxes. Parson Woodforde wrote in his diary about Andrews the smuggler scaring him by whistling under the window at 11 o'clock at night, but it turned out that the smuggler was bringing six pounds of tea.

✳ John Betjeman, Poet Laureate, described **Diss** as 'the perfect English market town.'

✳ Docwra's Rock Shop in **Great Yarmouth** is the world's largest rock shop. They make and sell over 80,000 sticks of rock a week.

✳ The Tuesday Market Place in **King's Lynn** is one of the largest and oldest market places in the country. It was known as 'Forum Martis' ('Tuesday Market Place') in the reign of Richard I during the 1190s.

✳ **Norwich** has an underground reservoir at **Lakenham**, built in 1871, which holds a million gallons of water. It has to be emptied and cleaned every five years.

✳ The bowling green at the Globe Inn in **Blofield** is the largest bowling green in the country and dates from before 1777. It was also used as an arena for Norfolk Wrestling on the first Tuesday after Whitsun, for matches between the 'collars and elbow' men. It is now the pub's garden.

✳ At 900 acres, **Narborough** airfield was the largest airfield in Norfolk during World War One. Captain W.E. Johns was stationed there, and his experiences formed part of the basis of his Biggles books. Biggles spent his childhood with his uncle in Norfolk and learned to fly at the fictional Number 17 Flying Training School in Settling, Norfolk.

✳ **Terrington St Clement** is Norfolk's largest village, covering an area of 13 square miles.

✳ Malcolm Sayer, designer of the E-type Jag, went to **Great Yarmouth** Grammar School.

✳ A slightly unusual form of sport found in Norfolk is snail racing. The annual world snail racing championships have been held over a 13-inch course in **Congham**, Norfolk, for more than 30 years. In 2008 the championship was won by a snail called Heikki which completed the course in three minutes and two seconds.

✳ **Melton Constable** Park was designed by Capability Brown in 1764–69. The church contains Norman work and many memorials to the Astleys. Sir Jacob Astley fought in the civil war and his prayer is still quoted by many: 'Lord, I shall be very busy this day. I may forget Thee but do Thou not forget me.'

✳ Boulton and Paul in **Norwich** produced the huts for Scott's Antarctic expedition.

✳ The **Haddiscoe** Hoard is the largest hoard of civil war coins found in Norfolk so far. They were discovered at Haddiscoe by a man working on the flood defence scheme in July 2003. There are over 300 silver coins in the hoard, ranging in date from Edward VI to Charles I, and they're on display in the 'conspiracy room' at the Elizabethan House Museum in **Great Yarmouth.**

✳ **Heydon** is one of only 12 privately owned villages to be found in the UK. The entire village, including Heydon Manor, belongs to the Bulwer family who have lived in the village since 1640. The newest building in the village was the pump-house, which was put up in 1887 to celebrate Queen Victoria's jubilee.

✳ In 1849, Charles Dickens visited **Great Yarmouth**, staying at the Royal Hotel on Waterloo Road and also at the Feathers Inn in **Gorleston**. A large part of his novel *David Copperfield* is set in Yarmouth.

✳ The Royal Agricultural Association of England was founded in 1837, and Norfolk is one of the oldest county associations. It was founded in 1847 when the West Norfolk and East Norfolk associations merged. For the first 15 years the agricultural shows alternated between **Swaffham** and **Norwich**, and then, until 1953, shows were held around the county at a different parkland each year. The Prince of Wales became president in 1872, and in 1908, when he became Edward VII, he gave the Norfolk Show its royal prefix. The permanent showground at Costessey was bought in 1952 and the first show was held there in 1954.

✳ Muhummad Ali visited **Norwich** in October 1971 as part of his promotional tour for Ovaltine. At a press conference afterwards at the Castle Hotel, Ali told reporters he had loved seeing Britain's 'little country towns' and said Norwich had been 'the most civilised place I've been to on the tour.'

✳ Daniel Defoe's most famous book, *Robinson Crusoe*, begins with a storm off **Great Yarmouth**.

✳ Florence the octopus made headlines after accomplishing the rare feat of breeding while in captivity. In December 2000, after she was brought from Florida to the garden centre at **Fakenham**, it was discovered that she was pregnant: she laid 60 eggs. In the wild female octopi stop eating while brooding their eggs and don't survive after the eggs hatch; sadly, Florence's 50th baby emerged on February 12 and Florence died later that afternoon.

✳ The Revd Wilbert Awdry is thought to have taken his inspiration for characters in his *Railway Series* (aka *Thomas the Tank Engine*) from the tramway that once ran from **Wisbech** to **Upwell** – particularly for Toby the Tram Engine. The tramway was built in 1882 and was mainly used for moving agricultural produce. It was closed to passengers in 1929 and was finally closed in 1966 as part of the Beeching cuts. Revd Awdry campaigned for a preservation society but sadly it didn't happen. The site of the station is now the car park for the doctor's surgery in Upwell.

✳ One of the most unusual names in Norfolk belonged to a young man in **Dereham**. The story was explained by the Reverend Benjamin Armstrong, the vicar of Dereham, in his diary entry for 25 December 1866: 'Married a young parishioner of the name of Mahershallalashbaz Tuck. He accounted for the possession of so extraordinary a name thus: his father wished to call him by the shortest name in the Bible, and for that purpose selected Uz. But, the clergyman making some demur, the father said in pique, "Well, if he cannot have the shortest he shall have the longest."'

✳ The world's last surviving steam-powered herring drifter is the *Lydia Eva*, which was built in 1930 and fished out of **Great Yarmouth**. It was the last ship to be built at the **King's Lynn** yard. The ship was put into dry dock in

2000, repaired in 2007 and finally refloated in March 2008. The *Lydia Eva* is one of only 58 ships on the National Register of Historic Ships.

✳ Laurel and Hardy once played at the Hippodrome in **Norwich** (now replaced by the car park on St Giles Street).

✳ There was once a royal station at **Wolferton**, which connected **Sandringham** with London King's Cross. When the station was closed in 1966 it became a museum and Queen Victoria's travelling bed was one of the exhibits. After the museum closed, the house was restored and is now a private home.

✳ In **Winfarthing**, a sword is commemorated in both the church window and on the village sign. The legend of the sword is told in Bacon's *Reliques of Rome* (1593): in mediaeval times, people came to Winfarthing to see the sword in the church. Women who wanted to get rid of an abusive husband lit a candle before the sword every Sunday for a whole year. It was also used to find stolen horses and items that were lost. The sword had actually belonged to a thief who had sought sanctuary in the church. He managed to escape past the watchmen but left his sword behind. It was placed in an old chest, and the vicar and his clerk made up the story to help swell the coffers!

✳ The first town in England to establish its mayorality was **Thetford**, in 1198.

✳ Camping was a form of football played in Norfolk and Suffolk. The *Promptorium Parvulorum* (see page 209) defined it in 1440 as: 'Campan, or playar at foott balle, pediluson; campyon, or champion.' It was usually played in a field specially set aside for the game, known as the camping ground or pightle, which was often near the church. In **Swaffham,** in 1472, the vicar donated lands next to the church for camping. It was usually a violent game (if played with shoes on, it was known as 'savage camp') and in the mid-18th century, after an inter-county match held at **Diss** Common, within a fortnight of the match nine had died from their injuries. The game died out in the early 19th century – a match recorded at **Kirby Cane** was said to be 'the first thorough boxing camping match that has taken place for the last 35 years', and the last recorded matches seem to have taken place at **Norwich** cricket ground and at **Stoke Holy Cross** in around 1831.

✳ Another Norfolk game with a murky past is logats. This was a game similar to bowls, but small poles or pins were used instead of balls. It was banned by Henry VIII. It's referenced by Shakespeare in *Hamlet*, during the gravedigging scene, when Hamlet says to Horatio, 'Did these bones cost no more the breeding but to play at logats with them?' (Bones were sometimes used instead of pins). The last inn where it was played in **Norwich** was the Hampshire Hog.

✳ The English folktale about the pedlar of **Swaffham** tells how, in the 15th century, a poor pedlar called John Chapman had a dream that if he went to London Bridge he would find his fortune among the stalls there. He put it out of his mind, but the dream kept recurring. So, in the end, he walked to London. Among the stalls a shopkeeper asked him why he'd travelled to London. When Chapman explained, the shopkeeper said that he too had had a dream: that he'd visited Swaffham and found gold buried beneath an oak tree in the orchard behind the house of a man called Chapman. Chapman duly returned to Swaffham, dug beneath the tree and discovered a pot containing coins. There was writing he couldn't understand on the pot, so he put it on sale in the market, where a visiting monk told him that the words meant 'beneath me lies one greater than I'. Chapman duly returned to the oak, dug a deeper hole and discovered much more treasure. The legend is commemorated on the town sign and also in the church, where there are carvings of Chapman and his dog on the bench ends. In fact, Chapman was a real-life character – a rich merchant, rather than a poor pedlar – and he paid for much work on the parish church.

✳ Another folktale, the *Babes in the Wood*, was originally a ballad published in **Norwich** by Thomas Millington in 1595. The story goes that two children were placed in their uncle's care after their parents had died. They were due to inherit their father's estate, unless they died before they were 21, in which case the uncle would inherit everything. The uncle paid two cut-throats to take the children into **Wayland** Wood and murder them, but they couldn't bring themselves to kill the children and instead left them in the wood, hoping that the children would find their way out. However, as the children were very young, they died of starvation and exposure underneath an oak tree, and the robins in the wood covered them with leaves. There was once a huge oak in Wayland Wood, which was where the children supposedly died, but it was destroyed by lightning in 1879; and hundreds of souvenir-hunters came to saw off bits of the remains of the tree.

The story has been associated with the de Grey family. Thomas de Grey was seven years old in 1562 when his father died and he became a ward of the queen. Four years later he died unexpectedly while visiting his stepmother, and his uncle Robert inherited the estate. It was said that Robert had murdered the boy. However, this is more than likely to be a political smear campaign as de Grey was a Catholic and had been jailed for not attending Anglican services.

✳ James Dyson, inventor of the bagless Dual Cyclone vacuum cleaner, was born in **Cromer**.

✳ The Wurlitzer organ at **Thursford** was originally installed in the Paramount Cinema in Leeds. It's the the fourth largest Wurlitzer in Europe and has 1,339 pipes ranging from ½ an inch to 16ft in length. The pipes are held in two specially constructed rooms.

✳ John Rolfe, who was born in **Heacham**, travelled to America in 1609. He was shipwrecked off Bermuda and ended up in Virginia. Four years later he married Pocahontas, the daughter of Chief Powhatan. Pocahontas is featured on the village sign at Heacham and there's also a memorial to her in St Mary's Church.

✳ William Blackstone, who was rector at **Attleborough**, emigrated to America in 1623. He's thought to be the first white European who settled in Boston and the first white settler in Rhode Island (in 1634). He's also believed to have planted the first orchard in Massachusetts.

✳ Willow worker Terry Bensley is the last remaining basket maker in **Great Yarmouth**, and is the only craftsman in the country who knows how to make the famous tall bearskin hat worn by the Grenadier Guards. The specification of the bearskins has stayed the same since 1830. They have to be made in a certain way, to a certain weight, size and shape. The frame is made from willow, held together with thin strips of willow cane which act like ribbon. There are only three nails in each hat, which are brass so they don't rust and ruin the bearskin.

✳ Peter Beales Roses in **Attleborough** is the holder of the National Collection of Rosa Species. The gardens have 1,300 varieties of roses, 300 of which are unique to them in the UK. In 2007 they were awarded their 15th gold medal from the Chelsea Flower Show.

Selected Bibliography

Blomefield, Francis (and continued by Charles Parkin) *An Essay towards a Topographical History of the County of Norfolk*, 11 volumes, 2nd edition, 1807–1886.

Kirkpatrick, John (ed. Dawson Turner) *History of the Religious Orders and Communities and of the Hospitals and Castle of Norwich, written 1725*, Norwich (Stevenson and Matchett) 1845, no ISBN.

Mortlock, D.P. and Roberts, C.V. *The Guide to Norfolk Churches*, 2nd edition, Lutterworth Press, 2007, ISBN 987-0718830649.

Page, William (ed.) *The Victoria History of the County of Norfolk, Volume 2*, 1906, London, no ISBN.

Pevsner, Nikolaus and Wilson, Bill *The Buildings of England – Norfolk 1: Norwich and North-East*, Penguin, London, 2nd edition, 1997, ISBN 0140710582.

Pevsner, Nikolaus and Wilson, Bill *The Buildings of England – Norfolk 2: North-West and South*, Yale University Press, 2nd edition, 1999, ISBN 0300096577.

Rye, James *A Popular Guide to Norfolk Place Names*, The Larks Press, 1991, ISBN 0948400153.

Sandred, Karle Inge and Lingström, Bengt *The Place Names of Norfolk, Part I*, The English Place-Name Society, 1989, ISBN 0904889157.

Twinch, Carol *In Search of St Walstan*, Media Associates, 1995, ISBN 0952149915.

Twinch, Carol *The Saint with the Silver Shoes*, Media Associates, 2004, ISBN 0952149931.

Williamson, Tom *The Norfolk Broads: a Landscape History*, Manchester University Press, 1997, ISBN 0719048001.

www.oxforddnb.com – website of the Oxford Dictionary of National Biography

Archived issues of:
Eastern Daily Press
Norfolk Chronicle and Norwich Gazette
Norwich Mercury
The Times